Dreamer's Dictionary

Dreamer's Dictionary

GARUDA

STERLING PUBLISHING CO., INC.
NEW YORK

Library of Congress Cataloging-in-Publication Data

Edinger, Roswitha,
[Träume. English]
Dreamer's dictionary / Garuda
p. cm.
Includes index.
ISBN 0-8069-5481-7
1. Dream interpretation--Dictionaries. 2. Symbolism (Psychology)--Dictionaries. 3. Dreams. I. Title.

BF1091 .E3513 2001
154.6'3--dc21 20011040080

Translation by Elisabeth R. Reinersmann
Published by Sterling Publishing Company, Inc.
387 Park Avenue South, New York, N.Y. 10016
Originally published under the title *Traume-Seelenbotschaften und Zukunfts-Visionen*
Distributed in Canada by Sterling Publishing
c/o Canadian Manda Group, One Atlantic Avenue, Suite 105
Toronto, Ontario, Canada M6K 3E7
Distributed in Great Britain and Europe by Chrysalis Books
64 Brewery Road, London N7 9NT, England
Distributed in Australia by Capricorn Link (Australia) Pty. Ltd.
P.O. Box 704, Windsor, NSW 2756 Australia
Manufactured in the United States of America

Sterling ISBN 0-8069-5481-7

Contents

"My dreams are the language of my soul, showing what
is in my heart in clear images,
revealing it in true prophetic form."

—*Fyodor Dostoevski*

Introduction

Dreams are part of our lives—from the moment of birth until death. These very personal "movies" originate in our soul and are symbolic images that need to be translated and interpreted if we want to understand their meaning and use them as a guide for and during our waking hours. Dreams present us with a world that is totally different from everyday consciousness. The soul of every person is richer and by far more expansive than his or her everyday world, and more than rational thinking can comprehend.

Dreams are messages of the soul, messages from the unconscious that are knocking at the door of our fate. It could prove very helpful to listen to this "inner voice"—even if it is not always easy to decipher its truth and message or to heed it.

Interpreting a dream means that we take seriously the whole person and what he/she says and expresses—not only the "active person" who behaves and acts consciously and deliberately during the day, but also the "passive person" whose unconscious, emotional life finds expression in his or her dreams. One third of our life is spent sleeping and what happens during those hours is not unimportant!

In dreams nothing is too small or too big. Dreams deal with the most insignificant things of life as much as they do with the biggest problems and important questions. Often a dream reveals matters that we are totally unaware of.

The world of dreams is as real and true as the world of our everyday existence. We experience emotions about all relationships and actions toward things and people as much during the night as during the day.

The History of Dreams

Knowledge and faith as well as the meaning of dreams have been with us for ages, and for centuries dreams have been the great mystery of human existence. The oldest document—a major papyrus roll from Egypt estimated to be about 4,000 years old—is kept in a museum in London. Many wise men and women in Egypt, Syria, Chaldea, and Phoenicia were masters in the interpretation of dreams and knew about their prophetic quality. It was this ancient knowledge and belief that served as a basis for the dream research that took place in Greece and Rome.

The art of dream interpretation reached new heights in the 8th century A.D. in the Arab world. After the aberrations of the Middle Ages, when people were obsessed by their belief in witches and came up with lopsided, demonic dream interpretations, a more sober attitude began to take hold. Sleep was seen as a simple physiological state, and dreams were thought to be the consequence of an overload of acidic substances in the stomach or dehydration in certain regions of the brain.

In the 19th century, however, influential people began to consider the phenomena of dreams, people such as Johann Wolfgang von Goethe, the great German poet; Friedrich Hebbel, German author; Gottfried Keller, Swiss author; Fyodor Dostoevski, Russian author; as well as philosophers Immanuel Kant, Arthur Schopenhauer, and Friedrich Nietzsche.

Pscychology and Dream Interpretation

A new phase of dream interpretation was launched by Sigmund Freud (1856–1936), a physician in Vienna. He believed that dreams and their symbols had much deeper meaning and were guided by a hidden order. He proceeded to use their content in the treatment of neurosis. Relentlessly, he insisted that almost every human dream hid sexual desire, a notion completely rejected at the time. While this was certainly an exaggeration, he was able to prove that the "manifest" dream (what we remember) is only a small portion of a far more extensive "latent" dream, whose content we can't remember when awake. Freud believed that our dreams are the *via regia*, the primary road to our unconscious.

Because our dreams are so much more than we remember, it behooves us to pay attention and carefully analyze even the small messages our soul is sending.

After Freud, who certainly overemphasized the sexual symbolism of dreams, came Wilhelm Steckel, who in the beginning dealt with the connections between a series of dreams (recurring dreams). Next came Alfred Adler (1875–1937), who saw the desire for power and recognition as a more forceful impetus behind all our behavior and dreams.

An even more far-reaching change in the research into our unconscious emotional life, as well in the interpretation of dreams, took place with the Swiss psychiatrist, C. G. Jung, (1875–1961). By going beyond the individual into the universal, which he called the "collective unconscious," he was able to show that our dream symbols are ancient, so-called archetypal human images. This enlarges the meaning of dreams. They could even be seen as a warning that evil or harm is lurking. They could alert us to future events, possibilities, or opportunities coming our way.

Dreams and Health

Scientific experiments conducted over many years have shown that every person dreams every night—and possibly every hour during the night. Most of us know nothing about it when we wake up. Is there a deep-seated reason for this? Are we afraid of the unconscious emotions, needs, or deeper urges and desires, and therefore choose to either forget or even deny our dreams?

For all higher-developed animals (and humans fall into that category), sleeping and dreaming is one of the basic, life-sustaining requirements, essential to our emotional, mental, and physical health. A human being deprived of dreaming for a sustained period will become ill.

Scientists at the University of Chicago observed two groups of students. One group was allowed to dream uninterrupted. The other group was prevented from dreaming. Whenever a measuring apparatus indicated that they were about to dream, they were awakened. The result was that the dream-deprived students became increasingly nervous and irritated, while the students in the other group—even though they needed to get up during the night—remained even-tempered. That seemed proof enough that humans need their nightly dreams to divert emotional stress in a natural way, and deal with unresolved feelings.

Those who explore the phenomena of dreams seriously will continue to be amazed! The richness of our "dream-scapes" is overwhelming, because the human soul is so much deeper and more profound than our everyday life suggests. Only the experience of our own dreams can convince us of our innate, hidden powers. Without paying attention to dreams, this power may remain unknown. We can learn a lot about ourselves when we begin to observe and analyze our dreams!

In spite of all we know today, dream research is still in its infancy. However, what is known is enough for us to use our dreams to stay "emotionally healthy," and with their help we can find our "own, real self"!

Dreams that appear again and again at certain intervals are particularly meaningful. They point to a state of "emotional pregnancy," a prolonged emotional process that could lead—piece by piece—to the resolution of a particular problem.

Dreams always bring about relief in our emotional life, because built-up tension, conflicts, feelings, and urges are dissipated, restoring emotional calm.

By now we know that the hormone vasotocin is responsible for dreaming. It is produced in the pituitary gland in the brain, harmonizing a disrupted sleeping/waking rhythm. According to recent research, the substance, in tablet form, does not produce unwanted side effects and is not addictive. By the way, alcohol represses dream activity.

Bach flower remedies have activated dreams, and vitamin B6 is said to strengthen a person's ability to remember dreams. Reading books about dream interpretation is also said to activate our dream life. However, the most important prerequisite is the acknowledgment that dreams are an important aid in maintaining emotional health—and this positive basic attitude, together with "joyfully looking forward" to dreams, is the best aid to remembering in the morning the "messages from your soul."

Dreams and Messages from the Soul

Current thought in dream research is that dreams originate in the unconscious, the "id." Our psyche is made up of three parts: the "ego" (our consciousness), the "superego" (our conscience), and the "id" (our unconscious). Important impulses, which determine thoughts, feelings, and actions, originate in the unconscious area, where we repress all disappointments, negative feelings, and bad experiences.

All these, however, do not lose their power, but appear again "disguised" in other forms. Such repressed feelings produce anxiety, prejudice, or various (unconscious) thoughts.

For instance, reacting vehemently to negative, almost

insignificant experiences during waking hours or in dreams, is a sign that a sore "spot" in the unconscious has been touched. It may be a disappointment from the past, or a frightening memory from childhood. The human soul uses dreams as a "mediator," so that all experiences and emotions from the waking hours, and also long repressed experiences and events, can be resolved.

However, our unconscious is not only the "garbage can" for negative experiences, but also a positive stimulus for important ideals and life goals, for creativity, innate talents, and the transfer of these positive gifts to consciousness and everyday life.

If we know nothing about our unconscious we will never acquire self-knowledge. And without self-knowledge we will never satisfy our basic human needs and desires—never reach *self-fulfillment*.

Dream interpretation can teach us why we are who we are, what possibilities reside within us, how we can solve conflicts in life, and how to best realize our goals. It is a way for people to get to know themselves. It is the best safeguard for mental and emotional health, and in that sense a valuable aid in life.

Dreams and Visions of the Future

Dream images, coming from the depths of our soul, are not only expressions of desires, hopes, and fears, they are also prophetic messages: hints of things and/or events to come and future developments.

Creative dreams and dream-like intuitions are not rare. Many examples exist where creative dreams suddenly gave insight and resolutions to problems and long sought-after ideas:

The chemist Friedrich August Kekule von Stradonitz credited a constantly recurring dream to the discovery of the molecular structure of benzoin (1865). He described the development of his formula for benzoin: "again and again an atom flitted in front of my eyes. . . . I could even distinguish different, larger structures . . . long rows, often tightly packed together, everything in motion, moving and turning in snake-like fashion. . . . And there it was: a snake caught its own tail . . . I woke up lightning fast and the solution came to me hours later!"

Mozart had similar experiences. He "found" melodies intuitively in strange ways.

Goethe, too, reported that many of his ideas came to him suddenly and in strange ways—without previous thought—in a sleep-like state!

Georg Friedrich Handel also clearly "saw" the conclusion to the Messiah in a dream and was wrote it down after he woke up.

During my 15 years as a therapist I have been able time and again to notice that about half of the experiences in dreams came as "visionary" messages and the other half were necessary to deal with emotional tension or to "digest" unresolved problems. Dreams are the most personal experiences of human beings. Over the centuries opinions about the nature of dreams differed widely: some thought dreams were true experiences of the soul, "leaving" the human body during sleep; others believed that dreams came from the gods or demonic powers; some thought that dreams were feelings not accessible to the human mind. But all agreed: dreams have meaning—even if we are not always able to understand them.

Correctly Interpreting Dream Symbols

To find meaning in our (often confusing) dreams, we need a key to interpreting them. In order to provide a helpful tool to the interested reader, this book has pulled together certain guidelines that have been developed over the centuries, organizing essential points and symbols in alphabetical order and understandable form.

However, it would be wrong to cling too literally to the written word, because the vivid symbolism of a dream is like a puzzle that needs to be put together—even seemingly unimportant details must always be taken into account.

A symbol can always have many meanings, and the personal situation in a dreamer's life plays an important role. When using this dream dictionary, I suggest that the reader not randomly line up one symbol after another, but pay attention to the finer points and to the connection they have to each other.

In order not to "lose" a dream, it is recommended that you keep a notebook and pen on your night table. It is sufficient to jot down just a few key points of the dream to keep it in your memory bank. At a quiet moment these notes will help to explore a dream in more detail.

Women and Their Dreams

Dream researchers in the United States have conducted large-scale studies and proven without a doubt that women are superb "dreamers." Their dreams appear to be more colorful and rich than men's. One explanation for the difference is that the retina of women is more sensitive to color than that of men. Women also hear music in their dreams. Generally speaking, they live more feeling-based lives and have greater imagination—all of which expresses itself in their dream images. Dream experiences seem to be evaluated and dealt with more from an emotional basis (that holds true for all women, even highly intelligent women). Women have a more intensive biorhythm cycle than men, which may account for the fact that their dreams are strongly influenced by the phases of the moon. Around the time of the full moon, women's dreams are more lively than when the moon is waning.

Women dream much more than men about people they love: husbands, lovers, friends, and their children. Many women report that their sleep is particularly restless and their dreams more intense a few days before their menstrual period. Afterward, dreams return to whatever is "more normal" for them. Since their sleep is lighter than that of men, women are more able to deal in their dreams with the experiences of the day.

A tip for men: if your wife or girlfriend has recurring dreams of tubes, narrow halls, or similar images, pay attention. You need to change your behavior in your intimate relationship and do it quickly. Your partner feels restrained by you and sexually frustrated.

Men and Their Dreams

Men have far fewer nightmares than women, and are much more active in their dreams. They tend to dream about cars, motorcycles, trains, or airplanes.

Men often get physical in their dreams and experience the need to defend themselves; they want to win and use their "elbows" to do it, because fights are usually a matter of survival. Most themes in their dreams are about their job, competition, social status, reputation, money, and possessions.

Also discoveries or technical improvement are themes in their dreams. The desire to became famous is much more prevalent in men's dreams than in women's.

According to C. G. Jung, men lie when they say they don't dream about sex: they dream much more than women about sexual desires or cravings. Furthermore, these symbolic dream experiences are much more aggressive in the dreams of men than in the more romantic and emotionally intense dreams of women.

Men are very good—more so than women—at repressing unpleasantness. They do it so well that they don't even dream about it! Difficult everyday events, for instance, at work, are resolved with logic and intelligence and seldom revisited in dreams.

A tip for women: if your husband or boyfriend has recurring dreams of empty rooms whose doors are wide open, pay attention: it might be a sign that there are other women in his life that keep a door open for him, and that he can't quite commit to you, or that his commitment is limited in some way.

An Example from My Practice

A client of mine told me the following dream: "I am standing at the edge of a lake. I see a boat. My husband is waiting on the other side and I know that I absolutely must get across the lake. Since I can see no other way to get there, I get into what turns out to be a boat in a state of decay and begin to cross the lake. Halfway across I see that above me and covering the whole lake is a shroud. The water begins to turn murky and suddenly my husband has disappeared. I start to panic and jump into the water. My legs get entangled by underwater growth. Somehow I am able to free myself. Then I realize I am on my back, drifting backwards in the murky water. Suddenly there is a dead body next to me and I realize that it looks a lot like me.

"Frightened and in panic I wake up. Time and again I have the same dream—more frequently in the last few months—and every time I am unable to get back to sleep."

In order to interpret the dream, it is important to look at the actual situation in the life of the client. The boat, being in bad shape, is the symbol of the journey of her life.

She wants to get to her husband on the other side of the lake. In depth psychology, a beach is a sign of vacillation, of not quite knowing where one wants to go and how to get there. The beach, however, is also a sign that things can't remain as they are. The client can't see her husband's face (she doesn't know what he thinks and feels). The couple talks only about mundane, everyday things. The lake (the emotions, the soul) is covered by a blanket (she is unaware of her feelings, covers them up) that looks like a veil (what is she trying to hide from herself or others?). She can see neither the sky (hope and solace) nor the sun (vitality and accomplishment).

Depth psychology believes that water is the universal symbol for life-giving energy, expressing the prevailing state of the dreamer's emotions. Murky water, therefore, points to depression or an emotional dilemma. Suddenly she jumps into the murky water and drifts (she doesn't want to face the present problems in her marriage; she wants to do nothing). However, the plants in the water pull at her legs (an erotic symbol—something wants to pull her down to the depth of her soul, to her true feelings, to make conscious her unfulfilled sexuality).

A dead body floating next to her looks like her. On one hand, it is a warning sign: stop going backward, floating in murky waters; stand up, look ahead, claim your true self, your life, and your needs. On the other hand, a dead body also is a sign that a present situation is coming to an end, is changing, or can be ended.

Depth psychology interprets a dead body as a sign of things unresolved, something that spoils a person's life; it also is a symbol for emotional rigidity.

Summary: the dream wants to show my client that things can't continue the way they are (the veil, a symbol for covering up reality), that it is imperative to make changes/end the present situation (dead body) in her personal life, so that her emotions, her spirit, her soul can be cleansed and life's journey (boat) can support her on the road to her personal goal (not backward floating but forward)!

This book will examine dream images in three ways: as dream symbols, as factors in depth psychology, and as visions of the future.

S = Symbol V = Vision D = Depth psychology

Acid

D: Dreaming about acid might be the sign of a fear so intense that it threatens to "dissolve" you. It could also mean that you are too distrustful or contemptuous of others, which, if you don't change soon, could "dissolve" your relationships.

Actor, Actress in Films

V: Dreaming about acting in a movie means you dislike false and hypocritical people—or you are pretending to be somebody you are not. Seeing others playing in a movie: be aware of treachery and lies. Seeing an actor in a dream: you want something you can't have, forgetting the good things you have. If you are the film actor, you don't feel comfortable around your friends. Find out who you really are.

D: People and actions in a "dream-movie" are usually a mirror of your emotions.

Actor, Actress on Stage

V: Seeing an actor: you will meet an intriguing person who will encourage you to take chances. Dreaming about playing the role of a person completely different from the way you are in real life: your behavior is in conflict with who you are and this "betrayal" is not good for your self-image. See **Film, Movie.**

D: Do you need more attention? Are you too ambitious?

Neither objective can be achieved through your present conduct. Are you playing games with others—or yourself? To what end? See **Stage.**

Ad

V: In a woman's dream, an ad may be a warning that, in the interests of others (family, friends, or colleagues), it is high time to make a long-overdue decision; otherwise, a problem may be made public. Reading an ad means you'll have to make a decision soon. Or you will receive news in the near future.

D: The ad either indicates skepticism and lack of enterprise or it is a symbol of new opportunities, possibilities, or contacts waiting for you. See **Advertising, Learning, Newspaper, Writing.**

Addiction, Addict

D: A dream about addiction is a symbol of your fears, emotions, and dependence on other people. Your life and your actions are influenced by external events and not freely chosen by you. You would do well to free yourself from your addictive behavior.

Admiring, Admiration

V: Dreaming about admiring someone means that you are too easily led by people and don't test their intentions first.

Adultery

D: Dreaming about adultery means you would love to have an affair; it could also means a bad conscience because of a past or ongoing affair. Sometimes it refers to conflicts among different parts of your personality (spiritual, physical, emotional). An adultery dream is also a sign of overpowering physical urges.

Adventure

V: Dreaming about risky, thrilling adventures are a sign of impending dangers; or you may be unsure about a present situation (or person). Dreaming about a pleasant adventure: it is high time (or the right time) to make long-range plans for a more active life.

D: An adventure points to your unconscious desire for more freedom and independence. A scary adventure means fear of uncertainties or skepticism about an actual event.

Advertising

V: Looking at an advertisement: be cautious about a deal you are offered—it could be a trap. Advertising something: you are not getting the applause or understanding you expected.

D: Something from deep in your unconscious is trying to get your attention. Maybe you have chosen to ignore or suppress it? See **Poster.**

Affection

V: Exchanging affection with someone in a dream is a sign of passionate feelings you have for a particular person—but the relationship won't last.

D: The dream is a sign of your unfulfilled need for affection. But are you too "thin-skinned," and easily offended, taking everything too seriously? Examine honestly which of the above applies to you. See **Love.**

Aggression

V + D: Hitting or shooting somebody expresses anger that has not been acknowledged during the day. Dreaming about being murdered or attacked: the murderer (a certain person in your life) makes impossible demands on you. If we can't fulfill the wishes, demands, or expectations of others, we feel guilty and our unconscious often "lets off steam" by way of aggressive attacks. See **Murder, Steam.**

Agony

V: Agonizing over something or feeling tortured: you failed to deal with something; or you have hurt someone and it is now coming back to haunt you. Chances are good that things will improve.

D: See **Pain.**

Air

D: Air is a sign that your spirit is motivating your emotional life. Are you gasping for air in your dream? Are you lacking air while running? Is someone or something stifling you? Do you have a tendency to build castles in the air? Be honest with yourself!

Alarm

V: An alarm going off is a warning to act swiftly on a present project. Setting off the alarm yourself: you are restless, impatient, and nervous; or you are getting unnecessarily worked up about somebody else's problem.

D: See **Signal, Whistle.**

Alarm Clock

V: If you hear an alarm clock go off in your dream: expect unpleasant surprises; it is time to replenish your energies. See **Clock.**

D: The alarm clock is usually a reminder—like the **Bell, Whistle,** or **Signal**—to be awake and not "sleep through" something!

Alcohol

V: Drinking a small amount of alcohol means you will

have interesting ideas. Drinking alcohol in secret: honestly examine your hidden desires.

D: Alcohol symbolizes secret desires. The meaning will become clearer when you examine other symbols in the dream. Were you just a little tipsy or outright drunk in your dream? Did the alcohol make you feel less inhibited, more courageous, more self-confident? See **Wine.**

Alcove

D: Seeing or entering an alcove: you are not quite honest in your love relationship or in an important friendship. Secrets are sabotaging the relationship.

Almonds

V: Eating a bitter almond: friends or acquaintances will disappoint you. Eating sweet almonds: you are loved and appreciated by your friends and they support your efforts. See **Nut.**

Altar

D: Dreaming about an altar: a project will turn out well. Lighted candles on the altar: certain plans will work out. Kneeling in front of an altar means you will receive help from "above," or a secret wish will be granted. It also suggests that humility might help in resolving a specific problem. An altar decorated with colorful flowers means a wedding is near. White lilies on the altar: death or burial of an acquaintance. If you are decorating an altar, it means fun and good luck!

D: Dreaming about kneeling in front of an altar is a symbol for your respectful and reverent ethics and the ability to sacrifice small desires on the "altar of your ideals." True, prayerful faith can make your desires and hopes come true. See **Praying.**

Ammonia

V: Smelling ammonia: you will get involved in a highly unpleasant situation.

D: See **Acid.**

Amputation

V: Dreaming about a hand or leg being amputated always indicates emotional loss in the near future. Undergoing an amputation means separation from a loved one. Amputation of a hand means your actions are restricted; or that you are not "sharing" enough with others. Amputation of a leg: you can't (or should) stop running away; you're heading in the wrong direction. Men dreaming about amputation means fear of "castration," or fear of impotence.

D: Dreaming about amputation means that your life has been torn apart and your peace of mind is under attack. The part being amputated usually refers to parts of ourselves that haven't been functioning properly. See **Arm, Leg, Left, Right.**

Anchor

S: The anchor is a symbol of hope, confidence, and health.

V: Seeing an anchor: a positive sign that dreams will soon be fulfilled. If the anchor is broken or only partially visible, it means a string of bad luck is about to start or something you had high hopes for is falling through. Anchoring in a harbor: you have again found solid ground. Throwing an anchor: you may be hoping that others will come to your aid, but it would be better to act on your own initiative!

D: The anchor is a symbol of your own, deeply rooted, and unwavering resolve, which you are about to exercise!

Angel

S: The angel is a temporary personification of divine revelation.

V: In the dream of a woman, the angel represents a strong desire for harmony, emotional connection, and guidance. Seeing an angel: good luck and shows your strength of character. Help "from above" or escape is in sight. Seeing oneself as the angel: you will receive love and friendship. Being surrounded by angels: you will find inner peace and satisfaction.

D: A dream about angels always means that you are reexamining your present attitudes. The angel, as a messenger, can lead you to new insights and be helpful in finding a new way.

Anger, Wrath, Resentment

V: Are you angry with yourself or another person? Are you struggling with yourself? Have you been unfair to someone? If you are fighting with somebody, remember, you will only reach a peaceful conclusion if you are gentle and understanding. If you are making others angry: an argument can be resolved but you won't be satisfied. See **Aggression.**

D: You are either having a conflict with someone right now or arguing with yourself. You could and should resolve the tension—and you will be ready to do so soon!

Animals

S: Animals represent, as **Archetypes,** the depths of our unconscious or our instincts. Animals in dreams are always repressed symbols of our urges—a dream language of the forbidden.

Bear: a symbol of vitality, power, and endurance (particularly in women's dreams). See **Bear**.

Fish: a fear of losing love; your partner is "slipping" through your fingers, but when the fish is alive, it is a sign of successful planning. See **Fish.**

Dog: extremely repressed sexual urges. See **Dog.**

Insects: repressed anger, emotional stress, family problems. See **Flies, Insects.**

Cat: a symbol of female eroticism, and sometimes a repressed desire for independence. See **Cat.**

Cow: female sexual urges—but always combined with patience and calm. See **Cow**.

Lion: glorified and powerful physical contact between men and women.

Mouse: a symbol of the female; the fear of mice is an expression of the dreamer's fear of a yet-to-be-acknowledged femininity. See **Mouse, Rat**.

Horse: aroused, but unrealized physical energies, or controlled vitality. See **Horse, Horseback Riding.**

Serpent: a phallic symbol; women who dream about serpents suffer from unfulfilled sexuality; a serpent crawling up your legs means sexual desires have been awakened. See **Dragon, Serpent**.

Small animals often symbolize a small sibling; large animals usually stand for the dreamer's own character traits and repressed cravings. Animals with human voices: a warning not to let other people hurt or take advantage of you. Dead animals are a sign of changes in your personal situation.

D: Animals are a symbol of primitive character traits, like greed, passion, or anger. The other symbols in the dream are very important.

Antlers

V: Antlers—particular in men's dreams—mean a painful disappointment in a love relationship. Several antlers stand for unrequited love or being dropped.

D: Antlers are often a sign of marital or partner conflicts. In a man's dream it usually indicates that he is afraid his partner is having an affair.

Ants

S: In the language of symbols, ants are an example of wisdom and hard work.

V: Dreaming about ants: a hint to be more industrious. Seeing ants on your body: expect good luck and success. Being bitten by an ant: take advantage of an opportunity in your professional life. Stepping on an anthill: your clumsy behavior is provoking a lot of frustration.

D: Seeing many ants is often a sign of a problem in your nervous system. The suggestion is to take a break and pay attention to health issues. If you dream about ants frequently, make an appointment for a physical examination.

Anvil

S: The anvil is a symbol of virtue, courage, and strength.

V: Somebody working on an anvil: you want to force an issue but with little hope of success. Seeing an anvil: friends are about to have a fight, or you will lose money gambling. Patiently working an object on the anvil: hard work and patience pays off in overcoming present difficulties; good work makes future gains possible.

D: See **Hammer.**

Anxiety

Being plagued by anxiety is often a sign that you are dealing with mistakes you've made. Feelings of guilt and lack of confidence are most often the reasons for nightmares. The dream may also indicate fear of chaos and problems—sometimes also a far-reaching change in your life. Being hunted by terrible images: you are harboring secret worries, or people you consider dangerous are the cause of the anxiety. If you frequently dream about being fearful and anxious: courage and being more assertive will make it easier to overcome hurdles. Making others fearful: a difficult situation or disappointment ahead. Sometimes anxiety-filled dreams are a sign of physical symptoms, like heart problems. Frequent anxiety dreams would suggest that you make an appointment with your physician for a check up. For women in particular, nightmares are often a sign of physical problems. The circulatory system may also be reacting to a heavy meal, too much smoking, too much alcohol.

Apple, Apple Tree

S: The apple—as far back as antiquity—is a symbol of fertility.

V: Looking at many apples in a tree: you have many friends. Eating a red apple: love will enter your life soon. If single, you will meet a new partner; if married, you will experience a renewal of your love life. If the apple has worms: frustration or separation. If it is full of worms: problems in your love relationship. If the apple is rotten: trouble is on the horizon. Biting into a sour apple: for better or worse, you must deal with an unpleasant situation. A golden apple: you are gaining self-knowledge. Giving a woman an apple: you will find a new female friend. Looking at an apple tree in bloom: business success. Looking at an apple tree just before harvest: chances for profit are good.

D: The apple, the biblical symbol of original sin, is always a symbol for love. The state of the apple indicates the state of the dreamer's love life. Since the apple always stands for sensual/worldly temptations, you might be thinking of giving in to them. See **Fruit.**

Apron

V: A man dreaming about wearing an apron: don't get into things that are not your business. It also means stop "running after every skirt"! A woman wearing an apron: your housewifely duties are calling you—take care of them now; or your partner is making a lot of work for you.

Archetypes

A number of archetypes come up in dreams again and again.

Mother image: including grandmothers, stepmothers, mother-in-laws, midwives, wise women, goddesses, the Church, universities, towns, countries, heaven, earth, oceans, fields, gardens, springs, baptismal vessels, the womb, ovens, cooking pots, cows, rabbits. All these symbols stand for childhood memories, emotional connection to our mothers, difficulties in growing up, our own character traits, and more.

Serpent biting its own tail: conscience and ego are in need of reconciliation (this is a reference to the fundamental struggle all human beings face—the polarities of good and evil, men and women, etc.).

Mandala: this symbol of circles and quadrants represent self-realization.

Aries

D: The symbol of Aries, the "horned" animal, the ram, represents masculinity and strength, but also enormous will power, courage, a certain toughness, patience—and, if the Aries is a man, sexual vigor. You either have most of these qualities already or need to practice them. See **Mars, Planets.**

Armor

V: Dreaming about armor: you want protection or to be shielded from strange influences. Are you looking for a "thick skin" to protect you from aggressive or nasty people? Wearing armor: you are afraid that others will attack you—you feel stifled by negative feelings. Has fear driven you to put on "armor"—hoping for protection from the influence of a parent or a "significant other"? Maybe you have protected yourself so much that others can't get close to you? Whichever applies to you, make changes, because walking in heavy armor makes moving through life difficult.

Arms

If somebody is hugging you: don't be distant because there is a good chance that these "arms" might be of help to you; somebody (a friend) might offer you a helping hand. Seeing yourself with arms stronger than they actually are: difficult times and hard work is ahead! If your arms or the arms of others are densely covered by hair: money is pouring in. Breaking your arms: family fights and squabbles and also a warning against careless actions. Dreaming about having one arm missing: you are suffering from painful inhibitions. Dreaming about being poor: be prepared for disappointments.

D: The image of the arm represents your ability to express your emotions, thoughts, or needs, and to either realize or destroy them. See **Right, Left.**

Arrest

V: This dream symbol indicates that you want to "arrest" a behavior or conduct, because it violates or endangers your moral principles (and conventional standards). See **Police, Prison, Sentence.**

Arrow

S: The arrow stands for the rays of the sun, and it is also a phallic symbol.

V: Seeing an arrow: present conflicts and arguments are partially your fault. Shooting an arrow: a warning—you are going to be the target! Because of your behavior you might lose a good friend; it points to a separation. Getting hit by an arrow: a breakdown or a catastrophe in the making. An arrow pointed in a certain direction suggests the direction you need to take in your personal and professional life. See **The Four Corners of the Compass.**

D: The arrow as a **Weapon**: you feel injured and take it out on others, or you suffer from the hurtful behavior of others, like meanness, spitefulness, or aggressive sexuality. See **Lance.**

Artist

D: This dream may indicate that you actually have artistic talents. It may also express "eccentricity" and a desire for more self-expression and fulfillment.

Ashes

S: The symbol of death, a grieving ritual, and penance.

V: Dreaming about ashes is not a good omen. Seeing or disbursing ashes in a dream is a message that someone is going to die. Falling into or stepping on ashes means a loss of money—be careful during financial transactions. Dreaming about seeing a lot of ashes: bitter disappointment and hurt. Collecting ashes: an increase in material goods.

D: The image of ashes is either a warning of impending hurt and disappointment or a promise of spiritual rebirth (the phoenix rising from the ashes).

Asparagus

V: Eating asparagus means that very specific wishes will be granted soon, particularly erotic desires. However, if the latter is the case, you might regret that you let your passions run away with you.

D: Since asparagus is a phallic symbol, the dream refers most of all to your erotic desires.

Assassination

Seeing or experiencing an assassination attempt means startling events are in you future, but "luck can be found even in misfortune"—things could be worse. You are assassinating someone: you are spending time and energy on a hopeless situation—you will not succeed. You see blood: you will experience personal and professional losses. Dreaming about being assassinated: you are in great danger—the utmost concentration is called for.

Asthma

D: Dreaming about having an asthma attack needs to be taken seriously. You are either living in a "suffocating" relationship, or your workplace, colleagues, or everyday existence do not give you room to breath. Waste no time finding the reason for this dream!

Astrology, Astrologer

D: Visiting an astrologer: you are looking for advice and help. If an astrologer is talking to you: you are examining a situation (and yourself) and are going to be successful. Dreaming about seeing astrological signs (signs of the zodiac or symbols of planets) means you are gaining insights into issues that have previously been foreign to you. Life will change for the better. See **Fortune-teller, Planets, Signs of the Zodiac, Stars.**

Attack

V: Being the victim of an attack: your projects are going to fail.

D: Character traits, cravings, or needs that you haven't been aware of until now appear suddenly and violently from nowhere, making you anxious and afraid.

Auditorium/Ballroom

V: Dancing in a ballroom: a fun-filled social event will lift your spirits. Seeing a large auditorium: you will have to deal with many people. Participating at a conference: you will be asked to solve a conflict.

D: Since an auditorium is a place where people meet, the dream implies that you are looking for contact, diversion, and companionship. Was the meeting fun or somber?

Aunt

V: Dreaming about your aunt: unexpected financial support or even an inheritance.

Auto, Car

S: Speed and things on wheels are favorite subjects in the dreams of men. A sports car represents sexual euphoria and a man's enjoyment of a female "chassis"!

V: Buying a beautiful car; a positive sign—you will quickly advance at your job. Driving a car safely and skillfully: success achieved through your own effort. Crashing into another car: a setback, because you are only concerned about yourself. The way we drive a car in a dream is an indication of how we direct our lives and what we still need to learn. Seeing only one car in a dream: you will soon receive news. Getting out of a car: setbacks and stagnation. Your competence is questioned. Dreaming about your car breaking down on the road: a business trip will not be successful. Winning an auto race: quick reactions on your part leave your competition "in the dust"; success on the job is almost guaranteed. In a man's dream, it means successful "elimination" of a (love) rival. Being involved in an accident: be prepared to be met by powerful competition.

D: Cars and other means of transportation are always

symbols of your life's journey. The car, in general, is a sign for positive changes at work. For men the auto is a symbol of masculine energy and always points to your present relationship with sexuality and desire for more intense sexual experiences (the more horse power, the stronger the urges).

Avalanche

V: Dreaming about an avalanche rushing down a mountain is a warning: you have set something negative in motion that is almost impossible to stop. Being buried by an avalanche: you are affected by an unhappy event.

D: The avalanche is always a warning about impending danger that can still be averted. See **Glacier, Snow.**

Avenue

V: Walking along a street or avenue: you are on a right path and focused on your goals. Seeing a house or a particular object: success is in sight. If the street or avenue stretches far into the distance, you can look forward to a long life. If you suddenly turn back: take another look at what you are doing with your life right now.

D: Avenues or railroad tracks are all symbols of life's journey. See **Road, Street.**

Axe

S: The axe may appear in dreams as a weapon as well as a tool and it usually means reckless action.

V: The axe is a sign of misfortune, usually a fight or a quarrel with people in your environment. You are not always the innocent bystander—particularly when you are the one using the axe. Splitting wood: a separation from your love partner is imminent. Picking up an axe: bad luck. Looking at a very sharp axe: terror and conflict.

D: The axe as a symbol of battle: quarrels or aggression

are imminent; or you are not dealing adequately with your own **Aggression** or **Anger**. An axe-dream is often a sign that your influence and authority is only a show and not based on the strength of your character. Working with an axe: you are successful at your job, but you have no consideration for colleagues or other people (you are the perpetrator). If someone else is working with an axe: you are suffering because of the inconsiderate actions of another person and you need to defend yourself.

S = Symbol V = Vision D = Depth psychology

Baby

V: Dreaming about feeding a baby: much hard work is ahead before you can reap the rewards of your labor. Rocking a baby in a cradle: good luck and happiness. Seeing a dead baby: someone is going to die. If you are giving birth, something new within you is being born—a new direction in life, a new idea, etc. If you are a woman dreaming that you are nursing a baby at your **Breast**: you desperately want to have a baby; or you want to help someone, take care of someone. Seeing a sleeping baby: your future looks bright. If a sick baby is crying: things are not going well at your job or business.

D: The baby is a symbol of your unconscious wish for a carefree, happy childhood; a need to feel more secure at present. Dreaming about a baby points to undeveloped character traits that need to be nourished so that you can grow to full maturity.

Back

V: Looking at someone's back: you will be shown "the other side of the coin." If someone is turning his back on you: an old friendship that had turned difficult is rekindled. The dream may also mean that some people are acting superior and clearly have a low opinion of you. Or is it the other way around?

D: Everything has two sides and can be judged from different perspectives. Are you afraid that something is going on "behind your back"? Are you unaware of something (maybe your own or other people's action)? Are you hiding something—if so, what is it? The only thing you can do is turn it around and take a good look. See **Front.**

Backpack

V: Carrying a backpack means that problems will weigh heavily upon you and interfere with your everyday activities. See **Luggage.**

D: How much responsibility did you take on? What experiences from the past are you still carrying around? Have they become a crushing burden? A dream about a backpack is very important and—together with the rest of the images—ought to be explored in depth.

Bacon

V: Dreaming about eating bacon is a warning about eating more sensibly and paying attention to your health. See **Ham, Pig.**

Bag

V: An empty bag indicates a low bank balance—and it will continue to be low for some time. Carrying a heavy bag: you have much work to do. A full bag: you will receive some money. Losing a bag: something is not working out, but the chance for success was low from the beginning. Rummaging in a bag and finding unexpected things: your unconscious is making you aware of character traits that you didn't know you had. See **Backpack.**

D: The bag contains character traits that can hinder or support you and, therefore, take a close look at what is hiding in the bag (your unconscious). If the content shocks you, don't "throw away the bag"—those traits would only come back later to haunt you.

Bailiff

V: A bailiff in a dream is usually a sign that you are dealing with some unfinished business. Don't worry, you will be able to take care of things—one thing at a time! A project already started will continue to go well. If you are the bailiff: a plan is going to be successful. If a bailiff is impounding something from you: good news, or an old worry will be resolved.

D: See **Court.**

Baking, Baker, Oven

S: Dreaming about baking means that something inedible is being changed into a palatable form.

V: Seeing a baker: a present worry is going to be resolved; something changes for the better. Seeing a baker baking bread: be careful, people want something from you. Seeing a baker's oven actively being used: you can expect improvement in a financial matter; the same is true also when you are the baker, baking. See **Cook.**

D: Dreaming about a baker or baking indicates that a change will take place for the better. So—don't stop dreaming about baking! The baker may reminds you of people with similar last names. The oven means that your financial situation will improve. Seeing embers stands for harmony in all areas of your life.

Balance

V: Dreaming about losing your sense of balance: somebody wants to "push" you around, rob you of your peace, or block your way. Doing acrobatic acts you would never attempt in real life is a warning: don't be too daring and independent. But the dream is also a symbol of your self-confidence.

Balcony

S: In a man's dream, a balcony is often a symbol of female breasts.

V: Standing on a balcony: your social status will improve. Recognizing another person on a balcony: a happy reunion with a dear friend. Waving to somebody from a balcony (somebody of the opposite sex): good luck in your love-life (a relationship already existing or a new one). A balcony crashing to the ground, maybe with you on it: you will have to bury many of your hopes and dreams.

D: A balcony often announces new friends—in a man's dream, it is usually expresses erotic desires and/or needs!

Baldness

V: Dreaming about being bald: you are missing something that you envy in others and you are suffering emotionally because of it. If you are very intellectual or wise, the dream could mean society's esteem for you is increasing. Looking at bald men: an invitation to a very interesting party or celebration. See **Hair.**

D: Being bald indicates a fear of being "found out." See **Hair**. It could also be a sign of feelings of inferiority—you think that others are more attractive than you are. Remember: the inside is much more important than the outside!

Ball

V: Playing with a colorful ball or child's balloon: while you may receive a disappointment, you will get over it quickly. Playing with a ball: a warning of a passing love affair. However, playing ball with many other people: expect a positive relationship with a new partner (personal or business). Playing ball with your life's partner: a good omen for your relationship, because you are learning from each other in a playful way.

D: The ball is a symbol of the whole person (of a fully rounded personality), but it is also a symbol of your destiny—fate sometimes plays games with us! See **Globe.**

Ball of Twine

V: Seeing a ball of twine: you are involved in an unpleasant situation and will have a hard time untangling a problem with which you are faced. You are looking at a gray or dark ball of wool: be more careful with how you use your energies. You will have to deal with many problems before you can successfully finish your work.

D: See **String, Thread, Wool.**

Ballet

V: Watching a ballet: be careful when it comes to the opposite sex. Disappointments or even betrayals are very possible right now. If you yourself are dancing in the ballet: you are easily seduced—or about to seduce someone. Don't make empty promises—you are much too frivolous right now. A man dreaming of dancing in a ballet: the "gigolo" or "Don Juan" in him is awakening!

D: See **Dance, Music.**

Balloon

V: Seeing a balloon: good ideas are forthcoming, maybe even a discovery. You might also have a love affair now—but beware—things will soon dissolve into thin air. If you are taking a ride in a balloon: you have lost the ground under your feet—lost sight of your goals. Watching a hot air balloon explode: somebody is really angry with you—and you have given that person every reason to be angry! See **Air, Ball, Helium Balloon.**

D: If a balloon is floating in the air: you are daydreaming

and will be disappointed; if a balloon is bursting: hopes and dreams will fail.

Banana

V: A banana indicates a desire for erotic adventures. Eating a banana: your erotic desires will soon be satisfied. Seeing a banana: you want a closer relationship with another person.

D: The banana is a phallic symbol. When the banana is eaten: sexual desires, particularly in women's dreams. Sometimes, however, it refers to disappointment in matters of love.

Band Aid

D: A band aid indicates illness, injury, or a bad conscience, because you have injured others. A band aid across your mouth is a clear sign that you should not talk so much. See **Bandage.**

Bandage

V: Dreaming about being bandaged means emotional hurts to come or hurts that happened in the past. It is also a sign of healing in process. See **Band Aid, Mummy.**

Bang

V: Hearing a bang: agitation and dread threaten you, and also nervous stress. Sometimes the dream is caused by a natural sound, like a door banging.

D: A bang in a dream is often indicative of sudden unpleasant events that have either occurred already or are imminent.

Baptism

S: Baptism means the beginning of new life.

V: If you are holding a baby who is to be baptized: you are

asked to accept a responsibility and you need to agree to it. You can now start a very important project. Being present at a baptism: you have a sudden desire to start a new life. Watching a baptism: you will find inner strength in a very difficult hour.

D: You are going through profound changes: you are more tolerant, gain new insights, cleanse your emotions, and awaken secret strengths—all of which is like getting a new lease on life. A wonderful dream symbol.

Barbed Wire

D: Barbed wire is a warning to beware of what you think are "little" love affairs—they could endanger your committed relationship.

Barefoot

See **Going Barefoot.**

Bark

V: Looking at the bark of a tree means you are protecting your personal space. It also suggests you keep your intimate affairs more private. If the bark is injured, your intimate space has already been "invaded." Carving something into the bark means that erotic dreams will come true. See **Armor, Shell, Tank, Tree.**

Barking

V: A barking dog is a warning: don't take unnecessary risks. Several dogs are barking: people around you are up to no good. Several dogs are barking at you: think first—then act—and keep calm. See **Dog.**

Barn

V: Looking at a full barn: your success is the result of the hard work you have done. An empty barn: the hopes you put in a certain matter were misplaced.

D: See **Grass, Hay.**

Barometer

D: Seeing a barometer with the temperature climbing rapidly: you are under great pressure. The barometer is destroyed: a change in your life can't be avoided. Examine who or what is putting you under so much pressure in real life and resolve the situation.

Barracks

V: Looking at barracks: the differences you have with your boss are creating a difficult situation and worries are becoming a burden. Living in barracks: your freedom is limited due to external circumstances or because of other people. Trying to find the barracks: you are doubting your lover's or husband's honesty and question whether your relationship will survive. You are leaving the barracks: you are finally moving toward a better future. See **Soldier.**

D: Barracks reflect your fear that you will be deprived of your freedom to make a personal decision.

Barrel/Keg

V: Opening a barrel: an influential person becomes your friend. Seeing a full barrel: a hint of prosperity to come. Looking at an empty barrel: you are dissatisfied with your life. Rolling several barrels into your basement: a good sign, meaning increased wealth and a secure future. Buying a barrel of wine: good friends are guests in your house. A barrel with the bottom missing: your efforts are futile.

D: The barrel—like the **Bucket**—can be seen as the "Vessel of your Life." It often has sexual meaning, but may also warn of physical illness.

Barrier, Obstacle

V: Dreaming about a barrier of any kind that is stopping you: unconscious scruples or inhibitions are keeping you from finishing a certain project. It is not that others are keeping you from it; you yourself are responsible for the situation! However, jumping a barrier means that you will overcome hurdles in real life. Standing in front a very tall barrier: a hint that you need to reexamine your plans—you've been too optimistic and idealistic; or you overestimated the situation. See **Wood.**

D: A barrier stands for inhibitions or hurdles that you need to get over soon. Or are you protecting yourself against impending changes and/or people?

Barrier (Railroad or Border Crossing)

V: Looking at a barrier: many obstacles are ahead. If something is stopping you, think about what it might be and make sure that you're on the right path. If the barrier is open: obstacles are in your way and they could turn into a serious problem. If the barrier is down: problems can easily be overcome.

Bars

V: Seeing yourself behind bars: you are either very dependent on others or are prevented from doing something. Looking at barred windows: you are isolating—show more interest in others. Maybe you are longing for a person far away. Seeing a huge iron gate: you have too many unrealistic hopes and wishes.

D: Bars are either a warning about unrealistic wishes or indicate your longing for a person who is far away.

Basement

V: Walking into a basement means you need a lot of patience and perseverance in the coming weeks. Living in the basement: lead a more thrifty life and curtail your spending habits—poverty is close at hand. Looking at a caved-in basement: bad luck.

D: The basement is a symbol of the unconscious, but also of the foundation of your life, where you keep what needs to be finished. Fear and danger lurk in these dark regions of your soul. The other images in the dream are very important. See **Cave, Grotto, House, Tomb.**

Basket

S: The basket is an ancient symbol for the womb.

V: Holding an empty basket: be prepared for a disappointment in matters of love. Handing a basket to someone else: you are denying someone's request or deciding against something. Looking at a flower basket: good times, great happiness, and a gift. Looking at a laundry basket: dishonest people are taking advantage of you.

D: A basket reflects an unconscious fear that you are going to be denied something or meet with rejection. The basket also represents "the harvest of life," the work you have accomplished.

Bass Viol

V: Seeing a bass viol or playing one in a dream: be prepared for a happy surprise or advancement in your job or profession. Listening to a bass viol playing: happy hours of fun. See **Music, Violin.**

Bat

V: Dreaming about a bat: be less fickle and don't take advantage of other people. Seeing several bats means you are worried about your debts, but business is slowly going to improve.

D: The bat is a symbol of the darker side of your personality, of which you are as yet unaware. If you do some investigating, you will learn a lot about yourself!

Bathing, Swimming

S: Dreams about bathing and swimming are always symbols of cleansing and renewal.

V: Dreaming about swimming outdoors: everything is looking up because you are gaining strength and endurance. Taking a bath in cold water: your health is good, but you need to be more active. Taking a bath in hot water: illness or problems. If the water in the tub is clear: a danger is passing, a situation is clearing up. Swimming in a lake with many waves: use your skills to solve a difficult problem and you will succeed! Swimming in murky water points to a negative environment. See **Brook, Foam, Water.**

D: Dreams about swimming or bathing always point to an emotional cleansing, like a rebirth. Even if other people are bathing or being bathed, the dream always means your own renewal and cleansing.

Baton

V + D: Either a project is not going well or you would like to have more influence over it.

Battle

V: In the case of older people, the dream might be a memory of past war experiences. Or are you are afraid of other people attacking you? See **Fight, War.**

Beach

V: Being on a beach; your goals are far-reaching. Seeing high waves crashing on the shore: expect difficulties and resistance on the way to your goals.

D: See **Ocean, Shore, Water.**

Beacon, Floodlights

V: Seeing a bright light: you will receive spiritual guidance, which will enable you to overcome a difficult situation. Seeing the headlights of a car: you are in for an unpleasant surprise. See **Light.**

D: Floodlights are a sign of your being very focused and alert right now. Floodlights shining on you: others have seen through you—you have been "found out." If the floodlights illuminate a road, it means a glimpse into the future.

Beak

V: Seeing a bird's beak; a suggestion to finally "speak up" or—depending on the rest of the dream symbols—to "shut up." Only you will know the meaning at this moment!

Beam

V: Seeing a rotten, old beam in a dream: expect losses. Somebody gives you a beam as a gift: good fortune for your family. Throwing away or giving somebody a beam: you are trying to unload your guilt on someone else, or blame someone for your bad behavior (be careful, sometimes this beam might turn on you like a boomerang). See **Barrier, Wood.**

Beans

V: Eating beans in a dream means frustration, either at the job or at home, and possibly also a downturn in your financial situation. Seeing bean plants in bloom: live more modestly. Picking and then eating beans means successful business dealings.

D: The bean is a symbol of the female sex organ (particularly in men's dreams). See **Vegetable.**

Bear

S: The bear is seen as an animal of strength, but in a much calmer sense than other wild animals. In a man's dream, the bear usually represents a controlling, overbearing mother, because the bear stands for the feminine power of nature. V: Seeing a bear: a sign of insecure feelings in interpersonal relationships, sometimes also gossip. Seeing a dead bear: uncertainties felt for some time are cleared up.

D: A bear often indicates deception and disappointment. Maybe somebody—perhaps a woman—is trying to deceive you. You are also not quite certain about a particular woman. See **Animals.**

Beard

S: A beard is a sign of male power, courage, and wisdom.

V: Seeing men with long beards: a positive sign for prosperity to come. A man dreaming about shaving off or otherwise losing his beard: an unconscious fear of losing his power, his masculinity. In addition the dream means that he must soon say goodbye to (or be abandoned by) a good friend. A man dreaming about a woman with a beard: be more careful with the opposite sex; the woman is "wearing the pants" and hiding her innermost thoughts. A white beard is a symbol of wisdom. See **Hair, Shaving.**

D: In a man's dream, the beard symbolizes masculine power. Shaving off a beard, however, means that he needs to let go of habitual behavior or prejudices. In a woman's dream, a beard means that she is unconsciously looking for a father figure and more protection and security.

Beating

V: Getting a beating: someone or something is putting obstacles in your way; or it is punishment for the wrong you have done? Beating someone else: in spite of the adversities you have to face, you will conclude an important project successfully. You will let nothing and nobody stand in your way. See **Brawl, Fight.**

Bed

S: The bed symbolizes regeneration, love, death, and birth.

V: Seeing an empty bed in a dream means bad news, perhaps news about a death. Seeing oneself in bed: pay attention to your health; the dream suggests that you need quiet and solitude (too much stress may lead to illness). Lying in a strange bed: exercise caution—don't be too trusting. Seeing a soiled bed: you are surrounded by negative people, be careful. If your own bed is in disarray: your hiddenmost secrets are about to be discovered and cause you embarrassment.

D: The bed in a dream always stands for your emotional situation. Also it stands for a need for quiet and safety. Sometimes it might even indicate denial and flight from reality. The bed can also express sexual needs—depending on what else is going on in the dream. Are you in need of more peace and quiet right now? Warmth, comforts? See **Intercourse.**

Bee

S: The bee is a symbol for industriousness and represents the way you are organizing your life.

V: Seeing a bee: a challenge to practice good habits and work hard. Watching a bee collecting honey: a deeper, more positive bond in your love relationship. Watching many bees flying about: you will be productive, work hard, and can look forward to a good harvest. Getting stung by a bee: great changes are in store (marriage, change in job, or residence, etc.). See **Bumblebee.**

D: The bee symbolizes hard work, endurance, love of order, but also social engagement and the ability to adapt to others. Are you yourself a "busy bee"?

Beer, Beer Glass

V: Dreaming about an empty beer glass (or several): you

are unconsciously looking for company. A full glass of beer, or drinking beer: your health will remain good. Several full glasses of beer: you are clearly satisfied with the way your life is going. Spilling beer: no more peace and quiet—get ready for some exciting days. See **Alcohol.**

D: Beer is a symbol of peace, serenity, and an unflappable personality.

Beetle

S: The scarab is a symbol of resurrection.

V: Looking at a beetle: a warning to be more humble if you want people to like you. Watching many beetles: losses are inevitable. Catching a beetle: a problem will be solved and you will make new friends. Killing a beetle: you need to come to terms with a mistake.

D: A beetle represents the "ups and downs" of life, your success and failures. Examine the rest of the dream images.

Beets, Turnips

V: Harvesting turnips: all your riches will soon be safely under your roof. Eating turnips: an opportune project—that you questioned initially—will turn out okay. Seeing turnips or red beets: good health and happy times with family and friends. A white turnip means complications in your love relationship.

D: A turnip may symbolize sexual needs, but generally it may be a sign of good luck, happiness, or sarcasm, depending on the rest of the images in the dream.

Beggar

V: Dreaming about a beggar walking into a house means a visitor is going to surprise you. Giving a gift to a beggar: a project will soon show positive results or you might get relief from an uncomfortable situation. If you are the beggar: social isolation, fear of your own weakness, or hiding something from yourself.

D: The beggar in a dream is the symbol of your **Shadow**, your dark side. You are denying part of yourself or hiding it. Sometimes the beggar might provide wise counsel. See **Guru.**

Being Awake, Watchman

V: Dreaming about being wide awake: your unconscious is reminding you of a problem that you need to recognize before you miss the chance to solve it. Seeing a watchman: hurdles will complicate a big project. People are throwing obstacles in your way, but you will recognize the danger in time. See **Police, Soldier.**

D: Your conscience is watching over your behavior. Does secret guilt "keep you awake"? Should you be more alert to what you are about to do? Are you looking for protection? You will know which of the above applies to you!

Being Cross-eyed

V: Is your view of reality distorted? Is it difficult to see yourself or others as they really are? Do you have a hard time making yourself understood? See **Blindness, Eyes, Glasses.**

Being Skinny

V: Seeing a skinny man: chances are not good for your dreams coming true. You are emaciated: your actions have made you unpopular; bad times and possible health problems may be ahead.

D: Seeing yourself emaciated: be prepared for losses. Seeing others emaciated: chances for success are improving. See **Losing Weight.**

Bell

V: Hearing bells ringing means pleasant events in your

personal life, with family or good friends. Ringing a bell: you are going to make someone very happy. Looking at a bell: you are pursuing a specific objective, but must solve a few problems first—do it quickly. See **Church Bell.**

D: A bell might indicate the beginning of a favorable phase in your life; it could also be a warning about disappointments and/or misfortune. Was the sound of the bell happy or somber?

Belt

S: A belt is a symbol of fairness, energy, faith, and truth.

V: Finding a belt: you are gaining the trust of another person. Losing a belt: misery in matters of love. Seeing an old belt: all efforts and struggles are for naught.

D: The belt is a symbol of erotic needs for power and influence over other people (particularly in a man's dream). Do you want to tie somebody to you? Or punish a person physically with a belt?

Bench

V: Sitting on a bench: you want to take a break, look at everything in peace and quiet. If the sun is shining brightly and people walk by: you will make a new acquaintance.

Berries

V: Picking berries: you are looking for a lover, but he/she will be difficult to find right now. Eating berries: having erotic desires. It could also mean that you are going to win something. Seeing unripe or dried berries: impending frustrations and conflicts—and no luck in love. See **Fruit.**

Bet, Betting

V: If you are betting: you are taking too many risks in money matters or at the game table. Winning a bet: you have become involved in a risky matter—you will have losses. Losing a bet: unexpected luck is coming your way. See **Games.**

D: Your unconscious is informing you that you are involved in a risky, uncertain matter. Think hard and reconsider your decision.

Bible

V: Reading the Bible, or someone else reading the Bible to you, means abundance and peace in your personal life—internally as well as externally. Dreaming about letting a Bible fall to the floor: a separation is imminent if you disregard well-meant advice. Buying a Bible: a familiar conflict is about to be resolved harmoniously because you are not trying to justify yourself!

D: The Bible is a symbol of the right path; you are at peace, have a good conscience, and live an ethical life. But it could also be a warning: are you too rigid?

Bicycle

V: Riding a bike: rein in your ambitions—trying to hurry would not work. Slow down and you will reach your goal unscathed. If you feel as if the bike is floating in the air (with you on it): you want to get ahead socially, to improve your financial situation, etc. Buying a bicycle: be more active and improve your physical condition. See **Wheel.**

D: A bicycle requires the strength and effort of the individual riding it—including the choice of direction. Dreams about bikes, therefore, mean that you are in charge of your actions and choices, including the choice of "taking a road less traveled." Bike riding often means that you are on a fun-loving, light-hearted, leisurely trip through life.

Bill

Being handed a bill: make a serious effort to be more fair

to others—no matter how hard it is. Receiving a bill: it is time to keep the promises you have made. Writing a bill: you are about to get involved in a risky business.

D: To men who have always taken their sexuality very seriously, dreaming about a bill is a sign of insecurity and fear of impotence. Life often "hands us a bill" for past mistakes, wrong decisions, and weaknesses. Did you get one of those bills lately? See **Check (Restaurant).**

Billy Goat

V: Seeing a billy goat: either you are stubborn and putting up a lot of resistance, or someone's stubborn behavior is making life miserable for you.

D: The male goat is a symbol of aggressive, stubborn behavior. Are you looking for a scapegoat? Are others trying to make you the scapegoat? See **Goat, Ram.**

Binoculars

V: Seeing a pair of binoculars, or looking through them: a satisfactory and secure future. Seeing a pair of broken binoculars: an unstable financial situation in the near future. Be careful with money and future projects.

D: Binoculars represent your desire to look into and find out about the future. Since binoculars enlarge everything, don't take a present situation too seriously—many things are actually much smaller than they appear to be in the beginning.

Bird, Scarecrow

S: Birds are a symbol of saved souls.

V: Seeing a bird: someone wants to cheat you. Seeing birds fly away: sadness and loneliness ahead. Seeing migratory birds in the sky: you are homesick or feel abandoned. Listening to birds singing: good news. Seeing predatory birds: your enemies are waiting for a chance to attack you. A scarecrow means that you can't see many positive character traits in a person.

D: The bird is a symbol of intellectual flight, ideals, and intuition. But the dream also indicates your desire to solve financial matters. Your thoughts are fluttering about like a flock of birds—you can't rest. Dreaming of being air-born reflects erotic desires. The scarecrow indicates negative character traits or a lack of affection—either your own or someone else's. Self-deception and a very negative attitude toward life often play a great part. See **Dove, Eagle, Owl, Raven.**

Birth

V: Dreaming about a birth could be a sign of the birth of a new idea, a new task, a new plan, or even an idea for a book (usually in a man's dream). In women's dreams, it refers to the birth of a new attitude toward life. If you are giving birth: a job change for more money. Having an easy birth; a long-held wish will be granted along with freedom from many worries. Dreaming about a difficult birth: you have to let go of something you love very much; sometimes it also refers to an illness. Watching an animal giving birth means a positive new phase and new opportunities.

D: Women's dreams about birth are a sign of personal growth, implying that the process will be painful. In men's dreams, it usually indicates the "birth of new ideas," new work, or extraordinary deeds. Dreaming about birth is always a signal of a new beginning or personal growth. It also is a sign of emotional health or of regaining emotional health. Birth is always a beautiful, positive symbol!

Birthday

V: Celebrating your own birthday: a pleasant surprise is in store for you. Celebrating the birthday of another person:

meeting other people will open up positive professional opportunities. The sum of the digits of the numbers of your birth date are connected to important experiences of either the past or the future . The meaning of numbers is discussed in the chapter "**Numbers in Dreams.**"

Blackboard

V: Writing on a blackboard: start managing your money better and don't borrow any right now. A blank blackboard: expect to receive a note—and pay careful attention to what is says! Wiping a blackboard clean: you have thought through your new approach to a project much better than before.

D: Are you looking at a blackboard for help and advice? Is the advice a warning to watch out for losses and risks? Is it a reminder from your unconscious to prepare a certain matter more carefully? You will know the answer better than anyone else.

Blacksmith, Forging

V: Seeing a blacksmith indicates that you should start working on yourself, developing your talents, accepting fate with courage, and thereby "forging" your true personality. Seeing a blacksmith at work: "strike while the iron is hot"!

D: The blacksmith is working on personality traits that are rigid and unbending. Blacksmith dreams are always a sign of change, of a personality being formed. What are you "forging" in the dream? Maybe the dream suggests you use your energies and creativity to solve your problems and reach your goals.

Bladder

V: Dreaming about having to "go to the bathroom" in public: quit being embarrassed or ashamed. Usually the dream comes from a simple physical urge to empty your bladder, but your need for uninterrupted sleep is still so great that your unconscious is trying all kinds of tricks to keep you from having to get up.

Blanket, Quilt, Covers

V: Wrapping a blanket around yourself means you're afraid of your enemies; but it is also a warning to be less open toward others. Looking at one or more blankets: company is coming. Sometimes the image of a blanket might announce a new member of the family on the way. See **Wool.**

D: What are you hiding from yourself or others? What are you ashamed of? Who do you wish would keep you warm? What would you really like to "cover up"?

Blaze

S: A blaze always means uncertainty, insecurity, and that you're in need of help.

V: Seeing a house engulfed in bright flames: a timely change for the better in a certain matter, or you can expect something new to take place. If the burning house is engulfed in dense smoke, and you are unable to recognize the people around you and their intentions, your own plans and actions have not yet "matured." If you are setting something ablaze: your fight against fate is futile.

D: Every dream involving fire needs to be taken seriously, because your emotional energies have—either through internal or external events—become destructive. The fire might also be a symbol for erotic passions or repressed urges. Sometimes a blaze signals mental problems or an obsession with an idea. Something is "burning" inside you—find out soon what it is.

Blessings, To Bless

D: Blessing someone in your dream is a sign of your generosity and willingness to help. Receiving a blessing: new, powerful energies are rising from within and will help you greatly.

Blimp

V: Flying in a blimp through clouds: it is not just you—but your plans and goals—that are up "in the clouds"—get hold of your imagination! Crashing in a blimp: the harm you will suffer is of your own making. See **Flying, Zeppelin.**

D: The blimp represents your sexual desires and appetites, indicating that your passions are stronger than your intellectually high-flying plans. That's the reason why you feel out of balance. Get back on solid ground, back to reality.

Blindness

V: Dreaming about being blind: start opening your eyes; you are turning a blind eye to a certain matter! With eyes closed you are running headlong into danger. Leading a blind person: a task you have taken on is impossible to complete. Meeting a blind beggar could possibly indicate a win in the lottery.

D: This dream is usually a warning: stop going through life with your "eyes closed." It is also a challenge to stop turning a "blind eye" to the opportunities and dangers of everyday life—open your eyes to reality. See **Deafness, Eyes.**

Blood

S: Blood, a symbol of life, stands for vitality and consciousness.

V: Seeing blood in a dream: be careful of other people in all situations. Losing blood: you are feeling weak at the moment; every frustration expresses itself in the weak parts of your body. Seeing blood on your hands: stop getting involved in the business of other people—you have enough to do with your own. Seeing someone else bleeding: you are afraid for a close friend. See **Vein.**

D: Dreaming about bleeding always points to emotional wounds that you are denying. Blood also points to your own belief ("it is in my blood"). Blood by itself is a symbol of your vitality.

Boar

V: A boar appearing in your dream is a warning: someone around you is hostile. Seeing a boar in the woods or meeting one: a specific incident will undermine and destroy your trust in another person. See **Pig.**

D: The boar in a dream stands for strong erotic desires. See **Animals.**

Boat

S: The boat is a symbol of your personality, part of what you need in order to move forward in the ocean of life!

V: Seeing a boat means a trip or a change in life. If the water is clear, things are destined to go well. Murky water means misfortune or a mishap on a trip or in your life. Getting hit by a storm while riding in a boat—or falling out of a boat: postpone a planned trip or action. See **Ship.**

D: Seeing a boat in a dream is a sign that your life is about to change. Since a boat usually is in the water, the dream mean that you feel you're on "shaky ground." A boat, like the **Auto, Train,** or **Airplane** might be a symbol of your life's journey. The condition of the "transport device" will show you what your actual situation is. In Greek mythology, the boat is a symbol of the journey "to the other side," to the "dominion of the dead"—or a symbol of your journey into a new phase of life. See **Water.**

Boat, Small

V: If you are crossing a raging river in a small boat: you are facing great difficulties right now, but things will get sorted out.

D: A small boat makes it possible for you to reach "the other side"—even if you have to depend on something or someone. Have you made reaching your goal more complicated than it has to be? Are you acting too slowly? See **Boat, Ship, Yacht.**

Boat Ride

V: A boat ride is an indication that you are not pursuing your goals forcefully enough. Dreaming about passing through a narrow spot means that you need to concentrate, pay more attention. Dreaming about two people riding in the boat may be a sign that a relationship is becoming too restricting, or that an emotional impasse needs attention so that both people in the boat can reach the shore.

Body

V: Seeing your own body is a good sign; you are in good shape and can be satisfied with your life. If you appear too fat or ill: you are dealing with either physical health issues or emotional burdens—get rid of them! If you are looking at a "growing" body—for a man: improvement in his social position; for a young girl: a secret love; for a young woman: pregnancy; for an older woman: receiving something of substance. Taking off your clothes: certain actions are making you feel ashamed. See **Nakedness**. Seeing someone else naked: in erotic dreams, it means you are longing for love. In an "unemotional" dream, it means a surprising discovery. Seeing an injured body: you will have to do with less or have to forego something. See **House.**

D: The body always represents sexual needs or the desire for an erotic relationship.

Bolt

V: The bolt on a door cautions you not to reveal the

secrets of other people—the result would be nothing but trouble and frustration. Locking a door with a bolt: you have been too gullible in your dealings with others—now is the time to change!

D: See **Key.**

Bomb

V: Witnessing an assassination attempt on a person of authority: you might be able to avoid (unknown) danger; or the danger has past. Seeing a bomb explode warns you not to act violently or aggressively. Throwing a bomb at somebody means hostility and aggression initiated by others or by yourself. Seeing a bomb on the ground means sudden and unfavorable events.

D: The bomb, more than anything else, is a symbol of impending danger where emotions are out of control or where you are gripped by fear. If repressed **Aggression** is the reason, try to prevent the **Explosion** as quickly as you can. This dream has to be taken seriously!

Bones

V: Looking at one or more bones: hard times are ahead—you are going to be "working your fingers to the bone." Chewing on a bone: you might lose your job; it also means real worries that there won't be enough to eat because of a lack of money. Throwing a bone to a dog: you are worried about someone and are actively helping that person—but your reward will be ingratitude. See **Skeleton.**

D: The bone is a warning about becoming hard and emotionally "fossilized." The dream also suggests being less rigid, not holding on so fiercely to old attitudes or social norms.

Bonus

D: Receiving a bonus; a reward for insights you have

gained due to your own efforts. Not very often, it is also the sign of a need to feel superior—or the fear of being inferior.

Book, Book Title

S: A book in a dream could be the "book of your life."

V: Sitting in the middle of a lot of books or being in a huge library indicates the fear of being stretched too thin intellectually, or living with too much stress. Buying a book means interesting news is on the way that will serve you and others well. Reading a book: you are creating something new from your experiences, memories, and insights. Reading a serious book: you are gaining wisdom. Writing a book: you are dissatisfied with your present professional situation; you would like to rewrite "the script of your life." See **Library.**

D: Books and book titles are metaphors for what is happening inside you. Main motifs or titles usually mirror your emotional situation. Or the book itself may hold many of your life's experiences, memories, and insights. Dreams about book titles contain messages that are particularly meaningful (analyze the title).

Border

D: A border always stands for the parts of your nature that play a secondary role in your everyday life. The dream might also indicate that you have reached or are defining your boundaries. See **Fence.**

Boss, Chief

V: Dreaming about your boss: expect something unpleasant in the near future. Having an argument with your boss: problems at work; you feel insecure and afraid you are going to lose your job. Shaking hands with your boss: you will change jobs. Receiving a gift from your boss might mean a loss or a change of job.

D: Dreaming about your boss usually means you're worried about problems at work or afraid of losing your livelihood.

Bottle

V: Looking at one or several full bottles means fun or an invitation. Empty bottles are a warning about an unpleasant event, or that you are at a disadvantage. A broken bottle or breaking a bottle means bad news. A full bottle of red wine is a good sign, promising prosperity.

D: A bottle is sometimes a symbol for sexual cravings, but it also indicates that personal and professional possibilities may be limited. Do you feel like an (empty) vessel? Did others imply that you are? Did you make a mistake, miss something? Do you have a tendency to put yourself down? Do others put you down?

Bouquet

V: Seeing a bouquet of flowers: you have good friends who will always stand by you. Being given a bouquet of flowers: someone is admiring you. Losing or leaving a bouquet somewhere: your love is not returned.

D: See **Flowers.**

Bowl (Serving)

V: A bowl filled with food is a warning: if you want to avoid hard times in the future be more frugal now and take better care of your belongings. An empty bowl means you are worried about the future, and you are waiting for an invitation that is never going to come. See **Vessel.**

Bowl (Small)

S: A small bowl is a symbol of abundance. It holds the essence of eternity.

V: Holding a bowl in your hands: someone will make an offer soon. Receiving a bowl as a gift: a happy family life. Seeing a full bowl: expect either an invitation or the visit of a friend. See **Armor, Container.**

D: An empty bowl: step back and think—is it time to replenish your depleted inner resources?

Bowling Pin, Bowling

V: If you see yourself or others bowling: avoid risky professional or business ventures in the near future—you could suffer great losses. Throwing a strike: you had courage and took part in a risky venture that was successful—but only at the last minute.

D: Bowling stands for the streak of luck we all hope for. But the dream is usually a warning: curtail your risk-taking habits. If you throw a strike: be bold and make a quick decision. See **Ball.**

Box (Small)

V: Looking at a box: you are wasting too much time grieving for the loss of your youth, and by doing that you are missing the advantages that are part of getting older. Holding a box in your hand: stop for a minute and think about whether—in the future—it will be worth sacrificing yourself for your relatives and friends. Seeing an open box: be careful, someone wants to steal from you. Somebody giving you a box: expect a pleasant surprise in the near future. See **Box, Crate (Large), Package.**

Box, Crate (Large)

V: Looking at a closed box: others are keeping secrets. Does the box have a lock and is there a key in the lock? If so: you are bent on finding out about other people's secrets. Looking at a box: you are either getting a present or will have a pleasant experience. An empty box is a warning: you are going to lose something or somebody is stealing from you.

D: A box is the hiding place for our secrets and experiences (as well as memories). Why don't you open the box and see what you find? See **Box (Small), Suitcase.**

Boy Scout

V: Seeing a Boy Scout: a warning to stay on the right path. If you are the Boy Scout: you are able to find happiness in secret places and need to keep it to yourself.

D: You are either looking for instructions for the future, or the Boy Scout is warning you to stay on the right path. See **Path.**

Bracelet

V: Wearing a bracelet: you will meet a good friend. Losing a bracelet: give up any hope of a romance with a certain person because the relationship will soon end. Receiving a bracelet as a gift: be aware of jealousy or too much passion. Giving a bracelet as a gift: good luck is in store for you. Wearing a beautiful bracelet: wealth is on the horizon. Seeing bracelets worn by others: you are spending too much money.

D: When dreaming about beautifully adorned bracelets, see **Jewelry.**

Braid

Braiding your hair: you have lost your senses in a romantic situation. Cutting off your braids: you want to get rid of bothersome habits—do it! Seeing a braid: you don't have the courage to try something new; you are holding on to antiquated ways.

D: You are hung up on the past, which keeps you from reevaluating things. This "old rope" needs to be cut off!

Brain

D: Dreaming about the most important organ of the human body is either a challenge to make better use of your intellect or a warning: don't make every decision with your head only. You know which is true in your case!

Braking

V: Dreaming about using the brakes (in a car) suggests that you quickly withdraw from a certain matter or deal with dangerous consequences. Putting on the brakes also means to stop immediately something you have initiated.

Branch

A branch (peace, olive, laurel) is used to honor a winner.

V: A green branch: your hopes will come true—you will successfully complete a project. Dry branch: your past still haunts you; or you are holding on to things from the distant past and your hopes are dashed. See **Tree, Tree Limb.**

D: Green, healthy branches symbolize your positive character traits or life experiences; dry branches are a sign of lost hopes, ideals, past experiences, and negative character traits that you have worked through.

Brawl, Brawling

V: Watching a brawl or participating in one: don't get involved in other people's business. You'll only end up getting the short end of the stick.

D: See **Beatings, Fighting.**

Bread

S: Bread represents essential human nourishment in every culture.

V: Seeing fresh-baked bread: a sure sign of good luck—and possibly good friends visiting. Watching others eat bread:

you envy other people. If you are baking bread: your efforts will be successful. Eating stale or hard bread means great difficulties need to be overcome. Offering bread to others: you are looking for a good friend. See **Baking.**

D: Bread is an everyday item, but it is also holy. It is always a symbol of "the food of life" and may be spiritual (Christian Holy Communion) or simply a wish for more social contact and more friends.

Break (as in "take a break")

D: Either you need a vacation or the dream is a sign that you no longer are finding the time for personal growth.

Breast, Chest

S: In a man's dream, a breast is an erotic symbol, but it also shows a strong need for tenderness and being connected.

V: Looking at the beautiful breast of a woman: good luck and a joyful love life. An emaciated breast: poverty and misery. Having hair on your chest: a positive sign—soon your financial situation will improve. Holding a **Baby** to your breast: a sure sign of homesickness; or simply that you have much empathy for another person. Watching a baby nursing on its mother's breast: much good luck in all your personal affairs. Having a large breast: prosperity is on the rise.

D: The breast usually expresses sexual desires, but also a need for love, safety, and security. If you frequently dream of cuddling against somebody's breast, you may be afraid of taking life into your own hands and seek to escape back to that protected state.

Brick, Shingles

V: Working with bricks: start putting your building or remodeling plans into action or make use of your intellectual talents.

D: Owning a lot of bricks: your future is secure. Looking at roof tiles or shingles: you are looking for safety and security (physically as well as emotionally). See **Clay, House, Roof.**

Bride/Groom

V: Seeing a bride in a dream is always a good sign and means something pleasant is coming your way. If a woman sees herself as a bride or with a bridal veil, it means positive developments in the romance department—maybe even marriage. A man embracing a bride: a warning to him about a foolish love affair.

D: Leaving out the fact that the appearance of a bride in a dream is a sign of your need and desire for love, it also can mean that the contradictions in your personality are now in harmony. Sometimes, in a religious sense, a groom stands for God, and a bride for the Virgin Mary.

Bridge

S: The bridge in a dream connects contradictions in your emotions and actions.

V: Crossing a bridge means reaching a new "shore" on your life's journey, changes for the better, and leaving behind old problems; also advancement in your private and professional life. A broken down bridge or going down with a bridge that is falling: a project will end in failure and a streak of bad luck—which you are partially responsible for. Seeing a number of bridges: frustration and anger. Walking across an old bridge in poor repair: overcoming danger at the last minute. Walking across a very long bridge: your future will be filled with many adventures.

D: A bridge is a sign of an emotional transition. It is usually a good omen—if the bridge does not break down. A bridge usually indicates that you will solve your problems and that contradictory opinions can be "bridged." You are on the way to new shores.

Briefcase

V: Seeing a briefcase means that someone has enough trust to share a secret with you. Losing your briefcase: all your secrets are being unveiled. Finding a briefcase with money inside: you would like to have money without working for it. Somebody stealing your briefcase: a warning to watch out for false friends. See **Purse.**

D: A briefcase is a symbol of your professional/business life.

Brook

V: Dreaming about a calm, slow-moving brook is a sign of good health, good luck, and success. Turbulent water moving fast: you are restless and stressed. Seeing a brook winding its way through a pasture: your life is complicated right now. Looking at a clear brook: your projects are going to move ahead without complications; you are peaceful, energetic, and able to concentrate. Fishing in a clear brook: you can count on increased financial rewards. Bathing in this brook: good fortune is coming your way because you are ready to accept it. This image is also a message: if you are ill, you are going to recover soon. Seeing, sitting, or walking along a brook where the water is murky: you will have to deal with worries and setbacks in the near future.

D: Water in any form is a symbol of the soul and of your life. The clearer the water, the greater the healing power of the soul. If the water is murky, try to find out what is "murky" in your life and work at cleansing your soul. The water flowing "within you" promises good fortune, success, and good health or misfortune and loss—depending on the state and direction in which the water is moving. See **River, Water.**

Broom

V: Seeing a broom: in future be more careful when dealing with others—you might run into some very unpleasant people. Sweeping with a broom tells you to take care of your responsibilities—or face losses. In a woman's dream, the broom might also be a phallic symbol.

D: The broom could be a warning about destructive attitudes or negative emotions—sweep out all spiritual and mental "garbage."

Brush

V: Using a brush to remove something from your **Clothes**: you are unconsciously longing for affection from a certain person. Seeing a brush is often a sign of frustration or ugly gossip in the near future. Buying a brush: other people envy you. Brushing/ polishing **Shoes**: Do other people treat you badly? Did somebody "step on your toes"? Seeing many brushes: arguments in the near future. Scrubbing the floor with a brush: you need to deal with problems; do you need to "get down on your knees" for some reason? See **Hair.**

Brush (Paint)

V: Looking at a brush: you are much too single-minded and naive in a certain matter. Painting with a brush: you have courage, adventurousness, and a creative mind. Painting with a small brush: don't let stupid remarks from others disrupt your plans. See **Painting.**

D: The brush represents strong erotic desires, but it may also mean that you are too simple-minded, or surrounded by simple-minded people.

Bucket

S: Carrying a bucket is always a symbol of efforts that will be rewarded.

V: Carrying empty buckets means disappointment. A full bucket means a sudden influx of money. If the water in the bucket is murky, it means worries and unpleasantness.

D: A bucket is a symbol of the "vessel of your life," and whatever is inside is a clear indication of the state of your life. Is the bucket filled with the proper substance? It is important to pay close attention to the rest of the dream.

Bud

V: Looking at a budding flower or leaf: the beginning of a love relationship.

D: A flower bud means feelings are "germinating" inside you. See **Flower, Germ, Sprout.**

Buddha

V: Seeing a Buddha or a statue of a Buddha means you are afraid of the influence someone has over you, but you are unable to escape it. A Buddha talking to you means an unexpected joyful event. Praying to a Buddha: you want to tell another person what is in your heart but lack the courage (make sure to do it first thing in the morning!).

D: The image of a Buddha in a dream means you are afraid of how the influence another person has over you affects you. It may also be that you are searching for spiritual or intellectual guidance. See **Guru.**

Bug

V: Seeing a bug: you have overbearing friends and need to let them go. Getting bitten by a bug: you can't get away from annoying people. See **Fleas, Lice.**

D: Is your nervous system in trouble? If not, the dream tells you to treat people that bug you like small irritations (or annoying insects). They are not worth your energy—let them go! See **Vermin.**

Building (as in building a house)

S: This symbol stands for building and expanding your life.

V + D: Building something—no matter how big or tall—using a lot of materials, is a good sign, because your plans will be successful. However, if you are adding on to an existing house that is in bad shape or falling down (the roof is caving in): a warning that plans or decisions you have made recently are going to hurt you or result in losses. In a woman's dreams, the house is always a symbol of her body. The roof stands for the head; doors and windows for the sexual organs; the ground floor and first floor for internal organs; the feet for the basement). Seeing a basement, for instance, might indicate poor circulation in the feet.

Bumblebee

V: Seeing bumblebees flying around means that you are wasting your time with absolutely unimportant matters. See **Bee.**

Burden

V: Carrying a great burden: you are going through a difficult time, but you are strong and up to the challenge. Throwing a burden off your back: you have enough strength to find a solution to an old problem. Watching others carry a burden: you are managing a difficult job at the moment.

D: A burden is the symbol of a responsibility that has become burdensome. Can you free yourself from it? See **Log.**

Burglar

V: In a woman's dream, a burglar shows what she wants to "steal" from life—maybe a few romantic adventures? Maybe a few hours of relaxation? The dream is an indication you want to get something on the sly, something you can't get openly. Are you doing this often? Handing a burglar over to the police: you might win in court or get a reward for something. See **Thief.**

D: The burglar is a shadowy figure threatening your emotional health. Do you have a bad conscience? Are you afraid (particularly if you are a woman) of sexual intercourse? Do you have secret desires for a sexual adventure?

Burglary

V: Dreaming that your house has been robbed always means that you are violating your body, which affects your vitality and health. Witnessing a robbery: expect an unpleasant surprise. It also suggests you let go of the old and follow a new course. In a woman's dream, a robbery often suggests a love affair. See **Robbery.**

Burial

V: Watching something being buried: unconsciously you mistrust God and the world. Dreaming about being buried: too much is "piling up" on you; get "out from under"—one step at a time—and start over again. See **Earth.**

D: Are you hiding from the outside world? The dream usually is a sign that you don't want to admit bad habits to yourself. Sometimes the dream means that you want to bury negative experiences, but that is not a solution! Dig everything up again and deal with it. See **Cave, Grave, Tomb.**

Burning

V: Seeing the top of a house, the roof, in flames (above you): a warning of impending danger. Walking toward a house where the roof is on fire: it is better to retreat in a present situation. (Sometimes the dream also signals a sinus infection in the making). Seeing smoke coming from a chimney: your affairs are taking a turn for the better. Standing in front of a (brightly burning) fire: success.

D: Fire and water always symbolize emotional energy. Fire is cleansing. Seeing bright flames means new ideas.

Burr

V: Seeing burrs in your dream: avoid being too close to your friends. You are irritated by burrs: don't let others take advantage of you and stay away from those who do.

D: Your unconscious is telling you to withdraw from unpleasant people (that stick to you like a burr) as soon as possible. But—are *you* sticking to someone like a burr?

Bus

V: The bus means that determination and ambition are the forces behind a need for advancement at work, particularly in a man's dream. Riding on a bus: being satisfied but still too hung up on old points of view. Riding in a bus that's going in the wrong direction: you are isolating too much.

D: See **Auto, Train, Trip, Truck.**

Bush

V: Seeing somebody behind a bush: be careful about people who gossip. If the bush is full of green leaves: good news and great joy in your house. Looking at a bush that is leafless, brittle, and bare: a plan of yours is condemned to failure and can't be revived. See **Leaf.**

D: A bush is a symbol much like that of a **Tree**, even though it is much smaller.

Businessman

V: Seeing or dealing with a businessman: your chances of winning are improving. If you are the businessman, you would like to go into business for yourself. If you are dating a businessman: an important conference in the near future.

D: The businessman is a symbol of your material outlook as well as financial—or intellectual—accomplishments. Sometimes such a dream might also be a warning that you are too egotistical and materialistic. What or whom do you want "to buy"?

Butcher

V: Dreaming about a butcher: pay more attention to your own behavior and do something about your negative habits. Watching a butcher at work: get away from "cold hearted" people. See **Battle.**

D: Aggressive (repressed) tendencies are coming to the fore; or you are afraid of other people's aggressive action. The dream about a butcher is usually a general warning about some perceived danger. Examine the rest of the dream symbols.

Butchering

V: Butchering an animal means financial success in a certain matter, but you could lose your reputation in the process. This dream is challenging you to examine your motives and decisions!

Butter

V: Fresh and delicious butter: everything is "in balance," Old, rancid butter: slander, intrigue, and hypocrisy. Eating butter means good health. Making your own butter: you want and need more love and tenderness in your life.

D: Sometimes, dreaming about butter is a sign of real worries, like: "will I have enough to eat every day?" The dream may also be a symbol of unacknowledged sexual needs. Or have you discovered the real reason why other people flatter you? See **Cream.**

Butterfly

S: The butterfly is a symbol of the immortal soul that leaves the body at the moment of death. It also represents infidelity, and being fickle and inconsistent—particularly in love relationships. Acting badly, being vain, or unfaithful are also connected with the butterfly symbol and are sure to bring disappointment.

V: Catching a butterfly: while you are happy right now, it may be for only a short time. Seeing a butterfly: either your partner is unfaithful or a friend will become fickle.

D: The butterfly can be a sign that you are going through an inner change—like the caterpillar becoming a butterfly. Make sure that the change is positive, even if the beginning (the caterpillar) was ugly.

Button

V: Losing a button: you are either really losing something or somebody is stealing from you. Sewing a button back on: things at your job are going to improve. Tearing off a button: be prepared for conflict.

D: The button is a sign that your life is becoming more stable. A lost button indicates imagined or real unfaithfulness (your own or your partner's).

S = SYMBOL V = VISION D = DEPTH PSYCHOLOGY

Café

V: Sitting in a café: a sign that you can't do anything at the present time. It is important to know what you are doing while in the café. Are you eating a piece of **Cake**? Are you drinking **Coffee**?

D: The café means that self-knowledge is easier to attain if you take a short break; or you are resting before starting something new.

Cabin

V: Looking at a cabin: you are very patient even when things don't go well. Walking into a cabin: you are looking for protection from the harsh responsibilities of life. If you are living in a very simple cabin: you are going to move into a better home.

D: A cabin is a reminder to be frugal. Providing you are not making exaggerated demands and have no unrealistic expectations, you might well consider yourself a lucky person!

Cactus

V: Looking at a cactus: you are isolating too much from people around you; you have become very "prickly." Getting punctured by a cactus: thoughtless actions on your part will cause you harm. Watering a cactus: you are much too nice to people who don't deserve it—they are "false friends." Looking at a small cactus on a windowsill: you are too stingy—with yourself and others.

D: The cactus stands for the injuries that others have inflicted on you or for disappointments caused by false friends. It might also be symbolic of your own "prickliness." See **Porcupine.**

Cadaver

V: Seeing a carcass in a rotting state can evoke disgust, dislike, or grief. Either an event provoking such a response is going to happen soon, or the dream is suggesting that letting go of a situation or a person is long overdue. Dragging a dead corpse in a suitcase: you are still carrying around things from the past—things that "died a long time ago," or your conscience is bothering you. Looking at a dead body: old problems will be solved successfully. The dream also suggests that a wedding or birth is imminent. Seeing yourself as the cadaver: a great burden has been lifted, you will live to a ripe old age. See **Skeleton.**

D: A cadaver represents past issues that need to be dealt with. The corpse you're rigidly holding onto may be old conventions. Have your feelings for another person turned "cold"? Are you afraid of **Death**? Do you wish that someone else were dead? A rotten cadaver—in the context of other images in the dream—indicates that a current situation is at a "dead end," but that something new will come along.

Cafeteria

V: Being a waiter or waitress in a cafeteria: you are surrounded by unsavory people; find new friends. You are the customer: a friend is having trouble—or needs help. See **Café.**

D: A cafeteria is a sign that you would like to have more

friends. How about inviting some people you like to your house?

Cage

V: Dreaming about a cage: be prepared for an unpleasant situation. Being in a cage: you feel imprisoned (by your surroundings, job, or marriage) and would like to "break out." A bird in a cage: a situation, unfavorable at the outset, is going to take a turn for the better.

D: A cage always stands for the limitations imposed on you by your upbringing, your surroundings, or by the compromises you have made. The rules you have established are too rigid. Try to break out of these restrictions. The cage is limiting your personal growth! Did you put yourself in the cage? Did someone else "lock you up"? See **Prison.**

Cake

V: You are baking a cake: you have a tendency to overindulge—this weakness needs to be reined in. Eating or looking at a cake: company is coming.

D: The cake has a meaning similar to that of **Bread**—only in a more refined form.

Calendar

V: Seeing a calendar means unpleasant surprises. Throwing out a calendar: after much worry and problems your situation is finally improving. Buying a new calendar: many friends will come to visit.

D: The calendar stands for how you use and plan your time and live your life.

Calf

V: Watching one or several calves playing is a warning: you are in the mood to do mischief. Feeding a calf: you are too generous toward the wrong people. Seeing a calf standing next to its mother: you are afraid to act independently, which limits your life; you depend too much on others or look to them for leadership. Watching a calf being slaughtered: a specific task is going to turn out badly. Dancing around a "golden calf": you are too focused on material goods and luxuries, Searching for a deeper meaning to your life would be very good for you.

D: The calf usually represents superficial amusement, a carefree, frivolous attitude. Pay more attention to personal growth and maturity and, most of all, independence.

Call, Calling

V: Hearing someone call: you will be asked to do an important task or you will be given an order. Make sure that your antenna points in the right direction so you won't miss anything—it could be important! Someone calling your name: either a distant friend is in need of help or it is a warning of impending danger.

D: Your own unconscious is calling for attention! It either wants to give advice or a warning of danger to come. Try to find the meaning of the dream—it could give you very helpful advice.

Camel

S: The camel stands for modesty and moderation.

V: Seeing a camel means anger and frustration, because problems you thought were solved are back. Seeing camels loaded with merchandise: a reward for your efforts and caring. Buying or riding on a camel: you would like others to take care of your responsibilities.

D: The camel represents patience, perseverance, and stamina. Are you the camel—trying to lighten the load? While it may make it easier to get through rough times, don't overdo it.

Camera

D: The camera stands for your memory and experiences that are stored on "the film of your unconscious." See **Picture.**

Canal

V: Dreaming about a canal: a business affair that is not quite above board might cause problems. Participating in the construction of a canal: the chances for your future are very good. Seeing ships moving in the canal: you might make new contacts or take a trip abroad.

D: The canal is a sign of your ability to consciously manage your cravings and passions, transforming them into intellectual or material goals.

Candle

S: The candle is a symbol of light—representing a connection between spirit and matter.

V: A brightly burning candle is a promise: in future things will turn out the way you have hoped. It could also mean an invitation to a party. The flame of the candle flickering or giving off smoke: the state of your health is not stable. A candle burning quietly and steadily is a sign of peace, prayer, contemplation, and a challenge to look within. Watching the flame of a candle go out: you may suddenly be informed of the illness or death of a person close to you, or it could mean that a close friendship is coming to an end.

D: The candle is a phallic symbol. Is there a flame of passion burning within you for another person? The candle also gives us light and warmth and expresses your desire for greater understanding, enlightenment, or wisdom. See **Light.**

Candlestick

S: A candlestick symbolizes spiritual enlightenment, life, and salvation.

V: A candlestick with burning candles indicates a happy love relationship, and perhaps a beautiful party ahead. See **Lamp, Light.**

Cannibal

D: The cannibal is the part of your personality that makes no effort to get somewhere on its own but wants to use others to do it. Unmask this freeloader and throw it out!

Cannon

V: Seeing cannons in a dream: either a lot of arguments or a deception will make life difficult for you. A cannon being fired: you have to face a highly unpleasant situation; be careful so you can avoid an accident. Hearing the sound of cannon shots: good news. Seeing a cannon ball: getting out of a dangerous situation. See **Ball.**

D: The cannon is a symbol of male aggression and reckless sexual passions. In a woman's dream, it means fear of sexual aggression or a sign that she lets her partner control and humiliate her. See **Weapon.**

Canoe Paddle, Paddling

D: A canoe paddle represents the energy with which you move through life—your desires, hopes, ideals, and even cravings. Are you paddling in place, or can you already see your goal? See **Boat, Rowing.**

Cans, Canned Food

V: Eating canned food: you seemed to be satisfied keeping mediocre company or sticking with a stale love affair, because you don't think you'll find anything better.

D: Canned food is a symbol of laziness or timidity that makes you hold onto old habits or relationships, which in reality are only holding you back. You are living "out of a can"!

Captain

V: Seeing or being a captain stands for the inner teacher (your true self) who is the guide of your life.

D: The captain is you—a symbol of the strength and talents that guide you safely through life. If the captain appears in your dreams frequently, it indicates a secret desire to exercise power and authority over others.

Caravan

V: A caravan stands for travels to unknown and faraway territories in the soul. It is also an indication that your travels through life will be calm. See **Camel.**

Carnation

S: The carnation represents passion and is seen in many pictures of Madonnas.

V: Dreaming about carnations: your love life is in excellent shape and your opportunities at work are good. In a man's dream, the image of the carnation—and flowers in general—often refer to women who can be bought. Maybe he is hoping for such an adventure—a desire he can only admit to himself through flowers. Picking a carnation: thoughtless actions on your part will create a crisis with a friend. Looking at a wilted carnation: a close relationship will come to an end.

D: The carnation is usually a symbol for the connection you have to other people. The color of the carnation is important. See the chapter **"Color in Dreams."**

Carp

V: Seeing one or several carps is a good sign, suggesting

that you might win something of substance, or substantially improve your overall situation. See **Fish.**

Carpet, Rug

V: Seeing a carpet is a warning: you will only be successful if you work diligently, improving your skills and talents. Cleaning a carpet: you will get an annoying visitor. A colorful carpet: your life will be exciting—no time for boredom.

D: The rug's intricate design is a mirror of your life. A valuable rug might also be a sign of arrogance or ambitions. Do you want to "sweep something under the rug"?

Cart

D: Your dream-cart holds all the worries, responsibilities, and conflicts you carry with you every day of your life. If the cart is heavy, unload some of your emotional baggage! If the cart is stuck in the mud, it is high time to reexamine the responsibilities you have taken on. Pay attention to other symbols in the dream.

Castle

V: Looking at a castle: you have too much imagination and unrealistic dreams—a recipe for disappointment. Living in a castle: "pride goes before a fall." Being a guest in a castle: you will meet a distinguished, influential person.

D: The castle is a warning of being too vain and ambitious. See **Fortress, Palace.**

Castration

D: Castration in men's dreams is a symbol of suppressed feelings and needs. You are plagued by feelings of guilt and inferiority; also you are afraid of not performing well enough sexually and being rejected. If these dreams appear frequently, you might consider seeking professional help. A woman dreaming about the castration of a man, a cat, or any other animal, usually indicates feelings of aversion toward male sexuality. Be honest: do you really want to castrate him?

Cat

D: In Egypt, the cat was the symbol of the goddess Bastet, but it also was related to the demonic.

V: Seeing a white cat: you feel great affection for someone. Seeing a two-colored cat: your feelings are passionate. A black cat: always a warning of impending danger. Seeing several cats: be careful, your lover is unfaithful. Dreaming about wild cats: you will have a fight with your neighbors.

D: The cat is, on one hand, a symbol of female sexuality, and on the other hand the essence of deceit. In the dream of a man, the cat stands for his present love life: he has—or would like to have—an intimate relationship with a woman, but a misstep on his side or hers is also part of the picture. A tomcat in a dream suggests male aggression, together with extreme sexual cravings and frequently changing love partners. See **Animal**. Seeing the claws of a cat indicates that either you have suffered emotional harm or you have injured someone else!

Caterpillar

V: Seeing a caterpillar: new possibilities will open up—pay attention but be cautious. Watching several caterpillars: some people don't have your best interests at heart, but be very careful. Things are turning out to be very different from what you expected. Catching or killing a caterpillar: your distrust in another person is justified—as you will soon find out.

D: You—or people around you—have hidden talents that will emerge later. The caterpillar can also point to physical cravings, because it is "blind to the intellectual and spiritual dimension."

Cave

V: Crawling into a cave: being overwhelmed by a present situation. Living in a cave: you have become unpopular. Digging a cave: a death in your family or circle of friends. Coming out of a dark cave back into the light: a long period of deprivation (unemployment, etc.) is slowly coming to an end; your economic situation is improving.

D: See **Grotto, Ditch, Tomb.**

Celery

V: Eating celery means you can look forward to many promising romantic experiences. See **Vegetable.**

Cellar

D: The cellar represents the place where all our memories, experiences, and our emotional garbage are stored. Dreaming about a cellar is a sign that we want to forget it, not think about any of it. However, our behavior and actions are still influenced by those energies. This "cellar" can be the source of strength as well as anguish. It is the depository of such emotions as hate, anger, fear, cravings, etc. The dream is challenging you to "clean out your basement"—to look at issues from the past that interfere with your life. This dream symbol appears frequently and taking the advice it gives is not easy—after all "cleaning the basement" is a dirty job! See **Basement, Cave, Grotto, Tomb.**

Cemetery

V: Women who dream frequently about walking through a cemetery have nothing to be frightened about. It only means they need more peace and quiet—the job, children, and the house are taking their toll. Lingering about the cemetery: you are hanging on to the past. Walking into a cemetery: you are too preoccupied with past experiences. Do you want to bury something so that you can start all over again? Bringing flowers to a cemetery: a death in the family.

D: The cemetery indicates anxiety caused by new or past problems, because you are forced to make a decision. See **Death, Grave.**

Ceremony

V: Taking part in a ceremony: you are taking your professional responsibilities seriously. See **Ritual.**

D: A ceremony is a mirror of behaviors and attitudes that give your life structure. Rituals sustain you.

Chaff

D: Separating the important from the unimportant (the wheat from the chaff): you are doing unimportant things. Don't take things or situations too seriously. See **Sieve.**

Chain

S: The chain is a symbol of the connection between heaven and earth, between two extremes, or between two living beings.

V: Seeing a person with a chain: you are unconsciously still chained to another person and are looking to break free. Being chained yourself: your way to freedom is going to be difficult. The dream is also a call to finally let go of the past. If you are pulling a chain apart: you will have the strength to free yourself from a confining relationship. If you hear the sound of chains: you will receive news that will negatively affect your future.

D: The chain represents either a burden you are still "chained" to, or of feelings and opinions that "chain" you to certain people, social norms, or beliefs that have become a burden to you. See **Shackles.**

Chair

V: The chair is a symbol of your social and professional position or an indication of your unconscious view of your standing in the community. The rest of the dream and your present situation in real life are also important. See **Furniture, Chair (Upholstered).**

Chair (Upholstered)

V: Dreaming about an upholstered chair: chances for a pay increase or a promotion at work are good. Seeing a worn-out chair: troubles and worries will spoil your happiness—particularly in your personal life. Sleeping in an upholstered chair means a present illness is taking longer to heal than you were hoping.

D: See **Furniture, Chair, Sofa.**

Chalice

V: Seeing a chalice: great sorrow ahead. Drinking from a chalice: joy and calm waters are yours right now. Breaking a chalice: bad news will spoil your fun.

D: The chalice symbolizes the "vessel of your soul," where all your emotions, hopes, and desires reside and of which you are only partly aware. It also is representative of the relationship you have with your feminine side and your mother. Often the chalice stands for the "cup of sorrow." See **Cup, Container.**

Chameleon

D: The animal is a symbol of you—being too flexible—which might easily turn into indecision and fickleness. Stop watching "how the wind is blowing" and develop more self-awareness and inner strength.

Chamomile

V: Dreaming about chamomile: you are about to get a

cold. Collecting chamomile in the garden: you will get sick but recover soon. Applying a chamomile poultice: your pain will soon be lessened.

Champagne

V: Seeing a glass/bottle of champagne means good fortune, even if small and short-lived. Drinking a glass of champagne by yourself: you are getting very little understanding from the people around you; you want more affection and tenderness. Breaking a bottle of champagne: an exciting event is imminent. Drinking champagne in the company of others: new experiences. The dream might also be a sign that you want exciting sexual encounters.

D: This bubbling drink may either be a symbol of overwhelming sexual needs that you can't control much longer—or a sign of your rebellion against social norms. In most cases, however, champagne expresses your need for happy companionship. See **Alcohol.**

Chapel

V: Seeing or being inside a chapel: you are not only enjoying inner peace and a place for reflection—but also God's guidance.

D: The chapel reflects your need for solitude and contemplation. This is the right time for religious reflection and the search for a higher power. See **Church.**

Charity

D: Receiving charitable gifts: help is coming from an unexpected source; also a long-awaited wish is being granted. Giving charitable gifts to others: financial matters are looking good for the foreseeable future; you want to give somebody a gift or be helpful. However, if you are well-to-do:

doling out money means your financial situation will deteriorate.

D: Receiving charity means you are afraid you can't make it on your own and will become a burden to others or be forced to beg.

Check

V: Writing a check: don't make promises you can't keep. Seeing or receiving a check: a promise made to you is probably not going to last. See **Bank, Money.**

D: Do not make promises you can't keep. Have others made promises to you lately?

Check (Restaurant)

V: Paying the check: don't take on responsibilities you can't fulfill. See **Debts, Money.**

D: See **Bill, Cafe, Proprietor, Restaurant.**

Cherries, Cherry Tree

V: Dreaming about cherries is a sign that your sexual needs are getting stronger. Picking or eating cherries: your desires are being fulfilled—even if in a superficial way. Eating sour cherries: experiencing disappointments in love. Rotten cherries: someone is slandering you. Seeing a cherry tree in bloom: happiness and good fortune. Climbing a cherry tree: you are starting a short-lived love affair. Falling out of a cherry tree: a happy adventure ends in disappointment.

D: Sweet fruits, like cherries, usually represent erotic feelings. The cherry tree stands for a disappointing love affair. See **Fruit, Tree.**

Chess

V: If you or someone else is playing chess: think carefully before you act. Try to increase your knowledge and then use it! Winning a chess game: your partner has given you an opening that you either haven't noticed or that you saw and did not act upon. Losing a chess game: your partner's intelligence could help you to achieve great success. See **Game.**

D: This game is a reminder to use more of your good sense and take advantage of the opportunities ("openings") coming your way.

Chestnut

V: Dreaming of picking chestnuts off the ground: you have enough ingenuity to make your lover believe that life without you would be unthinkable. Looking at chestnuts: you will either win big or conclude a profitable business transaction. Eating chestnuts means you have a chance to be successful. Sitting under a chestnut tree: after a difficult period, life is finally fun again and you are happy.

D: Who is "pulling the chestnuts out of the fire" here? Will it be to your advantage or does it serve someone else? Are others helping you?

Chick

V: Feeding a chick means a happy family life, because family members help each other. Eating a chick: melancholia is interfering with your sense of fun. Killing a chick: you are unfairly accusing an innocent person. See **Hen.**

D: The chick in your dream is a sign of your anxieties: you either think you are worth less than others (which is wrong), or you are playing the martyr. It is time to make some changes!

Chicken, Hen

V: Dreaming about chickens means good times are just around the corner. Seeing several chickens: don't waste so much time with pleasantries and idle talk. Plucking a chicken: you are not properly compensated for your work. Eating a chicken: your efforts on the job are going to be rewarded. Trying to catch and/or chasing one or more chickens—particularly in men's dreams: a warning about constantly chasing short-term love affairs—none of which provides satisfaction. You are watching a hen laying eggs: expect to receive money soon; sometimes it also means a new member is added to the family. Watching a hen sitting on eggs: your wishes will come true. Seeing one or more chicks means you are going to be blessed with children, many grandchildren, or a big family in general. Killing a chicken: your carelessness will bring you harm. See **Rooster.**

Child, Childhood

S: The child is a symbol of receiving unconditionally.

V: Watching healthy children at play: success and good times. Crying, screaming, and sick children, children that are falling down or undernourished, are all a sign of worries ahead. Giving birth to a child: a new job is opening up. If the child is being baptized: you are returning to your religious faith. Seeing a sleeping child: your future will be free of worries. When a child appears in a woman's dream, it usually means that she wants a child. The dream may also indicate that new plans, your job, or other changes are emotionally taxing. If the child appears time and time again, think about making some changes.

D: The child represents actual conflict situations that have become burdensome, and you are looking for a solution, a way out. This dream also means you want to "start over again" or avoid making a decision by going back home (being protected as a child). Dreams about childhood are usually an indication that you are trying to avoid responsibilities; but they may also be an expression of child-like character traits, or your dependency on others! If you dream about children frequently, make an appointment with a psychotherapist soon.

Chimney

V: Seeing a chimney or smoke stack: success and the promise of making money. If you are in love, your love is being reciprocated, and good luck is coming into your house. If the soot from the chimney is getting you dirty, don't expect your secret love affair to be a secret much longer. Seeing a chimney sweep at work: good luck, and a promise that your private and professional life will change for the better. Running into a chimney sweep and getting soot on your clothes: your love affair won't remain a secret any longer. See **Chimney Sweep, Fireplace, Soot.**

Chimney Sweep

V: The chimney sweep is not only a symbol of good luck in real life, but also in dreams.

D: A chimney sweep is a messenger who promises good fortune and success. See **Chimney, Fireplace, Soot.**

China, Tableware

V: Single people seeing china in a dream means they are soon to be married. Breaking dishes: expect family quarrels or unhappiness. Buying new china: your family or household will "expand." Dirty dishes mean family problems.

D: Tableware is usually a symbol of insecurity in dealings with other people or members of the family. Frequent dreams about breaking dishes means that—in real life—you are causing a lot of unnecessary trouble—or acting like "a bull in a china shop." See **Glass, Porcelain.**

Chives

V: A matter that seemed boring and unimportant is gaining in significance and beginning to look rather attractive. You are developing a taste for something. See **Herbs.**

Chocolate

V: Looking at chocolate: try to get your dependence on food under control. Receiving chocolate as a gift: you either have already or will gain a very reliable friend. Giving a gift of chocolate: you would like to have a certain someone as your friend.

D: Chocolate is a symbol of temptation, but it also stands for vitality and good health. Are you trying to bribe someone with chocolate? Is someone trying to bribe you?

Chocolate-covered Desserts

V: Eating chocolate-covered desserts means you love to exaggerate. Your imagination is running away with you! See **Chocolate.**

Christ

D: In a dream, Christ always stands for your own personality, for the wholeness you seek. The dream also suggests that you search for greater self-knowledge, new insights, new goals, all in the service of personal growth. In an indirect way, the image of Christ is like a **Guru**, there to help you discover your true self. The dream also indicates that you are living in harmony with yourself, your fate, the world, and that you are trusting in a higher power. A very profound dream!

Christmas, Christmas Tree

V + D: Celebrating Christmas: you can look forward to domestic tranquility and happy times with your family. A Christmas tree: expect a lot of joy and happiness.

Church

S: The church may represent many things: “a woman clothed in the sun,” the “bride of Christ,” “Noah’s ark,” “the ship,” “the vineyard,” “the net,” “the City of Heaven,” and more.

V: Walking into a church: do you have to make amends to someone? Watching a church cave in: you have lost your faith in God. Looking at a church: you will be kept from "going down the wrong path" or doing the wrong thing. Praying in Church: you will receive help from above, or a very important wish will be realized. See **Chapel, God.**

D: Dreaming about a church can be a sign that you are already emotionally mature or that maturity is still missing. It often indicates strong faith and, sometimes, your connection to others. The altar either expresses your spiritual strength or is a sign to make "higher spiritual aspirations" a greater part of your life. See **Altar.**

Church Bell, Ringing a Church Bell

V: If you hear a church bell ring: keep your eyes and ears open—you will get news that might be important and helpful. If you are ringing a bell: you will make someone very happy (without knowing it). See **Signal, Whistle.**

D: A bell always announces something—whether positive or negative depends on the rest of the images in the dream. Was it a happy or distressed sound?

Church Tower

V: Looking at a church tower from a distance: you are on the right path. Climbing a church tower: you are interested in your surroundings and your curiosity is creating new contacts. See **Church, Tower.**

Cider

V: Dreaming about cider is a warning about out-of-control appetites that run your life. Making cider: like a predator, you want to live out your fantasies by luring others into bingeing—but punishment is swift and the penalty high.

D: Cider is a sign of urges and passions "fermenting" inside you—but remember: cheap pleasures are usually followed by rude awakenings. See **Alcohol, Wine.**

Cigar

V: Smoking a cigar: be discreet right now in a certain matter and a business affair will be concluded successfully. See **Smoking, Tobacco.**

D: As a phallic symbol, the cigar is a sign of primitive sexual urges—and, at times, of masculinity as a whole.

Cigarette

D: See **Smoking.**

Circle

S: The circle is a symbol of completeness and symmetry.

V: Looking at a circle is a warning: "don't go around in circles" (you are only "chasing your own tail"). Standing inside a circle: your emotional energy is balanced and congruent; you could now reach a higher state of consciousness. Drawing a circle: you are involved in a situation that is going in circles and don't quite know how to extricate yourself.

D: Your personality is rounded and complete, but your thoughts are still going in circles, and that you can't see your way out of an actual problem. See **Cross, Crossroads, Ring.**

Circus

V: Seeing a circus: you are about to embarrass yourself. Watching a circus performance: beware—you might become involved in a very expensive enterprise.

D: You have special talents. Why are you still hiding them?

City

V: Seeing a small city: if your expectations are not too high, the outlook for your career is promising. Seeing a large city: life will become hectic and stressful. Seeing a city with many towers: you will have your own business in the near future.

D: The city often represents a desire for diversion. Are you looking for more companionship, contact with other people? Has your life become boring? Is there too little stimulation from the outside?

Civil Servant

V: Having to deal with one or several bureaucrats means worrisome times and problems are ahead. Giving money to a bureaucrat means financial or material losses. Fighting with a bureaucrat: a warning—conflicts or legal troubles are unavoidable.

Clam, Mussel, Oyster

S: The clam stands for the grave from which we will some day be resurrected; it is also represents fertility.

V: Looking at or finding clams: a pleasant, peaceful, and harmonious future (particularly for a female dreamer). Watching a clam being opened: a carefully protected secret is revealed or betrayed.

D: The clam, mussel, and oyster represent female sex organs, and the dream, therefore, expresses erotic desires (particularly in men's dreams). But the dream also suggests a rich emotional life and a vulnerability that is hidden inside hard shells. Maybe there is even a pearl hidden inside? See **Jewelry, Pearl**. Would you like to hide inside a mussel, or "clam up" and be silent? See **Crab.**

Clay

V: Looking at clay: progress in your personal affairs is possible only through sheer willpower and patience. You are stuck in a difficult situation. You need strength and energy to overcome the obstacles in your way. Working with clay: your position at work is secure. Building a house with clay: you are either establishing a household or enlarging the one you already have. Sculpting with clay: you have artistic talent or need to realize a creative project. You are "sculpting" your own destiny. See **Earth, Mud.**

D: Is your life built on a shaky foundation? Are you stuck in a difficult situation right now and don't know how to get out of it? Take heart: clay is pliable and can be shaped and made into many things! Clay may symbolize your body and your material needs.

Cleaning

V: Dreaming about cleaning: it is time to pay more attention to your relationships and to be more supportive. Cleaning and making yourself look better: be more humble and modest. Dreaming about cleaning is a challenge to always improve and polish your character, removing the stains that might cling to it.

D: Remove emotional, mental, and moral blemishes that are clogging up fragile spiritual connections. It is also important which objects are being cleaned or what is being "swept" out—pay attention to the rest of the images.

Cleaver

S: The cleaver is always a phallic symbol and expresses aggression (conscious or unconscious).

Cliff

V: Standing on a cliff: a difficult task is ahead and it can only be done by being very careful. Looking at a cliff at the seashore: hidden dangers and unconscious anxieties make a decision difficult. See **Mountain, Rock, Slope.**

Climbing

V: Dreaming about effortlessly climbing a ladder, stairs, or a hill means a successful conclusion of a project. If the climb takes a lot of effort or is difficult: many problems need to be overcome before you are rewarded for your efforts. Climbing a high mountain: difficult obligations in your life have to be concluded. In the case of men, this dream symbol often indicates fear of sexual dysfunction. Climbing a steep mountain with your intimate partner: you desire sexual climax.

D: This dream symbol is always seen as a form of spiritual renewal. If the dream has sexual connotations: you are longing to reach orgasm. The dream could also raise such questions as: are you climbing the social ladder? Do you find the climb difficult? What else do you see on your climb? See **Mountain, Rock.**

Clock

V: If the clock shows five minutes before noon: you are faced with an important decision—don't hesitate. If the large hand is moving quickly: you are dissatisfied with your life. Winding up a clock: you are starting a new phase in your life. Hearing a clock strike: you are faced with a life-changing decision. The clock has stopped: a relationship or situation is coming to an end.

D: The clock is a symbol of your fear that your life is going by too fast. Is it time to make an important decision? You will know what is best—what your situation requires.

Cloister

V: Seeing a cloister: you are emotionally confused. Don't

talk to others about it. Only solitude and silence will bring answers and relief. See **Hermit, Monk, Nun.**

D: A cloister stands for your idea of the "meaning of life." It is also a symbol of your faith, your trust in God, or your spiritual strength. See **Church.** Maybe you would like to pull back in order to renew your strength.

Closet

V: Seeing a closet: it's time to bring order into your personal and work affairs. An open closet is a warning: be more careful around people in your surroundings. A closed closet: be more accommodating and friendlier toward others.

D: The closet represents your body and its needs. Is your closet full and organized or empty? In case of the latter, you are either in need of more "emotional sustenance," or you need a rest so you can replenish your energies. See **Furniture.**

Clothes

V + D: Dreaming about clothes reveals how you see yourself. It might also be a sign of your need to hide from others (to disguise yourself). Different clothes have the following meaning:

Undershirt, slip: expresses your innermost, unconscious feelings.

Underpants, panties: your sexual needs, desires, and hopes.

Shirt or *blouse:* all feelings, cravings, or passions.

Pants or *skirt:* your erotic desires.

Coat: your "facade," how others react to you.

Shoes: your present situation, where you are at the moment.

Cloud

V: White clouds: for the time being things are pleasant and problem-free. Dark clouds: you have reason to worry, or something is bothering you—you are not having fun. A cloudburst: something unexpected is going to happen; someone is disappointing you.

D: See **Heaven, Weather.**

Cloudburst, Downpour

V: If you are surprised by a downpour: sudden difficulties will turn up—making life miserable. Soaked by a cloudburst: you have more luck than brains in a certain matter. Watching a downpour: good luck and maybe winning a large sum of money. See **Rain.**

D: A downpour announces unexpected good luck in a quandary that you could not have resolved with your head alone. That makes a cloudburst represent good luck—even if you get wet in the process.

Clover, Clover Leaf

S: The cloverleaf was a magical symbol for the Druids.

V + T: Looking at a cloverleaf is a sign that present problems will be solved and pleasant events will change your life. Seeing a four-leaf clover in a dream is also a sign of good luck!

Clown

V: Seeing a clown: sometimes you like making a fool of yourself, or you will do anything to be liked by others. The dream also indicates a fear of being ridiculed and points to a feeling of inferiority. You don't believe enough in yourself. If the clown appears frequently, consider visiting a psychotherapist. Meeting a clown is a good omen, meaning enjoyment and fun. It is also a sign that you will soon laugh about earlier problems, or that you are going to be able to solve present problems easily.

Club (Social)

V: Dreaming about belonging to a club: you would like more diversion and human contact. Maybe you shouldn't listen to others so much and take your life into your own hands.

Club (Weapon)

V: Holding a club in your hand: you will make a good decision. Hitting others with a club: you are trying to fight off your adversaries. If somebody is hitting you with a club: a friend is trying to thwart your efforts.

D: The club reflects your determination to use anything in your power to fight obstacles or adversity. You have made up your mind and nothing and nobody can keep you from carrying out what you're set on doing.

Coach, Coachman

V: Seeing a coach means a surprising increase in income. Driving a coach: you will reach your goal without difficulties. Getting in or out of a coach: a loss in the near future can be avoided only if you proceed with caution. If you are the coachman: your are making a fool of someone.

Coal

V: Handling coals is a good sign: you will be prosperous. Sitting on coals: you are waiting impatiently for something. Red-hot coals (in a fire): if the rest of the dream is positive, expect a happy event; if the dream is negative: you will feel deeply ashamed about something you did. See **Fire.**

D: Coals in a dream are a sign that you are using your experiences to gain insight and wisdom. See **Diamonds, Jewelry.** Coals may also stand for a desire for material things.

Coat

S: The coat is a symbol of protection.

V: Wearing a new coat: a new start in your life and your success at work. Wearing an old coat: your present situation is taking a turn for the worse. Tearing up a coat: you are angry and protesting against the hypocrisy and dishonesty around you.

D: A coat represents a disguise. Are you afraid that others will see through you? Is the coat supposed to keep you warm or protect you? Are you trying to hide something? See **Clothes.**

Coat of Arms

V: Seeing a coat of arms: look through old things, you will find a keepsake. Looking at a magnificent coat of arms: too much ambition can hurt and will make you unpopular. Dreaming about a stained coat of arms: you did something of which you are really ashamed.

D: The coat of arms is a symbol of your character and personality. It is a sign of what you have already achieved or want to try to achieve (if the coat of arms is beautiful). Seeing a coat of arms designated in the dream as belonging to your own family: if the coat of arms has the figure of an animal, look under the respective entry (for instance, see **Eagle**). See **Name.**

Coca-Cola

V: Surprisingly enough, if a man dreams about Coca-Cola, it symbolizes—because of the bubbling froth—the realization of sexual desires. Seeing a man drinking Coca-Cola might mean that it's time to take a break. See **Lemonade.**

Cock, Rooster

S: The cock stands for the "keeper of time."

V: In a woman's dream: hearing a cock crowing: be careful

when dealing with men. Seeing a rooster and a woman means satisfaction in all matters of love (for both sexes). Watching a cock laying eggs: play the lottery you just might win!

D: The cock is usually a symbol of masculine sexuality. Depending on how it appears in the dream, it is a warning about being too aggressive, or a sign of repressed masculine characteristics (if the rooster has been plucked). By the way, a rooster plays mean tricks in order to copulate with hens.

Coffee, Coffee Grinder

V: Watching others drink coffee: people are gossiping about you. Drinking coffee by yourself: get ready for a great vacation; or you will have a pleasant conversation. Grinding coffee: your family life is harmonious. Making coffee: pleasant guests are coming to your house. Looking at coffee grounds: worry about material things; or your happy life may be interrupted by an illness. Looking at a coffee grinder: a warning to avoid any and all gossip by changing your behavior; people around you can't wait for you to make a mistake. See **Tea.**

Coffee Shop

V: Sitting in a coffee shop: you are looking for a relationship with the opposite sex. Eating a lot of food in a coffee shop: all you will get is a stomachache! Serving someone in a coffee shop means losing your independence. See **Cake, Coffee, Waiter.**

Coffin

V: Seeing an empty coffin means that you will reach a ripe old age, or that you worry unnecessarily. A dead person is in the coffin: financial losses or setbacks at the job are a possibility. You see yourself in a coffin: you will live a long, wonderful life in good health. See **Urn.**

D: A coffin means that you need to say goodbye to something that has died. Something new is waiting for you, and you can only get it going if you have "buried" the past. See **Cemetery, Death, Grave.**

Coin

V: Looking at or receiving coins: a large sum of money will arrive unexpectedly. Giving coins to someone: don't be careless with your money. Foreign coins mean you will either receive money unexpectedly, or that a stranger's wealth will play a vital role in your life. Collecting old coins: you are involved in unusual pursuits or an extraordinary event. See **Money.**

Cold

V: Dreaming of feeling cold means that you are emotionally isolated and estranged from family and friends. Suddenly being in a cold climate: you will be disappointed by people around you, or they are reacting "cold-heartedly" to your wishes. See **Head Cold.**

D: A "cold" situation represents repressed or "cold" emotions. Are you cold? Are the people you meet cold? See **Ice.**

Colors

V: Seeing bright colors (particularly in women's dreams): emotions are churning. Colorful dreams are a promise of long life. Painting an object in bright colors: you are not quite honest with a friend. Coloring your face: others think your actions are foolish. Coloring a wagon: expect a surprise—pay attention to the colors (See the chapter on **"Colors in Dreams"**). Buying paint: you want more diversion in your life. Preparing the colors for a watercolor painting: you are facing an uncertain situation. Using oil paint: your life is going in the right direction.

D: The meaning of different colors in dreams is discussed in the chapter on **"Colors in Dreams."** Colors are an indication of mental attitude, inner voice, and depth of emotion.

Comb, Combing

V: Looking at a comb means family differences, differences of opinion, and confrontations. If the comb is broken: a serious rift is going to get worse. Combing your hair is a message: keep your affairs and house in order. Buying a comb: you are now able to take care of your own affairs. Combing long hair: a new friendship is beginning and will last for a long time.

D: These symbols are a challenge: keep your sexual cravings under better control, particularly if you are cutting, washing, and combing your hair in the dream, or if you are trying to tame an unruly head of hair. See **Hair.**

Comet

V: Seeing a comet is a warning: uncertain and difficult times are ahead. You will need to overcome poverty and danger.

D: A comet is a sign that a far-reaching change in your personality is about to take place, which is not due to external but rather to internal circumstances. This "new personality" in the form of a comet can seem either brilliant or dangerous—depending on the rest of the dream. See **Planets, Star.**

Companion

V: If you dream you are taking a walk and somebody joins you: you will soon find a new friend. Accompanying a friend to the airport or train station, etc., means illness or being separated from someone.

D: Being accompanied by a person you don't recognize: something in you, some part of your personality, has grown up and wants to "to go its own way."

Compass

S: The compass indicates hope and virtue.

V: Looking at a compass: you are confused, but the solution to the problem is at hand and it will change your life for the better. Losing a compass: you have lost sight of the direction you are taking in your life.

D: The compass shows your direction, self-development, and self-realization. Have you lost your bearings? Where is the compass pointing you? See **Four Corners of the Compass.**

Comrade, Buddy

V: Dreaming about having a buddy means you are leading a satisfying life. Going on a trip together: you will soon be pleasantly surprised. Saying goodbye to a buddy: you will move—or want to—to another house. See **Friend.**

D: Having a conflict with your buddy: you are emotionally torn. A compatible relationship: your emotions will soon be back in balance!

Concert

V: Listening or being at a concert means you want a better atmosphere and that your emotional well-being will enrich you. Being invited to a concert: you are well received and people have high regard for you. See **Stage.**

Confession

S: A confession is cleansing and purifying.

V: Being the person taking a confession: you will soon take part in a creative or charitable venture. You are confessing: you are admitting mistakes and forgive yourself for them. Somebody else is confessing: examine your behavior and correct it quickly.

D: Dreaming about confession means that you have

acknowledged your mistakes; it is also a sign that you have been forgiven.

Connection

V: Forming an intimate relationship: meeting a new friend. A wrong phone connection: you are being played for a fool, or the person you tried to call wants nothing to do with you. See **Telephone.**

D: The motto: "two heads are better than one" is an apt description here. But the dream means to reconcile and correct your different character traits. Sometimes the dream might be a warning against false friends—if the connection was "bad."

Constipation

D: Do you suffer from constipation in real life? Do you want to forget, "get rid of" memories from the past, "undigested" events, or experiences? If so, "work through" them—and the sooner the better! See **Intestines.**

Contract

D: Don't resist taking on a burdensome responsibility—any attempt to get out of it is futile and will only waste your energy unnecessarily. See **Learning, Paper, Writing.**

Cook, Cooking

V: Seeing a cook is a sign that you have adapted well to the toil of everyday life and are glad you did. Dreaming about dismissing your cook: be more careful with your money. You are the cook: a very pleasant surprise is ahead.

D: The dream reveals your need to make certain matters in your life easier or more palatable (experiences, disappointments, insights), allowing you to adapt better to responsibilities and demands. You will do so if the meal you are cooking in the dream turns out well.

Copper

D: Copper often means love and a happy, fulfilled life—sometimes also pride.

Corals

D: Looking at a pink or white coral symbolizes positive ideas, inspiration, intuition, and also pleasant experiences in a relationship. Nurture these traits. Red coral indicates feelings of love; black coral: invisible or unrecognized illness. See **Jewelry, Necklace.**

Cord

S: A cord is a symbol of entanglement and servitude, attributes of the devil.

V: Seeing a cord: your chances of carrying out a certain project are very slim. Or does someone want to set a trap, hoping you will stumble into it? Holding a cord in your hands: the relationship you have with another person will rescue you. However, whether this is in your best interests is not yet clear. See **Rope.**

D: The cord is a sign that your entanglement in a relationship is hindering your personal growth.

Corn, Cornfield

V: Planting corn is a positive sign of professional success. Grinding corn means joy and financial success. Looking at a cornfield: your future is secure. Seeing a lot of corn: you have invested your money wisely, your life is stable and secure. Small amounts of corn: poverty.

D: Corn represents the life experiences that have lead or

will lead you to maturity. It is also the reward you will "harvest" for knowledge born of sorrow. See **Grain.**

Corner

V: Holding on to a corner of a blanket, pillow, etc.: you need to hold on to what is offered—it will bring you luck. See **Bed, Pillow.**

D: Are you in a corner because of your own actions, or do you feel as if you have been pushed into it?

Corset

V: Looking at a corset: you will soon be free of a troublesome relationship. A man dreaming about a beautiful girl in a corset: a woman is going to disappoint you. Wearing a corset: your efforts are for naught. Taking a corset off: your old sorrows or problems will be a thing of the past.

Cottage Cheese

V: Seeing or eating cottage cheese: a matter that is aggravating you may turn to your advantage.

D: See **Cream, Milk.**

Counting, Slide Rule

V: Counting (adding and subtracting, etc.) numbers: can you really afford to have others living at your expense? Solving a mathematical problem is a warning about your spending habits, because you need to find a way out of a difficult situation—and soon!

D: Doing calculations: you can solve your problem if you start using your head. A slide rule is a sign that you have made a mistake and are looking for help. Sometimes very manipulative people dream about slide rules.

Court

V: Standing in front of a judge is a sign that you are trying to fight your bad habits. If you are the court judging another person: you feel injured by someone, but not yet ready to confront that person openly. If you are the spectator in a courtroom: unconscious memories have surfaced; you have a bad conscience because of a past mistake or action. If you are ordered to appear as a witness: a friend or acquaintance is in desperate need of help. Being served with a subpoena: a warning that others are trying to blame you for something. Being convicted: you are wasting your time waiting to be thanked for something you did.

D: The court is symbolic of many things: trying to make up your mind about somebody; trying to find a possible connection between things, or coming clean with yourself. Sometimes a dream about a court implies that you need to defend yourself against other people and their prejudice, slander, or hostility. See **Lawyer.**

Cow

S: In the Mediterranean region, the cow symbolizes the goddess of love and fertility.

V: Looking at one or more cows is a sign of personal good luck, unless the cows are malnourished, in which case it means bad luck. A cow barn means a recovery from an illness soon. Watching while someone else is milking a cow: you suspect that somebody is taking advantage of you. Being chased by a cow: through sheer stupidity one of your friends is becoming a danger to you.

D: The cow is a symbol of femininity, longing, and motherhood. In a woman's dream, it can indicate sexual desire that can be found only in the safety of a sound relationship.

Crabs

S: The crab symbolizes resurrection, since it renews/changes its protective shell regularly.

V: Looking at one or more crabs: your plans are delayed (one step forward—three steps back) and it will take time to get back on track. If you or others are eating crabs: your financial situation will improve. Having cancer: somebody wants to destroy your livelihood—expose this as quickly as possible!

D: This animal is a sign that some of your personality traits are in conflict with your values and/or the environment. Seeing a crab in your dreams often means you are too accommodating. If you dream that you have cancer, it is important to know where the cancer is located (the head, neck, chest, stomach, etc.).

Cradle

V: Seeing a cradle: single people might get married soon—married people can expect a happy event. A baby in the cradle: you are in a delicate position, trying desperately to keep someone from talking.

D: Your hope of having a child might be behind this dream. It can also be a warning: beware of people who would like to "lull" you into suspending your healthy suspicion or divert your focus from matters at hand. Or could it be the other way around?

Crash

V: Seeing a crash or crashing yourself: unexpected challenges interfere with your plans and the desire to get ahead.

D: Difficulties or sudden hurdles are thrown in your path. See **Cliff, Falling, Recipe.**

Crate

V: If you are looking at or owning a crate: you might

become wealthy. Looking at an empty crate means the opposite: poverty and worries are knocking on your door. See **Box.**

Crater

D: A hot, active crater is a warning about too much passion and cravings that are about to erupt. An extinct crater means you have largely overcome old, painful memories. See **Volcano.**

Cream

V: Seeing or eating cream: you have been given advantages; make sure that you don't act too selfishly.

D: See **Butter, Cheese, Milk.**

Cream (Face)

V: A woman dreaming about face cream means she wants to be more beautiful, well groomed, and desirable, because in real life she often feels left out.

Crib, Hayrack

V: Looking at an empty hayrack: your professional career desperately needs attention—you are confronted with a host of problems. A full hayrack is a positive sign: you can look forward to a carefree future. Looking at baby Jesus in the crib also promises a good future. From a religious point of view, the latter image is also a sign that you want to keep a secret.

Crime

V: Watching a crime being committed: an appalling matter or a legal argument needs to be cleared up. This dream is often a sign of unconscious brutality. See **Aggression, Murder.**

Cripple

V: Seeing or being a cripple: you have a lot of work to do on yourself before you will be "healthy" (emotionally and morally). However, the dream also indicates that help is on the way! Taking care of a cripple: you are caring for and feeling bad about an unhappy person. See **Invalid.**

D: The cripple represents the compassion you have for other people. It also is an indication of how much you depend on other people, or that you are in need of help.

Crocodile

S: The crocodile is a symbol of gluttony, deceit, and chaos.

V: Looking at a crocodile is a warning about evil-minded people around you. Getting bitten by a crocodile: a dangerous situation is developing. Killing a crocodile: you are able to defeat a powerful enemy—usually your own negative energies.

D: The crocodile represents dark, stifling energies or negative attitudes. Fears, greed, or passion could literally "swallow you up." However, with this dream your unconscious is saying that you can withstand these urges. Crying during the dream means you are crying "crocodile tears." See **Dragon.**

Cross, Crossroads

S: The cross is a symbol of the integration of extremes, the synthesis, and the moderation—the cross is the connection between time and space.

V: A cross is a sign of sorrow and misery to come. Praying in front of a cross: in a hopeless situation, unexpected help is on the way. A cross on the side of the road: a warning about hard times ahead, but if you rely on your own strength, you can do what is necessary to get through. Seeing Christ on the cross: good fortune. Standing at a crossroads: a long-overdue decision can't be postponed any longer.

D: The cross represents many things: it gives directions (since the cross always points at one of the four points of the compass, but it also stands for great sorrow as well as renewal. It is also a sign of "begging," of kneeling in front of someone. A crossroads indicates indecision, fear of taking the "wrong path." It also could mean that this is a time to make changes. The direction you are moving in the dream is important. Is it **East, North, South, West?**

Crossing

V: Crossing a large body of water means new, unexpected possibilities.

Crow

V: Seeing a crow in a dream alludes to someone's death. Seeing several crows in a tree: a family reunion is planned. Catching a crow: the future is going to be sad and fraught with conflict. Hearing a crow screeching: bad news to come.

D: The crow always represents a fear of failure. It also predicts bad luck or the death of a close relative.

Crowds

V: If you find yourself in a crowd with too many people: your job and everyday life is "swallowing you up." You are urged to distance yourself from the chaos in your life!

Crown, Crowning

S: The crown—or a jewel worn on the head—is a sign of royal honor.

V: Looking at a crown is a warning: "Before you become a king you must first become the servant of the people." The dream can also point to hidden ambitions and warn you not to set your sights too high. If you are being crowned: expect to be handed a great task in the near future. See **Emperor, King.**

D: The crown is a sign of vanity and the need for admiration. A damaged crown means your hopes have been dashed. Being crowned means imminent success.

Crutch

V: Looking at a crutch: you are about to have an accident, or you can expect help in an unfortunate personal matter. Throwing crutches away: you are now strong enough to deal with a difficult situation on your own. Walking on crutches: loss or delays in personal or business affairs. See **Limping.**

D: A crutch is a sign of your insecurities. You need and are in search of help. Are you using "crutches" in order to reach a goal?

Crying

V: If you are crying: you will get over worrying about another person and be happy again. See **Tears.**

D: Dreams about crying often indicate tension and fears. Are you crying because you regret something you did? Are you crying "crocodile tears"? Crying tears of sorrow: before you know it, something will make you laugh—a very hopeful dream!

Crystal, Crystal Ball

V: Looking at crystal glass is always a warning: be more realistic and don't fall prey to desires and illusions. See **Glass.** Breaking crystal glass: you are losing a good friendship because of your carelessness. Crystal jewelry is a positive sign for your inner clarity, concentration, and the fulfillment of your greatest hopes and desires. A crystal ball can forecast your future. Other images in the dream will provide important information. See **Psychic, Witch.**

D: Crystals show the basic personality traits that have "crystallized" over the course of your life. They also point to your intellectual strength. A crystal ball reflects the expectations and hopes you have for the future.

Cuckoo

V: Seeing a cuckoo means having to deal with a selfish person. Catching a cuckoo: gossip about yourself is driving you to distraction. Killing a cuckoo: your interference in other people's business might create unpleasantness.

D: The cuckoo represents immature eroticism and sexuality; it interferes with your love relationship, because you are looking to satisfy it in places other than home. The dream is also a warning about freeloaders who—when you aren't looking—will try to dump their responsibilities on you ("laying a cuckoo egg in your nest").

Cucumber

V: Seeing a cucumber in a dream: you are going to have to deal with nasty problems. Eating cucumbers: a friendship has been betrayed. Eating a pickle: others will be the cause of a bad experience.

D: A cucumber is always a phallic symbol, expressing sexual desires (particularly in a woman's dreams).

Cup

V: Seeing a cup: a friend will come to visit. Drinking from a cup: you will get together with another person, and something might develop from it. A broken cup: you will break up with a friend or a loved one.

D: A cup might be a sign of your sexual needs or your need for friendly companionship. See **Container, Mug, Vessel.**

Cupid

S: The god Cupid is always an erotic symbol.

V + D: Cupid is an ancient dream motif. Cupid shooting

an arrow at someone: stay out of the affairs of other people. Cupid shooting an arrow at you: a new romance is right around the corner and, while not permanent, will be a flirtatious, sexual adventure.

Curls

V: Seeing curls: you are overly dependent on your partner. Dark curls mean antagonism. Do you like the color of the curls? If so, you like the person. Many curls on someone's head mean your love life is rather confusing right now. Cutting off someone's curls: somebody is telling you "to get lost." Watching others cutting curls off: someone trusts you enough to confess a secret love affair to you.

D: See **Hair.**

Cursing

V: Cursing in your dream means you are not expressing your anger during the day! Repressed or denied anger will only make you sick! If someone is cursing you: change your approach. You have underestimated a person you thought you knew and that has caused problems.

Curtain

V: Seeing a curtain means a secret will be revealed. A closed curtain means a joyful event or a party.

D: See **Stage, Veil.**

Cutting

V: Cutting up food: your project will be completed successfully. If you cut yourself: the whole affair will end in failure—something you already knew beforehand.

D: Cutting something is a sign that you want to put your past behind you. Are you harboring aggressive feelings toward someone? Do you feel "cut off" from your emotions, ideals, and desires because of present adverse circumstances? See **Scissors.**

Cypress

S: The tree of the righteous, the cypress is a sacred symbol of life, connected to the gods of the underworld.

V + D: Seeing a cypress means a sad event or setback at work or at home. Planting a cypress: somebody is going to die.

S = Symbol V = Vision D = Depth psychology

Dagger

S: The dagger is a phallic symbol or one of **Aggression.** It is also a sign of your own weakness and hope that you will find strength and courage.

V: Seeing a dagger: you will soon "conquer" your rivals. Defending yourself with a dagger: suddenly you will be able to put an end to a certain matter. Being wounded by a dagger: means sad news. Seeing a dagger stuck in the ground: a warning that you are in danger. Seeing a dagger covered with blood: you have bitter enemies.

D: The dagger is a symbol of physical, mental, or emotional power. It can also mean impending destruction. If the dagger is pointing at someone else: you are unconsciously aggressive.

Damage, Harm

V: "Pain is often the best teacher." Learn from your experiences and put them to good use in the future. Maybe a past "mistake" will help you to find a solution for a present problem! See **Pain.**

Dance, Dancing

S: The dance is a symbol of freedom from earthly limits.

V: Dancing by yourself: you would like more attention

from a particular person. If you are dancing alone as if lost in a dream: usually it's a sign of being happy and in love—though sometimes only for a very short time. Being led to the dance floor, you will have to accept a certain situation, even if you don't like it. If you are dancing with a partner, who is leading? That would reveal the respective roles in a present or future relationship. If a woman is dancing "rings" around her partner while he is moving slowly, she needs to stop trying to have things always go her own way. If a man is dancing alone, he is dying to have a sexual adventure. See **Ballet, Music.**

D: The dream is either reflecting your present emotional balance or is a reminder to be more spontaneous. At times the dream, of course, also refers to sexual feelings and the need to have some fun and diversion. Frequent dreams about dancing might indicate you are too pleasure-oriented and lack seriousness.

Danger

V: Continually dreaming that you are in a dangerous situation means you either need a break or professional help. See **Fear.**

Darkness

V: Dreaming about being "in the dark" is a sign that you feel insecure at work and in life in general. You can't quite figure something out, can't understand it. If you are in a totally dark night, you are afraid of dying—and living—and you need advice from an objective person. Seeing a small light: you are distressed, but help is on the way. Being in a cave: you are unconsciously afraid of being attacked. Being in a dark closet: you recognize somebody's hidden intentions just in time to prevent the person from carrying them out. See **Night.**

D: Dreaming about darkness always refers to an emotionally dangerous situation or one that is unresolved. This may have to do with a specific experience with other people or yourself. Try to shed some light on the situation. Being in a dark passage: you are feeling unprotected from the intensity of others and yourself. It is a test: you need to prove yourself in order to come back into the light. Sometimes such a dream also suggests that you seek expert advice.

Dates

V: When men dream about seeing or eating dates, they want sexual experiences with more than one woman. Finding or eating just one date: you are going to meet an old flame. Giving a date as a gift: somebody will soon kiss you.

D: Dates in men's dreams are always a symbol of female sex organs, sexual desires, and the longing for love.

Daughter

V: Dreaming about a daughter when—in real life—you don't have one: you want to be accepted by a woman or hope that she will take care of you. See **Child, Son.**

Day, Diary, Journal

V: Every day is only a small part of your life, but the dream might want to remind you how quickly time passes. See **Clock**. The journal is a reminder of things past and events that were important enough not to be dismissed. Maybe you are confronted with past experiences with which you have not yet come to terms? See **Book, Learning.**

Deafness

V: Dreaming about being deaf: you are also "deaf" to what others tell you.

D: Are you "closing your ears" to reality, or to what others have to say? Don't you want to know what others think of you? Keep your eyes open and your ears peeled—you might be surprised what you hear. Are you also deaf when it comes to your own needs, feelings, or desires? See **Blindness.**

Death

S: A skull is a symbol of repentance and mortality.

V: If a woman dreams about her deceased husband: she has come to terms with his death. Dream-psychology has proven that we only dream about a loved one who has passed away when we have accepted the loss. In other words, when a deceased loved one appears in a dream, the grief process is complete. Seeing a dead stranger: you are thinking about a separation or you have dealt successfully with a difficult situation. Seeing an open grave: you have suffered a loss, but still hope that you can recover from it. Dreaming that it is getting progressively darker, and you are going (or want) to die, usually means that a particular phase in your life (children leaving home, menopause, etc.) is coming to an end. Seeing the "grim reaper" in your dream means a great burden is lifted from your shoulder. See **Sickle.**

D: Maybe something in you has died (your love for someone, an emotion, an old attitude) even if you are not even aware of it yourself. See **Cadaver, Cemetery, Dying, Grave.**

Debt

V: Deal with past actions and conduct now, and make changes (pay off the old "mortgages"); the reward will be peace and harmony. Sometimes the dream also refers to feelings of inferiority, because you are not living up to the expectations and demands of others, or the responsibilities you feel you owe them.

Decapitation

V: Seeing your own decapitation: either illness or shame and embarrassment. If you are decapitating somebody else:

you are possibly the winner in a conflict or a legal argument. Watching someone you know being decapitated: you are losing a person you love. Watching a stranger being decapitated: you might either defeat an adversary or create new enemies. See **Execution, Head.**

D: Decapitation is a sign that you are revising your present attitude about a specific event. Are you being ruled too much by your head? Maybe you should start trusting your intuition more and living accordingly!

Decay

See **Demolition, Rubble, Ruins.**

Deceased

V: Seeing a deceased person: the person has your best interests at heart and wants to tell you something that will support you. See **Death.**

Deer, Antelope

V: Seeing several deer or antelope: you want personal freedom. Since you have had very few opportunities for it, take the chance that is coming your way and run with it!

Delay

V: Dreaming about being delayed: you have chosen the wrong support—be better prepared next time.

D: Do you have the feeling that you missed a connection? Are you afraid that you will miss the right moment next time? Do you often avoid making decisions? Do you like to put off until tomorrow what you could do today? Do you like to "sit" on your problems, hoping they will go away? Stop procrastinating—get busy—and the dream is telling you to do it now!

Demolition

V: A house falling down or being demolished: relief from an old burden, if you are ready to start anew or give your life new direction.

D: Demolition of a house: the collapse of your hopes. Abandon old habits and attitudes so that something new can take their place.

Demon

D: Dreaming about demons usually refers to feelings you are denying, but that have, nevertheless, taken hold of you. See **Aggression, Disgust, Envy.** Frequent dreams about demons are warnings: make an appointment with a psychotherapist in order to avoid future emotional conflict and/or crises. See **Devil, Monsters, Mystical Creatures.**

Depths

V: The depths are usually a symbol of your deepest feelings or your unconscious. Sometimes they provide insight into the deepest layers of your character. But they might also reflect profound experiences from the past. You will know which applies to you.

Desert

V: Walking in the desert: professional success will come only slowly and with much effort; withdrawing from other people will bring loneliness. Seeing a desert: you are being deprived of something, or you are going to be very lonely for a while.

D: Your life is lacking feelings and intuition; you use too much logic and reason. The desert is a symbol of desolation and impotence. Your barren soul is desperately in need of water (emotions and feelings!). Do you believe that you are in a hopeless situation? Going into the desert: you will thirst—for affection maybe. Are you chasing a fantasy? Are you lonely? A desert dream wants to give you a "mental" push: think about what changes you could make to restore happiness and productivity to your life. Analyze your present situation honestly (take a close look at the rest of the symbols in the dream)—things can only get better!

Desertion

D: Dreaming about "changing sides" (becoming a deserter) is a warning: don't sacrifice your convictions because you are fearful and concerned about rejection. Remain true to yourself!

Destruction

D: Dreaming about destruction reflects dashed hopes, withered emotions, or loss of convictions. Sometimes the dream refers to negative influences (from people , work, or home) that could destroy you. For more information take a good look at the rest of the dream symbols.

Detour

D: Are you making things too complicated? You alone are responsible for the difficulties you have in reaching your goal. Are you too inflexible?

Devil

S: The devil is a symbol of confusion, darkness, and death.

V: Seeing the devil: you are either too preoccupied with negative thoughts or someone around you has a diabolical influence on you that is threatening your serenity. You are faced with temptations that could have serious consequences. Don't give in—even if your own weaknesses make it hard for you to resist.

D: Satan is a symbol of a purely egotistical side of your unconscious, or of your fears, passions, rages, or hates. These energies always lead to internal and/or external conflicts and need to be redirected—the sooner the better. If Satan appears in your dreams: while you reject some of these feelings, they are, nevertheless, reflected in what you do and how you behave (which you usually regret afterward). See **Demon.**

Diamonds

V: Sad to say, seeing such a brilliant treasure in a dream does not bode well. Wearing a diamond is usually a sign of an overly developed ego, or strong feelings of inferiority. Losing a diamond ring: separation from a loved one. Wearing a diamond ring/bracelet/ necklace: you are covering up a lack of self-worth with external "things" (sometimes also with bragging). Someone else wearing a diamond: watch out for false friends. Receiving a diamond as a gift: you will soon celebrate a happy event, an engagement or the like, and it might mean an improvement in your social status.

D: Dreaming about a diamond is a warning: don't be arrogant. Bragging is only a compensation for feelings of inferiority.

Diarrhea

You are in the throws of an emotional self-cleansing process. See **Intestines, Colon.**

Dice

V: Seeing dice: you are quite irresponsible and—with your eyes wide open—have taken risks that could result in losses and conflicts. See **Square.**

D: Playing a game of dice and winning: your chances for success are good. If you lose: your hopes will be dashed.

Dinner

V: Sitting at the table and eating dinner: good luck in something you're involved in at the present time. Eating dinner with other people: teamwork promises to be successful; it also is a good sign for joint decisions.

D: The Last Supper, in the Christian sense, means freedom from sorrow and worry. The dream bodes well for all of tomorrow's events and decisions.

Direction

V: Turning in a specific direction: See **East, North, South, West;** as well as **Four Corners of the Compass.**

Dirt

V: Seeing dirt in a dream, stepping into it, or getting dirt thrown at you is a clear sign of good fortune knocking at your door. See **Mud.**

Discovery, Discovering

V: Dreaming about finding or discovering something means either the loss of money or of valuable objects.

D: This dream indicates that yours is a restless, questioning, searching human mind. Dreaming about a discovery often means far-reaching changes in your life. It might also indicate that your views and your actions are too theoretical or idealistic. See **Uranus.** Finding or discovering something is a warning—don't rely too much on good luck.

Dissecting

D: You are attempting to get to the bottom of something by using reason and your intellect. Whether this is really necessary depends on the rest of the dream symbols. It might be best to choose the golden mean between head and emotions.

Distress, Emergency

V: Dreaming about being in distress: expect a happy event to take place. Helping other in distress: be assured that help for you is on the way. If you are indifferent to the affliction of others, expect great misfortune to knock on your door.

D: Dreaming about being in a serious, distressing situation is usually a sign that you are facing problems in real life. It also is a symbol of your own **Tightfistedness,** which you need to remedy. The emergency is an urgent warning to get out of a real-life situation immediately if serious losses are to be prevented!

Ditch, Hole

V: Standing in front of a hole in the ground: think again carefully about your plans—it might prevent you from making mistakes. Trying to jump over a ditch or falling in: this is about the worst time for business speculation and for spending money. Digging a hole and hoping a certain person will fall in: don't underestimate the intelligence of this person—he/she will sense what you are up to.

D: The ditch might be a trap someone has put in your path; or you may want to set a trap for someone. It points to past experiences and bad memories. Have you tried to "bury" some of your character traits—hiding them from yourself or others? Did you "dig your own hole"?

Diving

V: Diving under water: only diplomacy will you get out of a difficult situation. Diving into a calm lake: you want to get to the bottom of something and gain new insights—to straighten things out with yourself. See **Water.**

D: Do you want to "dive" into something unknown? Or should you "dive" into your unconscious—exploring the deeper layers of your soul?

Divorce

V: Dreaming about getting a divorce: you did something and are afraid of losing your lover or partner. Dreaming of other people's divorces: a warning to take your own vows more seriously.

D: Is this dream a sign that you are really in danger of losing someone, or is your unconscious warning you that an affair will endanger your present relationship? Only you can answer these questions!

Dizziness

V: Dreaming about being dizzy: you are unsure of what action to take.

D: You are afraid of losing control, because you are overwhelmed by demands and responsibilities. Sometimes the dream is a sign of actual physical problems that should be checked out. See **Balance.**

Document

V: Seeing a document: trouble with the authorities—you might have to go to court. See **Paper, Seal.**

Doe

V: Seeing a doe: a pleasant encounter is ahead. Seeing many does fleeing: you are offending your friends or running away from them. A tame doe: children will give you a lot of joy. Killing a doe while hunting: grief and sorrow in your love relationship. Seeing a buck: you are about to make a very stupid mistake. See **Deer.** Eating venison: you will either receive an invitation or a very distinguished visitor.

D: This gentle and shy animal symbolizes your soft and vulnerable side. Don't try to hide it. See **Animals, Forest.**

Dog

V: Seeing a dog in a dream: you will soon gain a new and faithful friend. Seeing a black dog: a friend is turning out to be dishonest. Seeing a red dog: you can't rely on your friends. See **Fox**. Hearing dogs bark: you may quarrel with your neighbors or they may be bad-mouthing you. Being bitten by a dog is a sign of a bad conscience. Dogs fighting over a bone means a family fight about an inheritance. Being attacked by a dog: be careful, you are acting more from instinct than logic. See **Poodle.**

D: The dog is a symbol of animal appetites and instincts. Being led by a dog means: you are aware of your inner strength and live in harmony with it. The "dog" in the dream will obey if we live in peace with our instincts.

Doll

V: Women who see a doll want a child of their own. When men see a doll, it means they want to have an affair, which will happen, even if nothing much comes of it.

D: The dream expresses your deep affection for someone, and a need for tenderness.

Donkey

V: Leading a donkey: be careful, your good-natured personality is being shamelessly exploited. Riding on a donkey: means unexpected difficulties, but be patient—in time you will reach your goal. Feeding a donkey: you are helping the wrong people—they think you're stupid. Hearing a donkey braying: you could have saved yourself the effort. Driving a wagon pulled by a donkey: people around you are using you for their own purposes and goals.

D: While the donkey indicates a lack of mental capacity, it also stands for patience and humility. Did you act like a "donkey" lately? Did others use or treat you that way?

Door

S: A door, a portal, or a gate—all three are always a symbol of transformation, a threshold between two places.

V: Stepping through a door: a matter is resolving itself without the interference of others. Standing in front of a closed door: you still have not made contact with your neighbors. If a man dreams about opening a door by force: he either wants to possess a woman completely or he is harboring violent tendencies. A man slipping through a door is a sure sign of wanting to have an affair. See **Gate, House.**

Door (Locked)

V: Seeing a locked door: poor conduct needs to be replaced with positive actions—it is the only way to avoid standing in front of a locked door in the future. Unlocking the door: the future will be pleasant.

D: A locked door is often a sign of sexual needs. It also could mean that, if handled reasonably—difficulties are manageable. See **Key.**

Dove

S: The dove in antiquity was the sacred animal of Aphrodite and one of the symbols of Eros. In Christianity, the dove is a symbol of the Holy Ghost.

V: Seeing doves: you are either lucky at the game table, or you will receive very pleasant news. Feeding doves: your altruism is much appreciated. Seeing doves on a roof: a warning to be satisfied with what you have. Hearing doves cooing: you are making peace with a loved one; also you will be given advice and you must follow it. Watching doves in the sky: your contact with important people makes new connections possible.

D: The dove is the bird of Eros, and also of Venus, a symbol of tender love. Are you longing for more peace, contentment, or harmony? Follow your inner voice! See **Bird, Flying.**

Dovecote

V: Seeing doves in a dovecote: be prepared for a long line of visitors. See **Dove.**

Dragon

V: Winning a fight with a dragon means that you have learned to master the powers of the unconscious. Being injured during the fight: you might get hurt by a powerful enemy. If a man dreams he is confronted by a dragon: he is unconsciously afraid of being devoured by a woman (spiritually and emotionally). Defeating the dragon means he wants to dominate women.

D: The dragon represents a person with cold-blooded power who will do anything in order to be successful. Killing a dragon: let go of shrewd and heartless attitudes. Or is there a "dragon" in your house that gives you grief?

Dragonfly

V + D: Seeing a dragonfly means you act too casually in many things. You are easily dazzled. See **Insects, Butterfly.**

Drawing

V: If you are drawing: pay attention to how you express yourself; often small efforts have great results. Seeing a drawing: people will present you with a "fait accompli." See **Painting, Writing.**

D: Here it is important to know what the drawing is about; is it about an actual event or subject, or a memory from the past that you're dealing with now? See **Picture.**

Dress

V: Looking at or wearing a beautiful dress: you are living comfortably, enjoying good fortune and popularity. If the dress is too short: you are lacking confidence or feeling inferior. Taking a dress off: don't be so trusting—keep some things to yourself. Wearing a white dress: people like you. A red dress is a sign of arrogance. A yellow dress stands for deception or intrigue. A green dress means that hopes will come true. A black dress brings sadness and grief. Tearing up a dress: you are overreacting in a certain matter. Wearing a dirty dress: your business is not doing well, and your behavior toward others leaves a lot to be desired. Washing a dress or bringing it to the cleaner: start being more financially responsible—immediately.

D: Dreams about dresses show how you present yourself or how you want the world to see you. Expensive dresses are a sign that you want better social conditions. They will bring good luck and success. Cheap dresses are a warning to be more careful with your money. See **Clothes, Shirt, Pants,** and the chapter "**Colors in Dreams.**"

Drinking

V: Drinking from a **Spring**: your health will improve. Drinking **Wine** means pleasant hours with good people. Drinking **Alcohol**: you have a tendency for self-delusion and running away from reality. You want to find courage in the bottle but achieve the opposite. Drinking **Milk**: enjoy life in a healthy and simple way.

D: You have a severe craving! Is it desire or passion or addiction? Are you trying to satisfy physical needs or spiritual desires?

Drugstore, Pharmacist, Apothecary

V + D: If you are about to enter a drugstore: a warning to

pay more attention to your health—if neglected, it might be in danger. Being sick and walking into a drugstore: recuperation is possible. This dream might also indicate your having to pay too much money for something. If you are the pharmacist: you would like to be wealthy.

Drum

V: Seeing or hearing a drum means unpleasant events and unrest ahead. Playing the drum: you are creating unnecessary excitement, or you want others to pay attention to you at all cost. See **Bass Viol, Kettle Drum, Trumpet, Violin.**

D: The drum is a symbol of your strength and vitality—similar to the **Pulse**. Sometimes it may be a symbol of self-gratification.

Drunkenness

V: Seeing a drunk: your present position is on shaky ground. Seeing yourself drunk: make sure you are stone sober during an upcoming negotiation. See **Alcohol.**

Duck

V: Seeing a duck swimming in the water might mean unfavorable news. If you are trying in vain to catch the duck: losses. Catching a duck: your plans will finally succeed. Seeing roast duck: your monthly "allowance" is being reduced. Eating roast duck: your family will have a great, fun party.

D: The duck stands for intelligence and wisdom, and might help you to get to a breakthrough!

Duel

Being directly involved in a duel means that you need to learn to keep your tongue in check (think first, speak later). Winning the duel: you will reach your goal, but only after you have faced and resolved your difficulties. You are challenged to a duel: great danger lies ahead! You see others fighting a duel: don't get involved in other peoples' squabbles; all you will get is a bloody nose for your trouble. Watching a duel from afar: you are jealous.

Dust

D: Dreaming about dust: you are being made aware of experiences from the past. But the dream might also mean that you want to simplify your life, even if it means dealing with discomfort. See **Dirt, Filth.**

Dying

V: Dreaming that you are dying: you are going through a spiritual renewal that will manifest in real life. Ancient dream books consider a dream about dying to mean a long life.

D: See **Death.**

Dynamite

V: Sitting on a box of dynamite is a bad omen, indicating impending danger; be particularly careful right now. Watching as dynamite is being laid: under no circumstance should you get involved in other peoples' business—things would only turn out to be very unpleasant. Wherever you look you see nothing but dynamite: new plans and goals wipe out old obstacles—but do not be reckless! See **Bomb.**

D: Dynamite is a symbol of a sudden impulse to develop new projects, set new goals; it might also indicate recklessness (physical, emotional, mental) used in order to reach a goal. If that is the case, the dream is a warning!

S = SYMBOL V = VISION D = DEPTH PSYCHOLOGY

Eagle

S: The eagle is seen as the "king of the air"!

V: Dreaming about an eagle means that you are yearning—unconsciously—for freedom. An eagle flying high in the sky: you have ambitious plans, and with courage and vision you will increase your independence. The eagle catching prey: you feel physically inferior in the presence of a stronger person. Seeing an eagle in a cage: you are feeling restricted by friends or by your environment. Being attacked by an eagle: either you are in considerable danger or you are interfering with someone's plans. Seeing an eagle land close to you: the impending death of a good friend. If the eagle is sitting on top of your head, you can't solve a current problem "in your head."

D: The eagle is a symbol of freedom and always points to a tendency toward intellectual "flights of fancy." If the eagle is flying high in the air: you want extraordinary intellectual powers; also far-reaching decisions are possible. See **Bird.**

Eagle-Owl (combination)

V: Hearing an eagle-owl calling: you are keeping company with questionable people who are the cause of your problem. Help is at hand in a difficult situation. The eagle-owl is a symbol of your cumulative experiences from which you could gain wisdom.

Ear

S: In antiquity the ear was thought to be the center of memory.

V: Seeing one or more ears: don't listen to the gossip around you, you might find out that it's about you. Looking at a donkey's ears: beware, you are about to do something stupid. Your ears are clogged up or you are deaf: you trusted someone and that trust has been abused. Cleaning your ears: your mistrust in a certain matter was completely justified. Someone pulling your ear is reminding you of a promise you made. If you are pulling someone's ear: a blunder someone else has made is causing sorrow and grief. Having your "ears boxed": beware of false friends, they can hurt you; or have you—maybe—done something wrong? Boxing someone's ears: keep your emotions under better control, so they don't lead to conflicts.

D: Dreaming about ears means you are easily impressed by others. Do you love to eavesdrop? Do you "play deaf" sometimes? Are you tired because someone is relentlessly "bending your ear"? Are you "lending an ear" to someone?

Earrings

V: Losing earrings means financial losses. Getting earrings as a gift: either somebody is in love with you or someone would like to be your friend.

Earth

S: The earth is the symbol of creation, "God's footstool."

V: If you are burying yourself: you are looking for your roots and your past. If you are looking at black soil: sorrow or grief. Dreaming of sunbathing suggests that taking a trip to the country will do you a world of good. Dreaming about climbing out from the earth (from a grave?) means either that a crisis in your life is over, or that you are reaching a new level of growth, almost a renewal. Turning over the soil (in your garden, a field, etc.): a reward for your hard work and a steady income. Sitting on the cold ground: pay more attention to your health.

D: The earth is a symbol for becoming and passing; it shows your past and your future. The earth stands for continuity, modesty, and being grounded, but also for inertia. Which of these applies to you?

Earthquake

V: Earthquakes usually mean sudden changes in your personal and social life. Watching an earthquake: a warning to remain steadfast even if you can't prevent changes. Suffering injury during an earthquake: the social/political situation in your country will take a turn for the worse.

D: Earthquakes are an ancient warning symbol. If you can withstand the upheavals of life (remain true to yourself), you will find a new place or starting point.

Earthworm

V: Seeing an earthworm: don't disregard other people's hard work. Be more frugal yourself (a very appropriate dream for people like bosses, politicians, and managers!). Using earthworms for bait: while you are following your own path, you are often inconsiderate, sometimes even unscrupulous.

D: The earthworm suggests that you be more considerate in the pursuit of your life's goals. It is time to change!

East

D: The East is a symbol for the spiritual, irrational, and mystical side of you. But it also represents your longing for light (the sun rises in the East), which represents rebirth. See **Four Corners of the Compass, Light.**

Easter, Easter Eggs

V: Searching for Easter eggs: the beginning of a new love relationship. Eating the eggs: you have very passionate feeling for another person, which can have biological consequences. Hiding Easter eggs: be honest—you are not playing straight with your friends and acquaintances. Giving Easter eggs: somebody respects and loves you and you will surrender. Receiving Easter eggs: a nice person will confess his/her love for you.

D: Easter eggs are a symbol of fertility and the desire for physical love. See **Egg.** Easter, on the other hand, symbolizes your longing for redemption in a certain matter.

Eating

V + D: Dreaming about eating means that you are sexually unfulfilled or looking to have sex. Eating at a large table: you want more social interaction. Eating a rich meal alone: recklessness and lack of empathy have made you unpopular. Eating very little food: you are remorseful. If you are hungry, but can't find anything to eat: a change in your life. If you are dieting, you will have frequent food and eating-related dreams.

Echo

V: Hearing an echo: pleasant company is about to visit. Hearing the echo of the words you have called out: be more careful of what you say—it might be fuel for embarrassing gossip. Hearing an echo in the woods: you may experience a time of loneliness.

D: An echo indicates an emotional reaction to an external event. Is the echo telling you something important? Or is it just repeating what you have called out—so you can hear what you're talking about all the time?

Eel

S: In a woman's dream, often a phallic symbol.

V: Dreaming about an eel: good news or the positive outcome of a project. Catching an eel: a new business deal is proceeding successfully, but people around it are envious. If you are ill, the eel may be a sign that you are getting well and will have more energy. If the eel is squirming: look out for a "smooth operator." Numerous eels in the water: a longing for sexual orgasm.

D: The eel is a sign of temptation and usually symbolizes hidden sexual desires. See **Fish, Serpent.**

Egg

S: The egg is a symbol of the life to come, of growth.

V: Eating an egg is a good omen for a permanent relationship. Seeing a lot of colorful eggs means many children. Finding a nest full of eggs: expect extra money either in the form of a win or an inheritance. Dropping an egg: losses in the coming weeks. Having eggs thrown at you: people around you are going to attack you. If you are the one throwing rotten eggs: you have done something wrong and it is going to boomerang.

D: Dreams about eggs are positive, because they always refer to your joy in life (unless the eggs are rotten). Beneath the eggshell are hidden your good and bad habits. Since the egg is also a symbol of rebirth, it could also be a sign of your own inner process of resurrection.

Elbow

D: Elbows are a symbol of your nimbleness, or a sign that you are strong enough to hold on. Seen in negative terms, it may refer to elbowing oneself forward. Are you using your elbows too much (as the perpetrator) or are you suffering from somebody else's use of "too much elbow"(being the victim)? Only you can determine which of the two possibilities apply to you.

Electrical Current

D: An electrical current could indicate a sudden "surge" of intellectual power. Are you feeling "electrified"? That would be a sign of erotic feelings or sexual adventure—even if you are not aware of this yet. If you see electrical sparks, the adventure will rapidly come to an end.

Elephant

S: The elephant is a symbol of sovereignty, power, and stability—in many places it is seen as a sacred animal.

V: In a woman's dream the elephant is a symbol of male strength. The elephant indicates that a job is going well, and success almost guaranteed. But the dream might also be a warning: don't be reckless, don't be a "bull in a china shop." Riding an elephant: good luck in your marriage; or you will meet a nice person. Seeing an elephant in a circus: people will think of you as foolish.

D: The elephant is a symbol of being steadfast, as it patiently carries a burden. It is also a sign of a sexuality ruled by rationality. The dream is a statement: you are strong enough to deal with any obstacles you might have to face. It is only a warning if you are thick-skinned and overbearing—if that is true, try to be more tactful.

Elevator

V: In a woman's dream, riding up in an elevator means social and professional advancement. Riding down in an elevator means the desire for sexual adventure. Seeing an elevator in your house: you want to get things done fast and without much effort—but that is wishful thinking.

D: Riding in an elevator means you are looking for help with a specific problem; or you want to reach your goals in life in a hurry without putting much effort into it (that won't work!).

Elf

D: The elf in a dream often represents your need for love and tenderness. A goblin or a dwarf is a sign of inferiority feelings. Do you suffer from inhibitions? Are you afraid? Or burdened by guilt? See **Nymph.**

Emaciated

V: Being or looking emaciated: losses and health problems. Seeing others as emaciated: a warning not to ruin others materially. Sometimes it can also be a hint of increased material gain. Dreaming of having put on weight can mean future prosperity.

D: Looking emaciated or very skinny: your inner center has "shrunk." You are being asked to take better care of yourself. Seeing others as emaciated: you hope for financial gain for yourself (this is how wicked the unconscious is!).

Embrace, Embracing

V: Seeing two people embracing: you are longing for a love relationship. Embracing someone: you will make a new acquaintance.

D: Someone is embracing you: a person wants to "possess you" completely, or vice versa.

Embryo

D: This symbol might point to a new emotion or a new idea that is slowly developing inside you. Sometimes you might also yearn to return to a pre-born state, or curl up in mother's lap again because the responsibilities for your life are just too much.

Emperor, Empress

V: The emperor represents your father. If you see both emperor and empress, they represent your parents. What the emperor or empress is doing is important for getting specific information about the dream's meaning. If you are the emperor or the empress: don't set your hopes too high. Being a servant at the court of an emperor means support from a person of authority.

D: Being the emperor or the empress: you are expecting too much and will face disappointments. See **King.**

End of the World

V: Dreaming about seeing the end of the world is, for people who have psychic gifts, a warning; for others, it means an imminent emotional crisis. See **Earth.**

D: Extreme problems and conflicts lead to separation from people you are close to you or from your own, outdated attitudes. The world as you knew it is coming to an end!

Enemy

V: If you are in a war, confronted by your enemies: conflicts and struggles. Meeting your enemies under any other circumstances: deceit and malice.

D: Enemies in a dream are a warning about conflict, arguments, and someone else's evil intentions. Be on guard and develop a healthy distrust.

Engagement

V: Dreaming about getting engaged: expect a painful disappointment from a person you love. People celebrating an engagement: single people may get engaged or make a commitment to someone, married people will find new friends.

D: If you are single, you are longing for love, marriage, or family; married people want to improve their relationship.

Envy

V + D: Dreaming about feeling envious means that your

relationship with your surroundings is not very good. You are faced with temptation and have a hard time resisting it. Right now you need considerable strength of character and to reduce tensions and feelings of envy toward other people.

Epidemic

D: A sign that you are materialistically oriented, which could destroy your serenity and even lead to illness. You would do well to transform your emphasis on money and property into spiritual values.

Escalator

D: Are you looking for advancement without doing your part? See **Career.** Or is the dream a sign that you would get ahead faster with help from others?

Euphoria

D: Euphoria in a dream is a short-lived illusion that—not unlike a soap bubble—usually disappears quickly in the harsh light of reality.

Evening

D: Evening in a dream might refer to the twilight years of your life, which, depending on other dream images, might be comfortable or full of fear. Or it might indicate that your energies are depleted (even if you yourself have no inkling of it), and suggest that you take a break. See **Morning, Noon.**

Evergreen

V: Dreaming about an evergreen means you are enjoying a very faithful friendship; but take care of it if you want it to last. Picking evergreen boughs and making a wreath: you will find a faithful friend.

D: Evergreens are a symbol of true and steady relationships—either you are looking for one or you have one already. Also, your faith in yourself is either strong or will be strengthened.

Exam

V: Hidden behind the dream might be the fear of having to make a long-overdue decision, or resolve confusion or tension on the job. Particularly in men's dreams, an exam symbolizes actual problems, such as the fear of standing up for yourself to your boss or on the job in general. These dreams are a challenge to face and resolve conflicts. They may serve to encourage us to learn and grow. A wrenching exam dream is meant to strengthen your self-confidence and provide the energy necessary to do the task. Taking an exam and failing: don't panic, the dream is a sign that you will pass. See **Learning, School, Teacher.**

D: The exam dream is testing your character and maturity. Passing the exam means you can move on to new tasks, be ready for the next test. Are you afraid of problems ahead? Do you doubt yourself? Is your belief in your own abilities on shaky ground? Build up your self-confidence!

Excavating

V: If you are digging up soil or a tree: a difficult task ahead. At the same time, such a dream indicates that you are working very hard and your task will be profitable. Dreaming of "unearthing" one (or more) dead people: a bad conscience. You are either surrounded by deceitful people or you are leading a less than honorable life. See **Death.**

D: The act of excavating can be proverbial in its meaning: the soul of the dreamer is "excavating" something from the unconscious, such as secret character traits—your own or someone else's. Suddenly you are remembering something that was forgotten or repressed, which is the reason for your emotional difficulties.

Exchanging

V: Exchanging something in a dream: get ready for a pleasant surprise—things are going to change.

Excrement

D: Dreaming about "playing" with excrement: you have regressed—psychologically—to an anal phase (sexual immaturity). Also, you have gained new insight from past experiences. Passing stool: you will get relief from an actual situation. Feeling dirtied by excrement: a fear of not being accepted (or feeling disgust about yourself). Handling your own excrement: you want to get rid of emotional ballast or unpleasant situations. Seeing or stepping in excrement is a good omen: personal matters are resolved in your favor and to your satisfaction. See **Intestines, Colon, Toilet.**

Execution

V: Watching an execution: you will either best your adversary or meet a new friend. Watching the execution of a person you know: you will lose a friend. Dreaming of being executed: others are putting you down and you feel ashamed. See **Gallows, Hanging, Murder.**

D: Your opinions or assumptions are going to change (or have already). A dream about an execution suggests revising an opinion you have had about certain events. Put your changed attitude to work.

Explosion

V: Witnessing an explosion: you are threatened by an alarming, unexpected event. Suddenly waking up immediately after a dream: a physical problem. Seeing an explosion: your present restlessness is temporary. Seeing dead people after an explosion: escaping at the last moment from a dangerous situation, unscathed. This symbol is a sign of severe tension that is about to explode. See **Bomb, Dynamite.** However, anxieties and tension will just as suddenly disappear. Why are you about to explode? What kind of volcano inside you is waiting to erupt?

Extinguishing, Quenching

V: Quenching your thirst: your dreams of finding love are being fulfilled. Extinguishing a fire: a passionate affair (thank goodness) is coming to an end—otherwise, it would have devoured you. Sometimes the dream means you will escape from an unfortunate situation at the last moment. Extinguishing a fire in your house: you are engulfed in actual difficulties, but you will prevail!

D: The meaning of the dream depends on what you have or are trying to extinguish. See **Candle, Fire, Lamp, Lantern, Light.**

Eyeglasses

S: Wearing glasses is a symbol of virtue, moderation, and balance.

V: Losing glasses: you will find intrigue and lies in your immediate surroundings. Somebody putting glasses on you is a suggestion to think honestly about whether you are too easily influenced by others; you are putty in their hands. Wearing glasses: you want to get a better understanding of your life and are doing just that. Someone else wearing dark glasses: someone in your immediate surroundings wants to hide his/her true intentions—be careful. See **Eyes.**

D: A pair of glasses is often a symbol of a distorted view of the world. The unconscious is making itself known: a matter or a person needs to be reexamined; it may also mean that you see the world through "rose-colored glasses." See **Blindness.**

Eyes, Ophthalmologist

S: These are symbols of spiritual and intellectual insight.

V: Dreaming about blue eyes: either somebody is secretly in love with you or you are secretly in love with someone. Dark or brown eyes: prepare yourself for a disappointing romance. Dreaming about an eye illness (eye patch, eye injury, or blindness): you are unable to see a situation in your life clearly, or you have a problem facing the real truth. An eye patch indicates that you can do your job even with your eyes closed! Visiting or seeing an ophthalmologist: you will soon see things as they really are. See **Cross-eyed.**

D: Dreaming about eyes means you are too preoccupied with yourself. The eye is considered the organ of light. Dreaming about eyes always has something to do with understanding life. Dreaming about an eye that is looking at you might be a warning from your conscience. Eyes by themselves are symbols of intelligence, spirit, alertness, and curiosity. Other events in the dream are important here.

S = Symbol V = Vision D = Depth psychology

Face

V: Seeing a person with a pale face means a likely illness or even death. Looking at an ugly face: you are worried, or bothered by conflicts you have with others. Seeing a beautiful face: hopes have a chance to come true. Seeing your own face in a mirror: pay attention to physical symptoms, but don't take yourself too seriously. Seeing a beautiful face reflected in the water means a long and agreeable life. Seeing a face with too much makeup: your friends are not what they appear to be—or they are lying.

D: Faces in dreams are the mirror of "the face of your soul"—the way the world sees you. Sometimes you might see the face of a stranger in a dream who will cross your path years later. What did you see in this face?

Factory

V: Seeing a factory is a good sign, promising business success. Working in a factory: you are dealing with a tense situation; things are hectic, but overall you are satisfied with your job. If you are the owner of the factory: you are spending great amounts of money and getting little in return. A smoking factory chimney is a sign of your sexual desires.

D: The factory is a symbol of new plans at the expense of

peace and quiet. Are you on automatic pilot? Would you like to change that?

Fainting

V: Dreaming you have fainted means a "dizzying" love affair ahead. The dream may also be a warning of personal loss and failings. Someone else is fainting: you will be asked for help. If it is money, be very careful.

D: Fainting is a sign of helpless feelings toward another person, but also that you are temporarily freed from your responsibilities. See **Dizziness**. Frequent dreams of fainting might also be a sign of poor blood circulation in the brain during the night.

Fair

V: Being at a fair: either a profitable connection or a good business transaction is in the making. You will see an infinite number of things at the fair, but don't let that confuse you. See **Shopping**.

D: Dreaming about a fair is a warning either about making unnecessary purchases or about being superficial. Is it hard for you to be alone? Do you need constant diversion or stimulation? Are you addicted to spending money, to shopping?

Fairy

V: Seeing a fairy in a dream always means good luck in personal matters and indicates that long-cherished, secret wishes finally will come true. For single people this dream means an engagement is possible.

D: The fairy is an ancient symbol of love for the opposite sex. It also means religious or spiritual guidance.

Fall, Autumn

V: Dreaming that fall has arrived means unpleasantness ahead. It also refers to unconscious fears about "the fall of life." Seeing a landscape of fall colors: love for a certain person is slowly dying.

D: Fall is a symbol of harvest—maybe receiving rewards for your past efforts. Are you letting go of frivolities, becoming more reflective? Ambitions and urges are slowly losing importance. In men's dreams, fall often expresses a fear of impotence. In a love relationship it is a signal that "the heat of passion" has passed.

Falling

S: A bad fall into an abyss often brings an undefinable feeling of relief.

V: For a woman, dreaming about falling is a metaphor for letting herself go. Falling means that you're stumbling into an unpleasant situation. Feeling the act of falling, physically, is not a cause for alarm. It is simply a case of "getting back into your body"—waking up too quickly. It might also be a sign of low blood pressure. Falling into a ditch: your reputation will suffer. Falling over something: a certain matter is made clear to you. Stumbling without falling: things could have been a lot worse. Watching others falling: you're going to unmask your enemies just in time. See **Abyss, Fall.**

D: Dreams about falling are a sign of the fear you have of people taking the "reins out of your hand," of losing control. Have you lost faith in yourself, lost your sense of self-worth? Are you afraid that others—for whatever reason—are going to "drop" you? Are you losing your good reputation? Or: have you "dropped" an old belief or opinion?

Farmer

V: Seeing a young farmer working means you are leading

a contented life. If you are the farmer, it means you are leading a burdensome life; or you have to work hard in order for your old age to be peaceful. however, you, your work, and your goals are on solid ground—promising great success.

D: The farmer in dreams is a symbol for a simple, natural lifestyle you are hoping for. If you are the farmer: you are a well-grounded person, in tune with the rhythm of life.

Fasting

V: Dreaming about fasting is often a hint that you are going through a health crisis. The dream suggests that you be sexually moderate.

D: Fasting can also indicate that you are trying to "cleanse" your character (from greed, impulses, instincts, and unrealistic hopes). The dream may also indicate an actual illness.

Fat, Obesity

V: Eating fatty foods in your dream suggests caution, possible illness. Greasy spots on your clothes mean possibly marrying into wealth. Being obese is a symbol of a gentle and natural death. It is also a symbol of feelings of inferiority—you believe people think you are disgusting. Preparing a heavy meal means impending loss.

D: Fat represents sensuality, cheerfulness, and a tendency to overdo things. It is a warning from the unconscious about excessive eating and drinking.

Father, Father Figure

V: Your father (or a father figure) is a symbol of your need for safety and security (particularly in women's dreams). For women who change partners frequently, the dream is the personification of a bad conscience (particularly if her father—when she was a child—was the primary disciplinarian). If you yourself are the father, it means you will "create" a life. Speaking to your father: you have a suppressed longing to lean on someone or to be guided by someone. Seeing your own father: you feel you are bringing shame to your family and owe your father an apology. Dreaming about your deceased father: help is on the way or someone is making you very happy.

D: A father figure in a dream means a confrontation with your boss or with a person in authority. See **Pastor, Physician, Priest, Teacher**. You feel imprisoned. Sometimes the dream reminds you of a person who has stood by you and has given you advice in the past. What has your father contributed to the person you are today? What do you have in common with him? See **Mother.**

Feather

V: Decorating yourself with feathers: you are too vain and egocentric. Looking at a feather used for writing: good news. A white feather means fun; or you are found to be innocent because an accusation was proven false. A black feather means bad luck (see the chapter "**Colors in Dreams**)." Seeing feathers fly: curb your money-spending habit—your hopes for getting money are futile.

D: Feathers represent thoughts and hopes, sometimes also vanity and false pride. Did somebody "clip your feathers" in a business matter? The color of the feathers as well as the other symbols in the dream are very important here.

Fence

V: Standing in front of a fence: with great skill you will overcome obstacles in your path. Climbing over a fence: now it will be a cinch to solve your problem. Getting hurt in the process of climbing: you will achieve your goal—with, alas, a few scratches—but once you have arrived, you'll be surprised how different things are from what you expected. See **Barrier, Wall.**

D: A fence can mean protection or an obstacle. If the fence is blocking your path, have courage and jump over it. Is a fence surrounding your property (house, garden)? Or is the fence a metaphor for the limitations imposed on you from the outside? Take a good look at the rest of the dream symbols!

Fencing

V: If you are fencing (with a rapier), it means a quarrel with friends and losing them.

D: Fencing might be a sign of wanting revenge, to get even. For now try to stay away from fights and quarrels! See **Dagger, Rapier.**

Ferry

S: A ferry, like a bridge, is a connection between two shores.

V: Being on a ferry crossing a lake or river: pay attention to the depth and width of the water. but in general the dream is not a good omen for your journey into maturity.

D: The ferry is an expression of your search for a new spiritual dimension. You have decided—if not, do so now—to let go of past emotional reactions and habits. See **Bridge, Ship, Shore.**

Fever

V: Dreaming about fever means that you are living out unconscious fears. Fever dreams mean that the unconscious is hard at work dealing with repressed emotions or fears. Sometimes it signals illness. Dreaming of having a fever means uncertain times for your love life or friendships. If someone else has a fever, it means losing a friend.

D: If illness can be excluded, you might have a case of "feverish" passion for someone, but beware—passionate fires burn out quickly!

Field

V: Looking at a fallow field: you have let an opportunity pass you by in your job. If the wheat is free of weeds and blemishes: good profits and professional advancement. A neglected field or a field devastated by hail and wind: a warning that great hardship is awaiting you. A field just sprayed with liquid manure means your venture will be successful!

D: Fields are primordial symbols for motherhood and fertility, for being connected to the strength and energies of nature. The field's appearance indicates how much you are emotionally rooted, and how strong and healthy you are. It also is a symbol for the feminine in you—the more beautiful and healthy the field is, the more vigorous you are. See **Meadow.**

Fig/Fig Tree

S: The fig tree is always a symbol of fertility.

V: Eating figs means expectations and hopes in matters of love will be fulfilled soon. Seeing dried figs means your assets are shrinking. Someone is giving you figs: a friendly relationship becomes more intense. Seeing a fig tree: hold your sexual urges in check. You see one or several figs: you are longing for love.

D: The fig is a symbol of sexual needs and erotic adventures. The fig leaf means innocence and chastity that you would like to parade in front of other people. The fig tree warns you about one-sided desires for purely sexual gratification.

Fight, Fighting

S: "The law of a sinful world is the law of fighting."

V: You are watching a fight: conciliatory words will defuse the tension between other people. Fighting on a battlefield: adversaries, enemies, hate, or envy make your life difficult, but you are able to defend yourself successfully. Witnessing a fight: don't use the old saying: "living well is the best revenge" as a motto for your life, because: "those who laugh last laugh best!" See **Beating.**

D: Dreaming about fighting reflects the difficulties you have in balancing conflicting personality traits. Decide which you want to nurture and which you want to minimize—it will restore your peace!

File, Filing

V: Filing a piece of iron: success will be the reward for hard work. Filing your fingernails: you are bored with life. Filing a piece of wood: you feel uncertain about a present situation.

D: The file serves as a warning: continue "working" on yourself, it is the only way to get control over bad habits.

Filled Up, Full

V: Feeling "all filled up": you are either hungry or are satisfied and in harmony with the world. In some cases, the dream is a challenge not to be so easygoing in the future.

Filth

V: Looking at filth: you want to distance yourself from something negative or from bad company—whatever it is, that's a good idea—follow through! Sometimes dreaming about filth only means that you need to solve a problem. Watching someone step into filth: you will cause trouble for someone—unintentionally. Finding money in a filthy spot: hold on to your wallet—somebody wants to steal it.

D: Dreaming about filth means you really believe you are dirty (physically or morally) or very plain (physically or spiritually). If the dream is a sign of feelings of inferiority, seek professional help. But remember, dirt is not always negative

(Earth, Manure, Mud) and is often an important symbol of personal growth.

Finger

S: A finger held over your mouth stands for silence.

V: Seeing a large finger in a dream: you have an unconscious hankering for love and sexual contact (particularly in women's dreams). A dirty finger announces quarrels and unpleasantness. Cutting yourself means mishaps or gossip. Are you missing a finger in your dream? Is one finger too thick, too thin? The interpretation of such images depends upon which finger is involved.

The *thumb* stands for courage, self-confidence, and a fighting spirit. The *index finger* stands for goals, patience, ambitions, pride, and intellect. The *middle finger* stands for success, profession, business, long-term plans, work ethic, and caution.

The *ring finger* stands for art, beauty, music, sense of community, emotions, and empathy. The *little finger* is a phallic symbol and represents sexual needs. Is a finger raised to admonish you? Is it a warning? Is it pointing at something? If a finger is missing, you are either missing the above-mentioned character traits or exaggerating them. Looking at fingerprints suggests you pay more attention to your individuality.

Fingernails

V: Filing your finger nails: you are very bored. See **File**. Fingernails are breaking off: deep down you hope that a certain matter does not succeed. Cutting your finger nails: you want to cut a person down to size. Seeing two hands with extremely long fingernails: a sign of powerful, aggressive emotions (conscious or unconscious). This dream may be a warning to you to hide those sharp "claws" or you may be bothered by someone else's sharp intellect. If these fingernails scratch anyone, beware—you are in danger of getting seriously hurt.

D: The fingernail usually symbolizes the "intellectual weapon" used to defend yourself against the attacks of others. Scratching someone means working off unconscious aggression. See **Cat.**

Fire

V: In men's dreams, a blazing fire is a symbol for a sexual high: his passions are on fire. Being afraid of fire means that he is afraid of total commitment. Enjoying watching a fire indicates a readiness to make a total commitment. Seeing a large fire without smoke: keep your passions in check. A heavily smoking fire may mean bad luck. Putting out a fire: dashed hopes. Lighting a fire: meeting a new friend or having a romantic relationship. Dancing around the fire: a party with friends. Seeing a fire in a stove: happy news—a child might be on the way. Putting out a fire in a stove: a warning of impending illness. See **Blaze.**

D: Fire is a very important symbol. Be careful if you see a house on fire (the house always stands for the dreamer), it can mean an impending illness. A brightly burning fire is a symbol of inner cleansing. A fire indicates hot passion, ideals, and desires. Fire can purify or destroy indiscriminately. Are you consumed by passion? Did you feel "burned out" after the dream?

Fire Engine, Fireworks

V: Seeing fireworks means the loss of your fortunes. Watch out for con men and unrealistic goals—you might have a rude awakening. Seeing a fire engine indicates hard times to come.

D: Fireworks mean you love attention and being the center of attraction. See **Fire.** The fire engine represents that part of your personality (self-control) that deals properly with all urges and passion.

Fireplace

V: Looking at a fireplace without a fire: a warning about losing something—either a good job or a good friend. A fire burning in the fireplace: expect carefree times in your family and in intimate relationships. If smoke is coming from the fireplace: worries and problems in your house or family. See **Oven, Soot.**

D: A fireplace stands for female sex organs. In a man's dream, it represents sexual feelings that need to be controlled (like the fire in the fireplace!). In a woman's dream. it is either a symbol of her search for human contact, affection, and warmth, or a sign that she doesn't feel safe.

Fish

S: The fish is a symbol of water, life, and fertility.

V: Dreaming about several fish in clear water might mean to try your luck in the lottery. Catching fish means success for a project started recently; or you might come into money. Pregnant women dreaming about eating fish means that labor will be easy. Men eating fish means good luck with women. Seeing or catching small fish: you are dissatisfied and sad. If the fish is cold or slippery: someone is flattering you and you are being taken advantage of. Dreaming of a fishing rod is a promise of hope and financial gain. Dreaming of being swallowed by a fish means you are in a deep emotional conflict and feeling helpless.

D: The fish often stands for sexual cravings or a desire to have children. You might also do well to fish around in your unconscious to gain more self-knowledge.

Fisherman

V: Dreaming of a fisherman suggests that something in your unconscious (water) wants to come to the surface. A hidden emotional matter would like to "see the light of day." See **Fish.**

Fishing

V: Casting a fishing rod: you long for a partner. Catching a fish in clear waters: good luck and success in an important matter. If somebody is throwing his fishing rod at you: pay attention, a deceptive person is in your life. Fishing at the shore of a calm lake: your emotional balance will soon be restored. Watching others as they fish: there will be an opportunity to make new friends. See **Fish, Water.**

D: If you are fishing: your emotional balance will soon be restored. Catching a fish: good luck is right around the corner.

Fist

V: Seeing a clenched fist in front of your face: an enemy is planning to attack you. If you are raising a fist against someone else: you want to be in the limelight, be in front. If you were able to remove an obstacle with your fist: you have the strength to make many things possible.

D: The fist is a symbol of **Aggression**, strife, and internal tension. It is a warning of danger, conflicts, and arrogance. See **Hand, Thumb.**

Flag

S: The flag is a symbol of victory.

V: If you are carrying a flag: you will gain respect. Looking at many flags: political power struggle in your country. Carrying a black flag: hostility. Lowering a flag: you have regrets about past action. To see many flags flying in the wind:

unpleasantness or even sorrow. Women seeing a flag pole or carrying a flag: reveals sexual desires.

D: The flag is a symbol of your life's goals and ideals. Are you contemplating new projects, new goals, or plans?

Flattery

V: If someone is flattering you, it is a warning about negative influences around you.

Fleas

V: Seeing a flea: you would like to take revenge on a certain person. Being bitten by fleas: you are bothered by persons of ill will. Catching a flea: all ordinary problems will be solved. Has someone put a "bug" in your ear? See **Bug, Flies, Insect.**

Flee, Escape

V: If you are escaping: you are avoiding danger at the last moment. Helping another person escape: a Good-Samaritan act will be the cause of future problems.

D: A dream about escaping means you are going to escape danger in time.

Flies

V: Pesky flies buzzing around you: gossip, and as a result, unpleasantness and aggravation. Catching flies: don't let others make you nervous; avoid stress at work. Killing flies: you want to avoid distasteful situations—but with little success. Flies in your mouth: problems with an impertinent person.

D: Dreams about flies usually are a sign of nervousness or something annoying (including people) in your environment.

Flood

V: Watching a flood: you are dealing with people who are bothering you with their pleas and petitions. A flooded room:

bad luck and fighting. Trying to outrun a flood: you are running away from yourself.

D: Some emotions and cravings are getting so strong, they are overrunning you, but your self-confidence will be restored. A torrential flood is a sign that you will have sudden, uncontrollable emotions, sometimes a big shock, or a nervous breakdown.

Flour

V: Grinding flour: you are bringing happiness to someone (consciously or unconsciously). Looking at a great amount of flour: your financial situation will improve considerably. Flour on your clothes: someone's deception may cause you pain.

D: See **Baker, Bread, Grain, Wheat.**

Flowers

V: Picking flowers means material success and a pleasant emotional experience. Seeing a bouquet of fresh flowers: good luck in love and friendship. Decorating yourself with flowers means the deepening of a relationship with a loved one. Tearing flowers off a plant: you are destroying (or have destroyed) your own happiness. In a woman's dream, flowers stand for great expectation and hope in matters of love. If the woman is picking flowers it means she is hoping that her secret wishes (sometimes the material kind) will be fulfilled.

D: Dreams about flowers point to something positive within you. It might also refer to a very private, personal experience that is, in real life, related to flowers. The more beautiful the flowers, the richer your emotional world and your ability to love.

Flying

S: When men dream about flying, it usually indicates their need for freedom. It also indicates cravings for sexual thrills.

V: Enjoying the flight means past events or situations have been successfully dealt with. Feeling anxious or pursued by something or someone could be a sign of physical illness (have your heart and circulatory system checked!). Flying high above other people: you have "high-flying" plans that you cannot always carry out. Flying low above the ground means playing it safe in life. Flying over land and oceans means you want total freedom. If you are married, it may mean you want a divorce.

D: Flying has many different meanings: sexual cravings, a better understanding about the past and insight into the future, or a wish to be lifted above the "demeaning" aspects of everyday life. Flying always is an uncertain undertaking because you are leaving the "ground" of reality. Hopefully, you will not fall back down to earth too harshly!

Fog

V: Being surrounded by thick fog: postpone all plans—right now you don't have the necessary information. Seeing fog: your personal situation is nebulous; right now you can only rely on your intuition and good judgment.

D: Fog is a symbol of your own insecurities and doubts about what course to follow in the future. Or are you trying to hide your intentions from others—or even yourself?

Fool

V: Seeing or being a fool: don't take yourself and others so seriously. But the dream is also a warning about making fun of others—it is much better to laugh at yourself. See **Laughing.**

D: See **Clown, Jumping Jack.**

Foot

S: The human foot represents being connected to the earth.

V: If you are running barefoot: come back to reality and

become more "earthbound," real, and sensitive. See **Going Barefoot.** If your feet are dirty: you have a bad conscience—unburden yourself. Washing your feet: an uncertain situation is clearing up—the small detour you made was very therapeutic. If you have fractured your foot: unexpected obstacles and misadventures are blocking your progress. Dreaming of having very big feet: you might buy a house—but be careful with your money. Dreaming of having very narrow feet: life is difficult, you are exhausted.

D: Dreaming about moving feet (walking, running, etc.): you are determined not to walk away from life's difficulties. Feet always symbolize the "foundation" of your life: your convictions, principles, and values. It is important in which direction the feet are running—**Left** (the feminine, intuitive, irrational, emotional) way, or **Right** (the everyday life, logical, "right") way, or if either foot is missing.

Footbridge

V: Walking over a footbridge: you have maneuvered yourself into a tight spot and are trying to find a way out. See **Path.**

Foreign Countries

D: Dreaming about being in a foreign country might mean that a situation, a person, a project, or one of your own character traits has not yet been acknowledged; you are still trying to figure things out. Maybe the dream refers to a past travel experience?

Forest

V: Seeing a beautiful forest: you have an unshakable faith in God and the future, and will experience prosperity and security in your old age. Seeing a forest fire: pay close attention to physical symptoms—your health is delicate. Seeing only the edge of a forest: a relationship is over.

D: The forest is a place where unresolved emotions and the shadow of the soul reside. Are you unable to "see the forest for the trees"? It is easy to get lost in the "forest of life"—the forest of so many experiences and so much information. See **Tree.**

Forget-Me-Not

V: Seeing a forget-me-not: a reminder that making up with an old friend is possible. Giving forget-me-nots as a gift: you feel a certain person is neglecting you. See **Flower.**

D: This little flower is reminding you of an emotional relationship from the past; or you feel terribly neglected by someone you like very much.

Fork

V: Eating with a fork: you are going to have a fight. Dropping a fork also means quarreling—a falling-out with a friend. Stabbing yourself with a fork: a dire warning—someone wants to deceive you. Stabbing someone else: another person is shamelessly exploiting you. Looking at a hay fork means increased prosperity.

D: The fork symbolizes disagreement and conflicts in your relationships, which is the reason why you're having trouble concentrating on your goal right now.

Fort

V: Dreaming about a fort means hostilities. A fort under construction: the government of your country is in a political crisis. A destroyed fort: the sign of a past unhappy memory, lack of self-worth.

D: The fort symbolizes your fear of difficulties or a need for security and protection. A fort in ruins is a sign of lack of self-worth.

Fortress (Castle)

S: A fortress is a symbol of security and safety.

V: Living in a fortress: you are satisfied with your present situation. Do you have a need for more safety? Do you need to protect yourself against the outside world? Seeing a fortress: a sense of adventure has been kindled. Standing in front of a fortress with the gates locked: your plans or actions will be met with resistance.

D: A fortress is a place of protection; for some, it might represent danger. Are you self-absorbed? Have you withdrawn from others? Do you feel comfortable in this fortress? Are the windows and doors closed? See **Castle, House, Palace, Rock.**

Fountain

V: A fountain in a dream challenges you to make use of the talents you have neglected so far. Make them shine in the light of day. See **Water, Well.**

Fountain of Youth

V: In a woman's dream, the fountain of youth is a signal that love is "wilting"—try to breath new life into your relationship. In a man's dream, it is a desire to be more youthful, to have more fun and a more active and intense love relationship.

D: See **Youth.**

Four Points of the Compass

V: Walking toward the **West** is a sign of awareness. The West is a region of extroverted (outer-directed) activities and order. Turning to the **South** means you are searching for warmth in the "land of emotion." The **North** is more cool—a place of premonition and intuition. The **East** indicates intensity and more introverted (inner-directed) thoughts.

Whichever direction you are traveling in the dream, translate its meaning into your everyday life.

Fox

S: Like many other red-coated animals, the fox is a symbol of deception.

V: Seeing a fox (or several): you are suspicious of your friends. A running fox: be careful, somebody wants to trick you. A tame fox: pay attention, a false friend wants to do you in. Catching a fox: you are going to uncover a secret plot. Participating in a fox hunt: you are outmaneuvering a woman. Or is it the other way around?

D: In men's dreams, the fox is usually a symbol of sexual cravings, intelligence, cunning, and instinctive behavior, but it is also deceitful. Does someone have it in for you?

Fragments, Broken Pieces

V: Looking at something broken or breaking something: your present pleasant situation will take a turn for the worse due to your own actions. Breaking porcelain: the "old" is swept away to make room for the "new."

D: There is a saying that "broken dishes mean good luck," and that is true for dreams, too, but sometimes the dream may be a warning against too much exuberance; hopes and wishes can be as fragile as glass. Was it broken **Glass** or broken **Porcelain?**

Frailty

V: Dreaming about being frail expresses your feeling of hopelessness or not measuring up to someone's expectations. Maybe you have a "weakness" for someone and that person is taking advantage of it? Or do you lack assertiveness? Frequent dreams of this nature are a sign of deep-seated anxieties that might need therapeutic intervention.

Frame

D: Looking at a frame refers to the parameters of your life (abilities or possibilities), but it is also, indirectly, a comforting sign, because if there are parameters that limit life in general, sorrow and grief must be limited as well. See **Picture.**

Fraud, Fibbing

V: Catching someone in the act of committing fraud: people gossip about you, but that is no reason to start fibbing—you will only be found out later.

Freckles

V: Seeing someone with freckles: you are afraid that people believe your mistakes and vices are "written all over your face."

D: Freckles are a sign that you are worried about your mistakes and weaknesses—you believe you are "marked" by them.

Friend—Girlfriend, Boyfriend

V: If you are lonely and dream about a friend, it means you want to have a better social life. Meeting a friend: a warning to think before you act! Seeing a deceased friend: surprising news. Helping a friend: you too will soon get help. Starting a new friendship means you have really good, true friends.

D: Meeting a person you know: the feelings you have for the person in the dream are the same as those you have for a friend in real life.

Frog

V: Seeing a frog means blessings in love and money matters. Hearing frogs croaking: repressed desires for love or sex will soon be making themselves known. Don't give people an excuse to gossip. As of now, your reputation is still intact.

Holding a frog in your hands: you are going to win in something. Killing a frog: you are going to harm yourself.

D: The frog stands for emotional and spiritual changes, like the changes that take place from spawning to the final form (the fairy tale "The Frog and the Princess" comes to mind). The dream is telling you not to be afraid of change. Hearing a frog croaking: these sounds are considered symptoms of emotional inadequacy; often they suggest that you are looking for a way out. You need to work more on your issues.

Front (as in Side)

V: Usually the front is showing you the "real, true side" one that is visible, a symbol of consciousness and reality. See **Back (Side).**

Frost

V: Looking at a frost-covered landscape: That certain matter is not going to work out, accept it. Also, stop mourning your past!

D: At the moment, now that your feelings for another person have cooled off considerably, there is hope that things will get better (when the sun melts the ice).

Froth, Bubble Bath

V: Eating something frothy or taking a bubble bath: you are very idealistic, and in your love life you are easily deceived.

D: See **Bath, Soap.**

Fruit

S: Dreaming about fruit is usually a sign that new plans are in the making.

V: Eating fruit: your hopes of finding love are going to be

fulfilled. Eating sweet fruit: a project is going well. Eating bitter or sour fruit: expect problems to affect a certain matter. Rotten fruit: your love relationship leaves you dissatisfied. Seeing many different kinds of fruit: an argument will be resolved to your satisfaction. Looking at a display of fruit in a grocery store: attractive business transactions are in the making. Offering or selling fruit: you are trying hard to win someone's approval. Picking fruit always indicates positive changes in relationships. Picking fruit off the ground: small efforts will bring great rewards. Holding a fruit basket: you are afraid your partner will reject you.

D: Dreams about fruit are often about sexual needs and are a good sign for new plans and romantic relationships. They also indicate rewards for past efforts. Rotten fruit, on the other hand, always means adversity.

Frying Pan

V: Seeing a frying pan: you will soon meet an old acquaintance. Frying eggs: you have taken on too much in your love relationship; taking a step back would be much healthier right now.

D: A pan is a utensil where "intense emotions" boil—you might burn your mouth or your fingers. Keep your "heated urges" under control without repressing them altogether. See **Cook.**

Full Moon

V: Seeing a full moon in your dream: your affairs are proceeding well and are successful—including your love life. See **Moon.**

Funeral

S: Dreaming about a funeral indicates a profound shift in your personality. It might symbolize fear of your own death (or that of a loved one), or letting go of old guilt feelings, or social isolation.

V: Don't be afraid if you dream about your own funeral: it promises a long and healthy life—the result of the shift mentioned above. Dreaming about the funeral of a friend who is still alive means problems with a friend and maybe a fight. Dreaming about the funeral of a stranger: good luck and joy for you, but bad luck for a friend or acquaintance. See **Death.**

D: The funeral is an indication that something inside you is in the process of "dying": feelings, hopes, wishes, an experience, etc. The process will be liberating; you will know you have overcome something and left it behind.

Fur

V: Seeing a fur coat: even good habits are not always properly appreciated by others. Wearing a fur coat: other people's efforts and hard work might give you a big win or good profits. Lying on a fur: your life right now is very comfortable; you don't need to work very hard. Receiving a fur coat as a gift: you will soon either marry for money or start a new business relationship.

D: See **Animals, Mink.**

Furniture

V: Dreaming about furniture: a sign of prosperity. However, your materialistic tendencies are blocking your path—like bulky pieces of furniture.

D: What kind of attitudes and convictions have you used to furnish your emotional house? Is the furniture heavy or light, old or modern, bright and beautiful, or damaged?

S = Symbol V = Vision D = Depth psychology

Gallows

V: If you see a gallows: you are surrounded by false friends. If someone is hanging on the gallows: your adversary will soon give up. If you are hanging on the gallows: a change in your life and fortune. Building a gallows: unexpected changes with positive consequences.

D: Gallows in a dream are usually a symbol of far-reaching changes in your life. However, there will be much suffering until then, because present problems won't be resolved in a hurry; major adjustments on your part are necessary. See **Hanging.**

Games, Playing

V: Dreaming about the lottery: be prepared for dishonesty and don't have too many illusions. Playing a game for money: deceit and quarrels ahead. Playing a game of cards: you are holding on to old clichés; or you are caught in the throes of an all-consuming passion that is "devouring" you. Playing a game of dice: your carelessness and naive trust in people is going to cost you dearly. Playing billiards: a planned meeting is running into difficulties. See **Chess.**

D: The dream may be a warning to change your careless lifestyle, which is interfering with your personal growth, or a challenge to lighten up and not take life so seriously. Other symbols in the dream will provide additional information and you know better than anyone else if you are too serious or too casual.

Garbage, Refuse

V: Falling over garbage: Let go of deceptive assumptions and double-check old attitudes. Replace them with new ones. If other things are falling on top of you and you can't make out what they are, but you feel good: you can increase your material possessions; if you feel bad, the dream hints that you will be wrongfully accused, that people are envious or resentful.

D: Treat garbage more carefully—meaning do a better job recycling your "emotional garbage," so you can create something new.

Garden

S: The garden is a symbol of paradise.

V: Women who are dissatisfied and unhappy often dream about a fenced-in garden with beautiful flowers they can't reach. Walking through a garden filled with beautiful flowers means emotional stability, satisfaction, and new friendships. An overgrown garden: a sign of remorse about past mistakes and things you failed to do. Taking a walk through a beautiful garden: pleasant experiences ahead. A garden surrounded by a high fence: someone will deny you an urgent favor because you have failed to show how you truly feel. The dream is usually a sign that you are isolating from the people around you.

D: The condition of the garden in your dream is a symbol of the state of your inner life, how seriously you take your responsibilities, and how well you use your talents and natural abilities. What does the garden look like? What is growing there? See **Flower, Grass, Pasture, Tree.**

Garlic

V: If you see or smell garlic: it is a good sign—you will recover from an illness soon. The garlic can also be a sign of robust health.

D: This smelly bulb is nevertheless a promise of good health for body, mind, and soul.

Gas

D: Negative thoughts are running through your **Head** and—over time, this will have destructive consequences. Develop a more positive outlook soon!

Gas Station

V: Getting gas at a gas station: you need a vacation and need to recharge your batteries. Take a break!

D: The contents of the gas tank are what you need for financial security; a gas station is the place where you recharge your "batteries." Maybe you're running out of "gas" and the dream is reminding you to take some time off.

Gate

V: Seeing an open gate: friends are looking forward to your visit (or vice versa)—don't disappoint them. A closed gate: you will receive a cold welcome.

D: The gate is the symbol of the boundaries and limits you need to overcome.

General

V: Seeing a general in your dream is either a warning about too much arrogance, a demand for obedience, or a sign that you will meet a person in a high position. Seeing yourself as the general means you will be given a responsible task. If you have contact with a general: a person in high position or a high official will sponsor you. See **Military, Uniform.**

D: The general in a dream is usually a sign of marital problems. Find out who is playing the "general," who gives the orders. It may also be the "general" inside you who makes decisions about how to use your emotional energies.

Getting Lost

V: Searching, wandering aimlessly, or getting lost symbolizes your present emotional state. You are looking for the right path—in matters of love as well as in other situations. Have you made a decision to go either **Left** or **Right**? Getting lost in the **Fog** or **Darkness** means you are ignoring the sympathy offered by a valuable person. Getting lost in the woods: See **Forest.**

D: You have maneuvered yourself into a difficult situation because you are on the wrong track or were led astray. Find a solution—quickly!

Getting Run Over

V: Being run over: in a man's dream, fear of being pushed into a passive role in a sexual relationship. The dream may also mean getting out of an unpleasant situation in good shape, but don't "run over" other people and expect that they will accept your plan or idea. Running over somebody with your car: your carelessness will cost you money.

D: Dreaming about being run over by a train, car, or machine: you have maneuvered yourself into a situation that you can't handle.

Ghost

V: Sometimes ghost dreams are about real encounters, but on an astral plane. This is because a part of us, during sleep, is freed from physical restraints and therefore capable of receiving information from other worlds. Often the ghost in a dream is a mirror of a part of our own selves. In some cases, dreams of ghosts are a hint that someone close to us is going to die.

D: The ghost in a dream may sometimes warn us about our fantasies. It may also indicate that spiritual/emotional development is in progress, though we are unaware of it.

Giant

V: Seeing a giant: if you can make friends with the people you hope will help, a major business transaction will succeed. If the giant is your friend: you are going to be very successful. If the giant is threatening you: in the end a risky transaction will fall through. See **Tall, Big.**

D: The giant, considered a symbol of male sexuality, is warning you to beware of uncontrolled instincts. Sometimes the dream is a sign of superiority (if you are the giant) or of inferiority (if someone else is the giant). This is a very important dream and should be analyzed further! See **Gnome.**

Gift

V: Receiving a gift: be prepared to face some losses. Open your heart to others. Giving a gift: you are prone to hasty actions and decisions. Also, someone will surprise you with a gift.

D: Dreaming about giving a gift or giving something away is a reminder to be more generous with your affection toward others. Or did you "give yourself away"? Maybe you have become so involved in a particular matter that you neglected your own interests? You are either an idealist or have too many illusions. You will know which of the above fits you! Sometimes a gift refers to your need for recognition and praise; or it is simply a sign of a positive state of mind. Who is giving the gift? To whom are you giving a gift? Did you give yourself a gift?

Glacier

V: Standing—as a man—with your wife or girlfriend on top of a glacier means that you will soon separate or divorce. Standing alone on a glacier: adversaries are behind you—now deal with your emotions. Standing at the foot of a glacier: your present situation is uncertain.

D: A glacier in a dream usually stands for repressed emotions and fears, partly of "frozen" feelings. Don't wait until an **Avalanche** comes crashing down, burying you. See **Ice.**

Glass

S: Glass represents light, transparency, and heavenly spirits.

V: Seeing a full glass indicates your positive attitude and success. An empty glass promises hard times. Adjust your lifestyle accordingly. Breaking a glass: your actions are the reason for a love affair breaking up. Cutting a piece of glass: the time is right to do some speculating. See **Bottle, Shards.**

D: The dream might indicate that you are "seeing through" another person or situation or you are afraid that others can see through you and discover your mistakes.

Globe

S: The globe is the symbol of the ideal universe and nonmaterial completeness.

V: The globe is a symbol of the unpredictability of "Lady Luck." Avoid risky projects or dangerous games—it is the best way to prevent bad luck. Holding a globe in your hand: good opportunities ahead. If the globe is falling to the ground: once lucrative projects are turning sour. Looking at a globe made of glass: you are still ambivalent, but a decision can't be put off any longer. If the globe is made of iron: you will face every challenge and conflict with great courage. See **Ball, Bowling Pin, Circle.**

D: The globe is a warning: beware, Lady Luck is fickle.

Gloves

V: Wearing gloves in your dream: receiving an award. Putting on gloves: good things for your love relationship. Receiving a pair of gloves as a gift: be more polite. Losing your gloves: frustration and quarrels. Dropping a glove: you are flirting with someone. Throwing a glove at somebody: you are testing your strength against a person who has become a problem for you; you are ready to fight. The gloves you have on are too small: you are dissatisfied at the moment. The gloves are too big: you took on more than you can handle.

D: Gloves sometimes mean you don't make friends easily and have a tendency to isolate. You have a strong need for protection. Or do you want to avoid "dirtying your hands"?

Glue

V: Dreaming about glue: you are too negative, particularly now when you could take luck into your own hands. You have glue on your hands: doing something that is forbidden means you must also take the consequences.

D: Glue in a dream is a sign that you are too negative: you think that bad luck sticks to you like glue. If you continue to program yourself this way, good fortune will surely pass you by!

Gnats

V: Dreaming of gnats swarming around you: trouble with a very irritating person. See **Fly, Insects.**

Goat

S: The goat stands for being alert and listening attentively.

V: Watching goats at play: try not to be too boisterous or foolish. Watching goats being milked: modesty will serve you well in a coming situation. Listening to goats: it does not matter how hard you try—someone will always find something to complain about.

D: The female goat is a symbol of patience, modesty, amiability, and the ability to resolve challenging situations without difficulty. The goat—as the sacrificial lamb—is also a sign of the sacrifices you have made in your life. Which description—modesty or martyrdom—fits your present situation? See **Billy Goat.**

God

V: If you are praying: your faith is growing stronger. If you see God or speak to him: you are receiving advice "from above" and would do well to act on it.

D: Dreams about God always convey valuable insights and are a promise of help. The dreams can be important road signs for your journey through life, promising harmony and abundance. God is the source of all there is and a symbol of the desire to live in harmony with all creatures, but God appearing in a dream might also be a sign of guilt feelings that we want taken away. It also indicates our desire for more wisdom.

Going Barefoot

V + D: Walking barefoot: you want to get in touch with your soul, or with the very essence of life! The dream can be a challenge to keep in touch; it can also be a sign that your health is improving. If you are walking barefoot in clear water: prospects for the future are good. Running barefoot through wet **Grass**: the possibilities are even more promising. Walking barefoot over gravel: a present issue can only be resolved with difficulty. **Stones** are thrown in your path.

Gold, Gold Treasure

V: Owning gold is a sign of building too many castles in the air and of trying to get ahead financially by sheer force. Giving away gold to others: try to be more discreet—don't talk so much. Dancing around the "golden calf": you are too superficial—develop your inner qualities. Stealing gold: you have absolutely no luck at games. Everything you try is doomed to failure. See **Money.**

D: Gold treasure is a symbol of your present or future level of energy. Gold is a sign that you have (or wish you had) influence, power, and wealth—and in a more stable form than money. Sometimes, gold may also be a symbol of your intellectual knowledge and talents; particularly when it appears in the form of a golden disk.

Golf

D: Would you like to be around wealthy people? Do you want to travel in "better company"? This dream is an indication of a superficial lifestyle that is ruled by money—and often cold calculations.

Goodbye (Saying)

V: Saying goodbye to others in a dream: take a step back for a while and examine your relationship with them. At the same time, this dream may also be a sign that you will always find new friends. Saying goodbye to your parents: they might be worried or ill. Saying goodbye to a stranger: your problems will soon be over.

D: A goodbye is always a sign of a new beginning. Was it a sad farewell or one that brought relief? From what or from whom would you like to separate at this time?

Goose

S: The goose represents alertness and incorruptibility.

V: Killing or eating a goose means receiving money or an increase in your income. Buying a goose: be alert, someone wants to take you for a fool. You hear geese gabbling: watch out, someone is saying bad things about you. Calling out to a goose: avoid the company of simple-minded people. Tending a flock of geese: you are forced to take care of an unpleasant situation. Fattening a goose: don't encourage another person's foolish behavior.

D: The goose—undeservedly—is a symbol of simple-mindedness or even stupidity. Sometimes seeing a goose means that you're being taking advantage of by your partner. Change it!

Gooseberries

V: A man dreaming about gooseberries: you either have a very combative wife or you will marry one. A woman dreaming about gooseberries: you are either unhappy in your marriage or your spouse is very aggressive. Picking or eating gooseberries: patience in your love relationship will pay off.

D: Gooseberries are always an indication of conflict in love relationships. They are usually short-lived.

Government

V: A dream about government is always a symbol of your belief that you will either live peacefully (if your government makes wise decisions) or in conflict (if your government makes bad or thoughtless decisions). See **Town Hall.**

Grain

V: Harvesting grain: actual worries will soon go away. Buying grain: a problematic future, because your own "supplies"—emotional and material—are getting low. If you have a lot of grain: you will continue to prosper. Having little grain means material as well as emotional losses in the near future.

Grandfather, Grandmother

V: If you are talking to either one: you have made a wise decision, and a specific project is going to be successful. If both your grandparents are deceased: expect to get help in a certain matter, or you have decided to live a more prudent life.

D: Grandparents represent the wisdom that is available to you. If you use good judgment in the things you do, everything will turn out all right.

Grape

V: Looking at ripe grapes: you are enjoying perfect health. Sweet, ripe grapes: you will be lucky in love. Sour grapes: an argument will "sour" the days ahead. Picking green grapes means good fortune for your family. Red grapes: the next few days will be difficult and the outlook is not good.

D: The grape is a sexual, erotic symbol. The urges that drive you are not yet under your control. Grape wine symbolizes the spiritual strength that gives meaning to your life. See **Alcohol.**

Grass

V: Seeing fresh, green grass: financial improvements are possible. Seeing dead grass: worries or even illness. Looking at tall grass: avoid "uncharted territory" when making a decision; rely on tried and true methods—reduce everything to manageable proportions. Eating grass: your actions make you look foolish. Lying in the grass: you have great hopes, but be careful—don't build "castles in the air." See **Lawn, Meadow.**

D: A dream about grass contains a message: exchange material goods for intellectual strength. Seeing a lot of grass means you think too much!

Grave

V: If you are being buried: don't worry, the dream is dealing with your spiritual growth, not telling you your life is in danger. The dream might also indicate changes, and sometimes may be a message of an impending death. If you are digging a grave: what you are doing right now could destroy a lifelong friendship. If you are standing in front of an open grave: you need to let go of something or admit your part in a certain matter—it could finally free you from guilt and worry.

D: A grave indicates your desire to solve a problem, but you are still uncertain and quite helpless. You want to let go of a past issue and you are looking for a way. See **Cemetery, Death.**

Gravity

V: Feelings of being pulled down: your preoccupation with material things is keeping you from reaching a higher spiritual plane. It is time to change.

Greed

D: A greedy person is one who hates to lose money, security, power, and sexual prowess, and stockpiles it all. As a result, such a person is unable to form a true emotional relationship to anyone else. Life will be the poorer for it. Dreaming about greed is a warning that we would be better off to use and share everything we have!

Grinding, Grindstone

V: Working on a grindstone: try to get to the bottom of things and "grind off" your bad habits—otherwise, people will find you very irritating. Looking at a grindstone: you are going to fight with other people. Sharpening a knife: you will "speak with a sharp tongue."

D: See **File.**

Grotto

D: A grotto dream is an expression of your sexual desires. It might indicate that you're afraid of being "swallowed up" by your partner's love, or that you want to retreat ("crawl into a hole"). These feelings might be the result of past experiences.

Guest

V: Dreaming about guests in your house means new friends. See **Friend.**

Guinea Pig

V: Seeing a guinea pig in a dream means happy, fun days are ahead.

Gunpowder

V: Seeing gunpowder is a warning: stop whatever you are doing or have planned to do right away. Handling gunpowder: you are about to get involved in an adventure that is inherently dangerous. See **Cannon, Shooting.**

Guru

V: Connecting with a guru is a good omen: you are forgiving yourself and establishing new goals in your life; or you are changing the course of your life. Meeting a guru: you will find guidance, new insights, and new direction. See **Hermit, Old Man.**

D: The guru in your dream is not a stranger but a symbol of your inner strength. It means you are looking for spiritual guidance, knowledge (including self-knowledge), and wisdom. Trust and accept the guidance that is offered because you will view your life from a "higher" plane—the guru is truly a wonderful symbol!

Gypsy

V: Seeing a gypsy: you have an unconscious longing for freedom. Speaking to a gypsy: your assessment of a certain matter and how to proceed was correct. Paying a gypsy to predict the future: someone is making a fool of you. Listening to gypsy music: a romantic adventure is in the wings.

D: Gypsies are a symbol of freedom, individuality, and intuition (beyond the control of logic). Are you trying to ignore the conventional standards of society? Sometimes the dream is a warning about conniving people. See **Astrology, Fortune-teller.**

S = Symbol V = Vision D = Depth psychology

Hailstorm

V: Getting caught in a hailstorm: disputes with relatives, family members, or people who are out to hurt somebody. Observing a hailstorm from a distance: financial losses in the near future or a separation.

D: Hailstorms are always a sign of dissatisfaction, or a warning about family disputes or material losses. When worries and problems come "down like a hailstorm," it's time to let go of the matter or person, or to seek shelter (or look for protection or help) from others. See **Storm.**

Hair

S: Hair is considered a man's finery and a woman's veil.

V: A man getting a short haircut indicates his fear of subjugation and repression. Dreaming that he has lost all his hair: fear of becoming impotent. Seeing himself with long hair: he wants more independence and freedom—from moral as well as sexual taboos. Dreaming about a woman with beautiful hair (dark or red): he wants to find a sexually vibrant partner.

For a woman dreaming of losing her hair: she is afraid of losing energy; she also might feel physically and mentally overextended. Dreaming about a haircut: fear of losing her good reputation and also a sign of repressed feelings of sexuality. Dreaming about unkempt hair: being sexually careless and unsafe. Carefully groomed hair: she is disciplined in sexual matters. Hair falling out: losses are imminent.

D: Dreaming about hair might point to sexual needs, or to sensuality in general. Are you trying to hide your tendency for "splitting hairs" or overemphasizing your intellect? Beard, underarm hair, or pubic hair always indicates sexual urges. Or are you facing "a hairy situation" right now?

Hairdresser, Barber

V: If a hairdresser is cutting your hair: don't let others influence you—it would cause harm. In the case of a young woman or young man, the dream means an engagement or a wedding; for older people it means material good fortune. Women dreaming about getting their hair cut very short: they are keeping their feelings under control.

D: Dreams about hairdressers and barbers mean you want to look good, are a bit vain, and hope to have sex appeal. Don't be so concerned about your appearance that your love life becomes superficial.

Halter

V: Seeing a halter means going on a wonderful trip. If somebody is taking a halter away from you: somebody is going to haggle with you.

D: A halter could represent self-discipline and suggest that you keep greediness and urges or feelings and emotions under control (as when the halter is very tight).

Ham

V: Buying a ham: you are looking for material wealth. Eating ham: you have deprived yourself of something and you are still hurting. Deep down you would like to have more (things, food, etc.).

D: The dream is a warning against too much materialism

and gluttony—you are overdoing it to an extreme. Sometimes the dream refers to sexual gluttony. Which is it in your case?

Hammer

S: The hammer indicates trying to accomplish something by force. With more sensitivity you would have reached your goal long ago—and done so without difficulty (that is particularly true for men!).

V: Somebody showing you a hammer: you are absolutely correct, but are forced to defend your position. Working furiously with a hammer: you are very angry right now, but you can manage the present situation.

D: The hammer is a symbol of power and influence. In a man's dream it is often a sign of thoughtless insistence on having sexual needs met. The dream is always a warning to curb negative attitudes.

Hand

S: The hand is a symbol of control, activity, power.

V: Looking at a hand: make sure your dealings are honest. Looking at clean hands: you have honest friends. Looking at dirty hands: a clear warning to beware of false friends or dishonest people around you. Wringing your hands means suffering from the demands of others; also worries and conflicts. Don't be passive and whiny—get a grip and change! Burning your hands: others envy you, or you got burned recently. Looking at several hands: great wealth through your own efforts. Holding your hands in front of your eyes: forgive someone for a mistake and be more tolerant. Losing your right hand: possible death of the father (if the left hand, possible death of the mother). Looking at beautiful, strong hands means wrapping up a very good business deal.

D: The hand is a symbol of "action," energy, drive, and competence. A hand that looks injured, crippled, or is missing always indicates a difficulty in taking action. Is it the right hand (the masculine side) or the left (the feminine side)? See **Left, Right.** What do the fingers look like? See **Finger.** Do you want to "take somebody by the hand"? Or vice versa?

Handcuffs, Being Handcuffed

V: You are handcuffed: meeting a former lover makes you sad, but feelings of regrets are too late. Putting handcuffs on someone else: you can't force love—it will only break your heart.

D: Shackles are sign of being captivated by illusionary love. Sometimes a dream about shackles or handcuffs indicates nervous tension, less often masochism or sadism. Who or what holds you in shackles? From what shackles would you like to free yourself?

Hanging

V: Dreaming of having committed suicide by hanging is a warning that other people are taking advantage of you. Participating in the hanging of someone else: a warning not to act hastily or make hasty decisions. Dreaming about hanging laundry on a line: your situation is taking a turn for the better.

D: Dreaming about a hanging indicates that you are presently in a very important developmental stage. See **Death, Gallows, Murder.**

Harbor

V: Dreaming about an ocean harbor means building a solid foundation for your life and the promise of a worry-free old age. Seeing a lot of ships in the harbor: news that you can put to use to make a good profit. Being on a ship that is about to enter a harbor: good financial opportunities or hopes coming true.

D: The harbor is a sign of fear about daily struggles. Are you looking for a safe "harbor," away from the struggles and worries of life? Do you want to rest for a while? See **Ocean, Ship, Shore, Yacht.**

Hare

S: The hare is a "moon animal" and a symbol of fertility and renewal.

V: When women dream of stroking a hare they are longing to have children. In men's dreams it is an unconscious need for love. Watching a hare at play: don't spread rumors about others. Shooting a hare: losing a good friend. Men chasing a hare: they are ready and willing to engage in sexual adventures.

D: The hare, as a symbol of fertility, may be a sign that a child is "on the way." It might also be a sign of "mental fertility." In a man's dreams, it often means he wants to have a love affair.

Harp

V: Looking at or playing a harp means disappointment ahead. Watching someone else playing a harp: you will fall head over heels in love.

D: A harp is a clear sign of an overtaxed nervous system. You need to relax more. Or do you want to start a love affair right now?

Harvest

V: Dreaming about a rich harvest means rewards for your efforts and success at your job. A harvest disrupted by bad weather: family arguments and frustrated relatives. Taking in hay: being fond of a certain person and a deepening relationship.

D: A harvest often symbolizes discomfort if the dreamer is

in the autumn of life. It could also indicate the need for recognition. If the harvest is plentiful: you will receive the "real fruits" of your labor.

Hat

V: Dreaming frequently about wearing a hat: you would love to be the center of attention wherever you go; more humility would be in order. If you are wearing a very extravagant hat: your actions or your behavior make you look like a fool. Making a hat: you will soon be offered an interesting job—or someone is going to make an interesting request. The wind blowing the hat off your head means a loss of profit. Watching a hat floating on water may indicate a friend's suicide. Wearing a straw hat: your lover will be unfaithful. Wearing a hat with feathers: you are too vain and too desperate for admiration. See **Top Hat.**

D: The hat represents opinions and attitudes you would rather hide from others; be brave—speak your mind. Who are you suspicious of? Take off your hat and show the world who you are!

Hawk

See **Eagle.**

Hay

If you are lying in a haystack: your tastes are simple and you know how to enjoy the small things in life. If you are loading hay on a wagon: you are working hard and getting little in return. Dreaming about the smell of hay: you are enjoying good health. Cutting hay: a slow increase in your wealth.

D: Hay points to past experiences and emotions that you remember and now are able to deal with. See **Grass, Meadow, Straw.**

Hazelnuts

V: Looking at hazelnuts: right now don't argue with your neighbors or colleagues. Cracking hazelnuts: it will take a lot of effort on your part to successfully finish a certain task. Eating hazelnuts: make an appointment with your dentist.

D: Nuts are a symbol of difficult problems, but the results—"in a nutshell"—will turn into an asset. Tackle the problem, "crack" the nut!

Head

V: Seeing a head in a dream is a warning: be more attentive and alert. Seeing a torso without a head: you have run headlong into a situation from which you need to extract yourself in a hurry. If the head on your body belongs to someone else: whether you like it or not, others will decide for you what to do next. If the head on your body faces the back: thoughtless actions and wrong decisions have created severe problems for you!

D: The head indicates that your good sense is controlling the rest of your body. Smashing your head in a dream means many problems and conflicts with no resolution in sight. Did you "lose your head"? Why, to whom, and in what circumstances? Are you running around like "a chicken with its head cut off"? Dreams about the head may also be a sign of an actual illness in that area. Decapitating another person: you are now ready to use your head to solve your problems. One-eyed head: dreaming about eyes might be a hint that you are too occupied with yourself. If the image has the right eye missing, you might try to gain more insight in emotional areas. Prominent teeth: you are looking for material things or "biting" into them.

Head Cold

D: A head cold indicates that troubles are about to

explode. Sometimes it also points to difficulties that it would be wise to avoid. Do you feel that people around you are emotionally "cold"?

Hearse

V: Watching a hearse drive by means saying goodbye to a person, to old habits, or to a particular position that has outlived its usefulness. See **Grave.**

D: A hearse might also be a suggestion to take old feelings, past hopes, and desires to a grave and bury them.

Heart

S: The heart is the symbol of life and emotions as well as affection, yearning, love, and hate.

V: Looking at a heart in a dream means that someone loves you deeply. A bleeding heart means making a great sacrifice for someone else—and getting insulted in return. The condition of the heart is a symbol of your actual emotional state. Dreaming about a heart in pain or a heart beating fast: anxiety and depression. Dreaming about having heart trouble: might be a signal of actual physical problems.

D: The heart is a symbol of tenderness, affection, and love, and sometimes also of fear. "Is your heart burning with passion" for someone? Have you taken something "too much to heart"?

Heat

D: Heat represents your sexual urges and "heated emotions"—and should be regarded as a warning: getting too close to the fire is bound to burn you. See **Fire.**

Heel

V: Seeing your own heel: you are afraid that other will discover your weaknesses. Your heel is injured: your weaknesses are already exploited by others.

D: We always try to hide our "Achilles' heel" from others. What is your most vulnerable point? See **Foot.**

Hell

S: Hell is the symbol of darkness and the devil's domain.

V: Dreaming of hell reflects great distress. You have lost all hope and don't know what to do or where your life is going. This painful situation is going to continue a while longer until—through a purification—you can recognize the right path. If someone else is in hell: great changes are ahead. See **Demon, Devil.**

D: Hell represents fear, anxieties, guilt feelings, and other negative energies, but it is also a place of "purification," and promises serenity in the end. Don't deny emotional pain but accept it and live through it—things will change. What is this "hell on earth" doing to you? What kind of purgatory are you going through? Is hate devouring your happiness?

Herbs

V: Seeing or collecting herbs: you have cared for a sick person or dealt with a difficult situation. Eating herbs: a long, joyful, and healthy life.

Hermit

V: Seeing a hermit in tattered clothes: bad news in the near future; your efforts are fruitless. Seeing one hermit means you are looking for advice. If you are the hermit: you have lost faith in your fellow men and would like to withdraw. Living with your partner in an isolated place: your relationship needs a major overhaul—in some cases, only a separation will do.

D: A hermit often symbolizes a wise counselor; sometimes it means you have lost faith in a person or in humanity and that you would like to "get away from it all." Are you feeling lonely right now? Do you need peace and quiet, to find a place where you can think about the world, yourself, and your life? See **Guru.**

High Tide

V: Seeing a large expanse of water in a dream means that earthly desires are taking a backseat for the moment. Watching waters rise or being in the water at high tide: you are seriously distressed and worried. Watching high tide with large waves coming in suggests that you make a long-overdue decision now—or suffer the consequences. Watching the tides come and go is a reminder that life and fortunes always change! See **Low Tide, Water.**

D: High tide represents an emotional eruption, like a surge of love, or fear, or a shock, etc. Any of these things may happen or you may have just experienced one of them. See **Flood.**

Highway

V: Seeing or walking along an endless highway is not a good sign: you must deal with and overcome many difficulties on your job or in business. Success is far in the distance.

D: See **Avenue, Street, Walkway.**

Hike, Hiking

V: Dreaming about hiking: progress on the path through life will be slow, but with patience and determination you will do fine. Meeting a poor hiker: your present path is the wrong one—you can reach your goal only if you change course.

D: Pay attention to how you feel: are you walking with purpose and having fun? Are you tired and feeling worn-out?

Are you going up or coming down? Is the trail easy or difficult? See **Cliff, Climbing, Mountain, Path, Slope.**

Hippopotamus

D: Seeing a hippopotamus: while you present to the world a picture of authority (in behavior and appearance), deep down you feel that you are standing on "wobbly" legs. See **Animals, Whale.**

Hole

V: Looking at a hole means someone is setting a trap for you. Falling into a hole: you are harming another person, but in the long run it is you who will suffer. Seeing holes in your clothes: it is time to start paying your debts. Mending a hole: you are either settling an unpleasant argument or finding the solution to an old disagreement. See **Precipice.**

D: The hole is usually a warning of danger or that someone is setting a trap for you. It could also be the memory of a past mistake that is bubbling up. Are you seeing the world only through a very small "hole"? Are you falling into a hole? Do you have a "hole in your head"? In a man's dream, it might indicate a female sex organ and refer to your erotic desires.

Home, Apartment, Dwelling

V: As was already mentioned earlier, dreams about a home where the doors are open always symbolize, in men's dreams, their relationship to women. If the home is primarily furnished with wooden objects, the man is looking for a more motherly type. Living in a beautiful home: your future looks exceptionally good.

D: See **House, Moving, Room.**

Homeless Shelter, Homelessness

V: If you are looking for a shelter: you can count on people to support you in an unpleasant situation. Losing your shelter: you are feeling unprotected and helpless, but courage will save the day.

D: The dream is a symbol of your fear; you are looking for support, safety, and emotional warmth. Dreaming about remaining homeless: your hopes will not come true.

Homesick

V: Dreaming of returning home: happy hours to come. Leaving home: you are worried about the future of your family. Being homesick: in spite of your present love relationship, you now know what you lost when a past relationship ended.

D: Being homesick is a longing for the past. Much has changed in your life, and you now can admit that much you held dear (in relationships) has been lost.

Honey

V: Looking at honeycombs means good fortune in business matters. Eating honey means a lack of self-knowledge, the reason for your emotional complications, but recovery is in sight. See **Bee.**

D: Honey in a dream promises "sweet rewards" for emotional work you did. The rewards are the direct result of the profound self-knowledge you have been able to achieve. Honey is also a symbol of serenity (which in itself is a symbol of emotional healing)!

Hood

D: Dreaming of wearing a hood indicates your need for safety; you may want to hide your true personality from others. See **Hat.** Would you rather have a mask than a hood to hide behind? Or is the hood a sign that you want to stay warm?

Hook

D: Are you squirming on a hook? Are you "hooked"—addicted to something? What happened to making your own decisions, to maturity, to freedom? Get off the hook!

Hoop

V: Seeing a child's hoop: you are longing for the carefree games of your childhood. If the hoop is large: nurture new relationships in your life.

D: See **Circle, Ring.**

Horns

V: Seeing others with horns on their forehead: conflicts and clashes with other people. Looking at horns or having horns on your head—particularly in men's dreams: you are afraid that someone is cheating on you. Your wife or lover does not think much about being faithful.

D: See **Antlers, Cow, Stag.**

Horoscope

V: If you are in the presence of an **Astrologer**: pay careful attention to the information you receive.

D: Unlike newspaper and magazine horoscopes, a dream about a horoscope should always be examined carefully. It can provide valuable insights into your personality, which—in turn—can increase and strengthen your intuitive abilities. See **Signs of the Zodiac.**

Horse

V: Seeing a horse and a rider, or riding yourself: taking the reins firmly in your hands and remaining steady will bring a project to a successful conclusion. Falling off a horse: let go of a project you had planned—it is guaranteed to crash. Seeing a horse in the pasture: you want more freedom and independence. A horse pulling a wagon: you have to depend on another people and would love to free yourself. Many horses in a pasture: you are regaining your independence or planning on working for yourself. A restless, bucking horse: you overcame great difficulties and will be rewarded with lasting success. Leading a horse in a halter: take time and evaluate an important decision you are about to make for your future. Then move slowly but with determination toward success. Looking at a foal: expect a very happy event to take place soon. A white horse in a dream heightens the meaning of the positive symbols, a black horse adds to the negative symbols. See **Racetrack.**

D: The horse is a sign of intensified cravings, sexual needs, and passions rising to the surface—the more wild the horse in the dream, the stronger these energies. A rider on the horse means your urges are governed by your intellect. A calm horse: you have reined in and are controlling your physical urges. A black horse means death or separation. A white horse, most of all, has spiritual meaning, but it also stands for ambitious goals, intellectual strength, and the ability to create. Holding tightly to the reins: you are allowing the above-mentioned energies to come to the fore. A stallion is a sign of masculinity, potency, strength, and aggression; a mare of femininity, gentleness, and the need for harmony in life—also fertility. Pegasus, the winged horse, is a symbol of your imagination and a sign that you have transformed your instincts and urges into creative energies. See **Animals.**

Horse Racing

V: Watching a horse race: you are about to indulge in a luxurious pleasure. Being a jockey in a race: you need a great deal of luck, but being too carefree could be a mistake.

D: Participating in a horse race: the success you enjoy is

due more to a lucky coincidence than to your own efforts. The dream suggests you keep this in mind because "Lady Luck is fickle."

Horseshoe

V: Seeing a horseshoe is a very good omen: your hopes and desires will be fulfilled. Everything you do these days will be successful or proceed without a hitch; you might even win in a game of chance.

Hospital

V: Seeing a hospital means good news, or visiting a sick friend. Lying in the hospital: a good friend is getting you out of a difficult situation. You are very sick: take a moment and rethink plans you made—they won't work! Leaving a hospital: you are going to start a business; you are emotionally independent.

D: The **Illness** in a dream is a sign of your anxiety. If you are not actually sick, the dream may refer to a conflict between your feelings, thoughts, and actions. The hospital represents the help you receive in solving problems and overcoming obstacles. See **Sanatorium.**

Hotel

V: Seeing yourself in a hotel: a trip you have planned will be much more expensive than you thought. If a married man sees himself in a hotel: he has to continue to keep his love affair a secret.

D: You are dealing with emotional confusion—the hotel is a metaphor for your flight from yourself. Are you about to explore unknown places? The hotel also represents your present attitudes and actions; sometimes it is a sign that you want more comfort and luxuries.

Hourglass

S: Sometimes a symbol of death, the hourglass is also a primary image of moderation.

V: The hourglass reminds us how swiftly time passes. It might mean separation from a loved one or that you are "running out of time."

D: The hourglass reminds you that life passes "like sand through your fingers." It means time is marching on and you feel that you haven't achieved anything significant. Figure out what the lesson is in this dream.

House

S: Like a town or temple, a house stands for the center of the world and a reflection of your universe.

V: The condition of the house represents your present situation. The *roof* of the house refers to the state of your health, the *exterior* to your external appearance. The *upper floor* stands for your forehead (and brain); the *middle floor* the area of the chest, the *first floor* the intestines, and the *ground floor* and *basement* the legs and feet. If you dream of old houses frequently, you are afraid of old age. Building a house together with other people: you have good friends at your side. Looking at an empty house: you have missed a few opportunities. Tearing down a house: you are strong enough to deal with the obstacles that come your way. Living in a run-down house: pay more attention to your health. Watching a house collapse: you won't reach your goals—be prepared for losses. In a man's dream, the house (it does not matter if it is a luxurious villa or a farmhouse) represents ambitions, professional advancement, security, and safety. In a woman's dreams, the *balcony* is the chest.

D: The house in a dream is the symbol for the **Body** and what happens with the body. A house in ill repair, destroyed, or even on fire, points to your poor health and should be taken seriously. The *foundation* is a symbol for the mental/intellectual "foundation" on which you have built your life. The *basement* is the symbol of the unconscious, where repressed urges and cravings hide. The *kitchen* is the place where "life is lived" every day and where diversion can be found. The *bedroom* represents attitudes toward sex and emotional connections to other people. The *living room* stands for recreation, rest, and relaxation. The *bathroom* is the place for moral cleansing and the "washing away" of disappointments. The toilet stands for "letting go" of emotional ballast, tensions, and the past. The *roof* (and attic) stands for your mental/spiritual part, and symbolizes protection from the outside world. See **Door, Furniture, Stairs, Window.**

Household Items

V: Looking at household items: you like having your own home. It might also refer to a wedding or being a guest at a wedding. Cleaning implements mean improvements in your economic situation. See **Dishes.**

Hunger

V: Being hungry is a sign of a "hungry" soul. Try to find out what your soul is longing for.

D: Hunger is a symbol of the need to be accepted, including your opinions and judgments. Even if life is secure, this dream may refer to a maybe unfounded fear of poverty. This fear needs to be held up to the light of day and reality. Are you in need of "spiritual nourishment"? Are you fasting right now? Could actual hunger be behind the dream?

Hunt, Hunter

S: In men's dreams, both images often indicate a woman chaser.

V: Going on a hunt: you, too, need to learn that only

patience makes success possible. The dreamer is looking for a relationship. An unsuccessful hunt means disappointment. Seeing a hunter: you have much work to do on yourself to develop better habits. Being invited to go hunting means a good hand in a card game.

D: Hunting is a symbol of your hunt for material things—success, money, and joy—which is the result of greed, ambition, and expectations. The "hunt" is a challenge to reexamine your life's goal and make important corrections. Who or what is hunting you? Who are you hunting? The hunter and the hunt are both very masculine dream symbols (hunter and collector!).

Hurricane

V: Watching or experiencing a hurricane is a very bad omen for all plans, business transactions, and private affairs. Be glad if all you lose is money—the hurricane can do a lot worse! Take this dream very seriously! See **Storm.**

D: This dream is meant to be a warning, because a hurricane always points to an impending crisis. Old opinions, ideals, and out-of-date beliefs and values are being shaken. Nothing will be in the same place afterward. The dream suggests you start shaping something new within you now, so that the expected hurricane won't damage your personality!

Hyacinth

V: Looking at a hyacinth means receiving a gift; you are very popular—people like to be in your company. Getting a hyacinth as a gift: you will fall deeply in love. If the hyacinth is wilted, your expectations of another person are disappointing. See **Flower.**

Hyena

S: The hyena is a symbol of stinginess.

V: Seeing a hyena: a warning not to expect protection or support from a certain person—that would be a great mistake on your part. Being threatened by a hyena: you will have to face a desperate situation—maybe even an attack.

D: See **Animals, Wolf.**

Hypnosis

V: If you are hypnotizing another person in a dream: be careful, you are trying to influence others in real life, to get somebody over to your side. If you are hypnotized: be very careful here too; others are trying to influence you. Are you already being controlled by another person? Being hypnotized: right now you are not sure what to do or what not to do. You are unsure about the consequences of your actions.

D: A dream about hypnosis is a warning: you are about to give up on yourself and are too much influenced by others. Hypnotizing someone else: you want to have more influence over others and events. Have you already too much influence in real life? If so, this dream is a warning. At present you seem confused! Where is your will power? What happened while you were "in a trance"? Other dream symbols are very important here!

Hysteria

D: Hysterical actions in a dream are a sign of severe anxiety and intense feelings—you are unable to think and act rationally and logically. If you have these dreams frequently, consider seeking professional help!

S = Symbol V = Vision D = Depth psychology

Ice

V: Falling on the ice: a project that was headed for success is turning bad. Looking at ice crystals on the window: frustration in your love life; emotions are beginning to cool. Falling through the ice: a secret adversary wants to harm you. Seeing an iceberg: search your unconscious, the part of the iceberg that is below the surface. See **Snow.**

D: Ice and snow are a symbolic expression of loneliness and poverty. Both reflect coldness—that feelings are cooling off (either your own or another person's). Have your feelings for someone gone cold, "turned to ice," or have the feelings someone had for you? See **Cold.**

Ice Cream

V: Eating ice cream on a hot day: a very exhausting love affair will satisfy your cravings but not bring happiness.

Ice Skating

V: Seeing an ice skater: you can expect quick success—as long as you act ethically. Watching others ice skate: Copy what others do. If you are shaky on skates or fall all the time: you are doing things you know nothing about and the outcome will be disaster. Skating in an ice skating rink: be careful—you are involved in a very risky enterprise.

D: If you are ice skating: with the right "tools" you will go far. Your expectations are reasonable—you will have good relationships and exercise good judgment. Getting injured or injuring others while ice skating: your emotional coldness will harm you or others. See **Ice, Snow.**

Illness

V: If you are the sick person: you will soon be comforted and have a friend at your side. Visiting a sick person: joy and good luck. See **House.**

D: Illnesses in dreams always represent the emotional state we are experiencing at the moment. Things from the past that we have denied or repressed and past emotional injuries should now be healed. See **Hospital.**

Impotence

V: Dreaming about impotence reveals the dreamer's fear of being sexually inadequate or losing his masculinity or her femininity. Are you feeling particularly weak right now? Do you have little influence over others? Are you feeling inferior? Try to find the reason for your anxieties or seek professional advice!

Incineration

V: Watching something being incinerated: it is high time to clean up a matter that has bothered you for a long time. If you are being incinerated: it is a warning not to get involved in something where you could get burned.

D: What is most important in this dream is what and who has been incinerated. Pay attention to the rest of the dream symbols. See **Burning, Fire.**

India, Indian

V: Seeing India or seeing a person from India: you still

have very romantic ideas; you also have a tendency toward the mystical, but in practical matters you keep your feet securely planted on the ground. Seeing Indian figurines or Indian people: you are getting seriously involved in spirituality and studies of that nature. Seeing or speaking to an Indian guru: See **Guru.**

D: People who dream about India often have difficulty managing their lives because they are constantly "living in another world." More self-criticism and realism would be in order. Are you trying to deceive others or yourself? Do you often float too much in a"mystical dimension"?

Inflation

V: Dreaming that the country is in a period of inflation: a warning to be smart right now or lose all your money. If you dream that inflation is imminent: your life is in crisis; your value system needs a radical overhaul.

D: Inflation dreams are an indication that what has been important to you is losing its value. You face a profound crisis and feelings of emptiness, which are keeping you from making the necessary radical changes in your life. Make sure you get through this time of deep change without suffering permanent emotional harm. Other dream images are important here because they will point to the kinds of changes you need to make.

Injury

V: Seeing an injury: a warning to be careful when dealing with people or instruments/tools. Here it is important which part of the body has been injured. See **Body, Operation.**

D: Somebody has hurt you (through an insult, unfairness, or disappointment), and you need to come to terms with it. Or was it you who injured someone? See **Bandage, Pain, Wound.**

Ink

V: Seeing ink suggests that you make peace with someone—no matter the cost. Don't sign any written agreements right now, it is premature and the consequences could be serious. Writing something in ink: an important document is on its way. Spilling ink: an arrangement you have made recently turns into a problem.

D: Ink is often a symbol of things hidden in your unconscious; you are upset by recent events that have taken a turn for the worse. An ink spot is a sign of feeling guilty or a bad conscience. See **Writing.**

Inscription

D + V: Seeing mysterious inscriptions that can't be deciphered: you are seeking guidance. Look carefully for additional signs that might tell you what the dream is trying to convey. If you see inscriptions containing names or dates, be prepared for the death of someone in your immediate circle of friends.

Insects

V: Being surrounded by insects means unpleasant and irritating people or events ahead. Are there spiders among the insects you see? Be very, very careful: somebody is spying on you from a distance. Looking at insects: some annoying person is bothering you with empty gossip. Being bitten by a large insect: you need to deal with a loss; or your soul—because of either future or past experiences—is reacting by bringing on an illness.

D: Seemingly insignificant events turn out to be more important than you thought. Guilt feelings or a bad conscience is bothering you. See **Bee, Fly, Spider.** The insect represents instinctive actions and conduct. Whether your actions are beneficial or harmful can be determined by looking at the rest of the dream images.

Instrument

V: Looking at medical instruments is a warning about the possible danger of an accident or a sudden illness. See **Music.**

Insult

V: Somebody insulting you: you are needlessly afraid of something; you lack self-worth. Insulting another person: find out if you have been too timid in an important matter. You might be resentful toward a person in real life, but lack the courage to tell him off. Being insulted by a stranger: clear up a misunderstanding at work—have courage!

D: Insults in a dream are always a sign of your lack of self-worth—be brave, stand up for yourself and you will get much further.

Insurance

V: Buying an insurance policy: you need more self-confidence, because more possibilities are waiting in the wings than you thought.

Intercourse

S: For younger people, dreaming about intercourse is a symbol of (sometimes unconscious) sexual desires; later in life it means new, creative plans.

V: Dreaming about having intercourse with a lover: the prospects are good for a love relationship. Having intercourse with several people: your way of life may be lax or your sexual desires extreme and this could harm you!

D: Intercourse indicates sexual desires that you sometimes don't want to acknowledge, even to yourself. The dream might also symbolize a new beginning, a new project. See **Bed.**

Interrogation

V: If you are being interrogated: you have a bad conscience—take a good look at yourself. Sometimes it indicates that others are inquiring about you.

D: This dream suggests more self-examination and self-knowledge. It would be a good idea to get more information about a certain matter or person. See **Speaking.**

Intestines, Colon

V: Dreams about intestines are a sign that you are trying to "digest" something; or you have learned from past experiences and are moving on. See **Excrement.**

Invalid

V: A woman, dreaming about an invalid means her partner is not as strong as she would like him to be, or he is about to give up on something. If the latter is the case, be supportive and give a helping hand. Being the invalid: you are losing your professional or personal freedom. Sometimes your unconscious is warning you to slow down at work.

D: The invalid wants to warn you about the danger of losing your intellectual independence. At times the dream also indicates a negative emotional connection to other people. What or who do you think is limiting you?

Invitation

V: Being invited by someone: a matter of concern will soon be addressed favorably. If the invitation is in writing: you want to enlarge your circle of friends.

D: An invitation represents isolation and loneliness, which you would like to—and can—change for the better.

Iron

V: If you are at a forge shaping iron: arguments, quarrels,

and frustration. Seeing a piece of red hot iron: your passions are red-hot (particularly in a man's dream). Looking at an iron gate means obstacles and difficulties ahead.

D: Iron is a symbol of strength and resilience, but also of your distaste for certain plans. Are you suffering because of a person's rigid personality?

Island

V: In a man's dream, the island stands for frustration at work; you are anxious to be involved, to create something new, to make use of your pioneer spirit. Or you are simply stressed out and want to (or should) take a break from your hectic lifestyle. When you return—maybe from a vacation—you can again set the world on fire. Being alone on an island: you want to be left alone or feel lonely. Seeing an abandoned island: you are traveling in uncharted waters—or you have no clue where to go from here.

D: An island reflects fear about the responsibilities of life and—in that sense—is an attempt to take flight from reality (or to retreat from the world). Sometimes it might simply be a matter of needing some peace and solitude after a particularly hectic period. The dream can also be a warning about not isolating or withdrawing.

Italy, Italian

V: A man seeing an Italian woman means he is about to have a passionate love affair.

D: Italy is the symbol of heightened sensuality, beauty, and creativity. Sometimes the dream is a warning of too much emotion, superficiality, or a craving for pleasure *(La Dolce Vita)*. Looking at Italian art means your own creativity wants to be expressed.

Ivy

V: Ivy growing around and up a tree trunk: be careful, false friends are under foot and they are very "clingy."

D: This climbing plant is a sign that you are looking for good, solid friendships, or a love that is based on faithfulness.

S = Symbol V = Vision D = Depth psychology

Jack-o'-Lantern

V: Seeing a jack-o'-lantern is always a warning: stop what you're doing—you're on the wrong path. "The light at the end of the tunnel" is a deception. The same is true if in your dream you are lost or the road ahead is the wrong road.

D: Jack-o'-lanterns and interesting but deceptive road signs (representing your ideas and goals) are always tempting, but they will lead you astray. This is an important dream and a warning. Get past illusions and tricks and try to get to the bottom of it! Pay attention to the rest of the images in the dream.

Jacket

V: Getting into the wrong sleeve of a jacket: you are baffled about something or have been given wrong information.

D: The jacket indicates the kind of affection you can give and receive. The state of the jacket is a metaphor for your feelings. See **Shirt, Pants, Clothes.** A jacket that is old, worn-out, or has holes means you have been emotionally harmed, but it also suggests that you are finally letting go of old, negative responses (throw the jacket away)!

Jasmine

V: A bouquet of jasmine means you will soon get a visit from a very dear person.

D: See **Flower.**

Jellyfish

V: Seeing a jellyfish: there is either a health problem, or people around you can't make up their minds, but the support you expected is not forthcoming.

Jewelry

V: Wearing jewelry: don't be vain and arrogant—it does not make for good friends. Seeing other people wearing jewelry: you are easily taken in by others and are prone to misjudge them. See **Precious Stones.**

D: Are you "decorating" yourself to gain attention or admiration? Giving jewelry as a gift to someone: is jewelry an indication of the "precious" feelings you have for someone? Receiving jewelry as a gift: does someone have "precious feelings" for you?

Jewels, Gems

V: Looking at or buying precious stones is a recommendation: learn to live without many of the things you have been taking for granted. Losing a precious stone: unexpected good fortune will come your way.

D: Precious stones represent the untouchable center of your personality. Dreaming about owning jewelry says much about you. See **Diamonds, Jewelry, Precious Stones.** Here is some of what they symbolize:

Amethyst: intellectual flights of fancy, without losing a sense of reality, however.

Diamond: spiritual awareness/perception, but sometimes also impersonal, emotional coldness, or drive for power.

Lapis lazuli: sensibility; but also it stands for your friends and your physical vitality.

Opal: your imagination, your dream life, and the purification of urges and greed.

Pearl: serenity but also depth born of suffering.

Ruby: emotional warmth, true humanity, true love, and positive interpersonal relationships.

Sapphire: religiosity, renouncing the carnal and sexual to the point of being too intellectual.

Emerald: the power of consciousness and emotional balance, because you have "found yourself."

Jockey

V: Being a jockey on a horse: you are a person who takes great risks and loves nothing better than to win every "competition in life"—or you would like to have others depend on you. See **Horse Racing.**

D: The jockey stands for the ability to use your instincts and vitality (your own and those of others) and to translate them into success—whether for your benefit or harm will depend on the rest of the dream images. See **Horse.**

Judge

V: Seeing a judge: don't be so anxious—speak with care and deliberation. If you are the judge: consider a decision carefully before you act. Dealing with a judge in an official matter: you will soon get a "just reward" for bad conduct. See **Court, Lawyer.**

Jumping

V: Jumping hurdles: the chances for professional advancement are good. Jumping over a ditch or hedge: you will be able to overcome all obstacles in your path.

D: Dreams about jumping mean that you are a risk-taker and grab at opportunities before thinking of the consequences. It might be a suggestion to tackle your problems in one courageous leap, or that you're afraid of the challenges you might have to face.

Jumping Jack

V: Looking at a jumping jack is a sign of instability—at work and/or financially. Seeing yourself as a jumping jack: what is missing? Make an honest account of yourself. What happened to you—are you "spineless"?

D: The jumping jack stands for insecurities and feelings of inferiority. You are afraid that people around you won't take you seriously, that you're only a toy in the eyes of others. Have you made a fool of yourself lately? Who in your relationship is the "jumping jack"? What about your assertiveness? See **Clown, Fool.**

Jungle, Rain Forest

V: Being in a jungle: life is pretty chaotic right now—you don't know where to go and are fighting a bitter battle.

D: The jungle is a symbol of confusion and uncertainty, but also of living conditions in a big city. Are you confused right now? Angry about someone's unpredictability? Are you unsure today about what will happen tomorrow? Are you unpredictable? Has life in the big city become too much, too nerve racking, too confusing? Is it a jungle out there? Which describes your present situation?

Juniper Bush, Juniper Berries

V: Eating juniper berries means you are making good

progress and your health is stabilizing. Seeing a juniper bush: you have a faithful friend. See **Berries.**

Jupiter

D: The planet Juniper means good fortune, growth, wealth, great plans, intellectual stimulation, prosperity, and tolerance. The dream might also express certain appetites (cravings for food, drink, and sex), and you will satisfy them by hook or crook.

S = Symbol V = Vision D = Depth psychology

Kernel

D: A kernel always stands for your essence (the moral center or truth), which is the guiding force in your life. See **Nut.**

Kerosene

V: Looking at a can of kerosene: meeting a certain person might be useful but unpleasant. Lighting a kerosene lamp is a warning about too much foolishness. Spilling kerosene: a relationship based solely on opportunism is coming to an end. See **Oil.**

Kettle Drum

V: Listening to a kettle drum: in the case of legal or other conflicts, be very careful and try to reach an amiable compromise. Playing the kettle drum: be less heartless and arrogant—that will only get you negative attention. Doing a "drum roll": either announces that you are a miserable loser or declares you a victorious hero.

D: Are you playing the kettle drum with too much zeal only to get you negative attention? Are you hiding too much ambition behind such zeal? If not, expect good news soon. See **Drum, Trumpet.**

Key

S: The key symbolizes your ability to open and close doors.

V: Looking at a key: someone will either tell you a secret or you will find the solution to a puzzle. Unlocking something: a warning against getting involved in a risky adventure. Losing a key: you have been careless and the consequence is a missed opportunity. Finding a key: your chances at work and love are excellent. Finding a key that belongs to an unknown person: you will discover a secret. See **Door.**

D: With logic, reason, and intelligence you can solve everyday problems by yourself. Sometimes, in women's dreams, the key, a phallic symbol, represents sexual needs.

King, Queen

V: Seeing a king or a queen: your business affairs are going well and your income may increase. If you are the king or the queen: you are either thinking too highly of yourself, or trying to hide your feelings of inferiority. Being crowned: a significant goal can be reached in a short time.

D: The king is a symbol for the "father" in you, and also of conflicting feelings—superiority on one hand, inferiority on the other. The queen is a symbol of the "mother" in you, but also your desire to make others dependent on you. See **Emperor.**

Kiss, Kissing

S: A kiss represents love, respect, friendship, unity, and forgiveness.

V: Dreaming about kisses indicates unfulfilled love with a hint of eroticism. Dreaming you are kissing a stranger (man or woman): is a warning that a short-lived acquaintance will bring you nothing but trouble. Kissing a person you know: the relationship to that person will get even better. Kissing your mother: you are longing for tenderness. Kissing an old person: disappointment in a love relationship.

D: Kisses mean that you long for love, tenderness, affection, or passion.

Kitchen

V: Looking at or being in a kitchen: take better care of your house and the well-being of others and yourself. Looking at the stove in a kitchen: you are developing maternal talents, taking care of and pampering your loved one. See **Baker.**

D: The kitchen is the internal place where the **Cook** works the experiences of your life into a palatable whole, making them easier to digest and enjoy.

Knee, Kneeling

V: If you are kneeling: you need to be humble in order to clear up a certain situation.

Seeing an injured knee: things will take a turn for the worse. If the knee is swollen: you don't know what to do next. Seeing someone else kneeling: you have wronged someone and now feel guilty.

D: The knee represents erotic desires, cravings, and passion. It may also be a sign of humility or even a humble attitude (particularly if you are the one kneeling). Sometimes it represents guilt for having harmed someone. If that is the case, make amends now. See **Legs.**

Knife

S: The knife is an instrument of sacrifice and also of execution. See **Court, Death, Revenge.**

V: Looking at a large knife: an unpleasant situation is ahead—a situation to which you have contributed. Seeing a sharp knife: a difficult decision or separation. Looking at a knife and fork: expect a friendly invitation. In a woman's dream, the knife is either a phallic symbol or represents hidden aggression. What did you do with the knife? Did someone threaten you with the knife? See **Cutting, Pocketknife.**

D: The knife is a symbol of primitive but dangerous eruptions of violence.

Are you finding yourself on the edge? Who is attacking you with "cutting words"? See **Dagger, Weapon.**

Knight

V: If you are the knight: your friends are going out of their way to support you in your present difficult situation. Seeing a knight: be prepared for a fight—in your personal life as well as on the job.

D: The knight is either a sign that you need protection right now, or that you are very chivalrous toward another person. See **Armor, Castle.**

Knitting

D: If you are knitting: a boring task will take time to complete; or you are making something simple complicated. See **Stocking.**

Knock-knees

V: Seeing someone with knock-knees: someone's criticism is causing you great embarrassment. You are knock-kneed: someone is blaming you for a problem that you did not create.

D: A dream about knock-knees is a sign of everyday problems that need to be solved.

Knot

V: Looking at a string with many knots: your situation is all "tangled up." Undoing the knots in a string: it will take a lot of effort to straighten out a difficult matter, making it possible for a long-held wish to be realized. See **String.**

D: Depending on other actions in the dream, the knot symbolizes the problems and complicated relationships you have with other people—problems that need to be solved or quickly untangled. Simply "cut through" the knot if it won't give or appears too daunting. Looking at loose knots in a dream: the relationships you have with certain people need more attention.

S = SYMBOL V = VISION D = DEPTH PSYCHOLOGY

Laboratory

V: Looking at or being in a laboratory: you are reexamining a situation. If you pay attention to all the details, you will conclude a personal or business matter successfully. Working in a laboratory: you have maneuvered yourself into a difficult situation.

D: You have worked yourself into a difficult, tricky situation. The outcome of the dilemma will depend on the rest of the dream images.

Labyrinth

S: The labyrinth is a symbol of human life in general: its challenges, delays, and complications.

V: Looking at a labyrinth: you are in over your head! You have been sidetracked and have lost perspective. Stumbling around in a labyrinth: you are looking for the security of your childhood; you would do better to search for an exit from your current behavior.

D: In the search for self-knowledge, you have met the chaos inside you (maybe in your unconscious?). It confuses and frightens you. Look for the exit!

Ladder

S: The ladder is a symbol of the way to heaven: climbing a

ladder means you are humble—falling off, you are arrogant.

V: Climbing a ladder: you are desperate for a promotion. Climbing high up on a ladder: you are missing opportunities at work. Falling off a ladder: you are too ambitious, which makes you unpopular and will only harm you. Someone else is falling off a ladder: you have been deserted by a person you thought would always be there for you. Looking at a ladder: you've been given an opportunity—don't miss it. Looking at a broken ladder: let go of whatever you have planned—pursuing it further would only harm you.

D: The ladder means you doubt that you will be successful. Are you willing to "take one step at a time" on the ladder of success? Are you avoiding climbing the ladder in order to escape danger? Have you asked too much of yourself? See **Stairs.**

Ladybug

V: Seeing one or more ladybugs means the same thing in a dream as it supposedly does in real life: they will bring you good luck.

Lake

V: Seeing a calm, clear lake: you are going to be calm and peaceful. A stormy lake: troubles ahead, but the reason for them lies within yourself. Swimming in a lake: "still waters run deep"—that means *you*!

D: See **Ocean, Water.**

Lamb

S: The lamb is the symbol of humility, innocence, and sacrifice.

V: Seeing a lamb: you are much too good-natured—be more assertive. Shearing lambs: beware, you are taking advantage of people! Watching a lamb being slaughtered or slaughtering it yourself: your reaction to a certain matter is not as heartless as it seems. See **Sheep.**

D: The lamb usually represents tenderness, innocence, and purity, but are you perhaps the "sacrificial lamb"? Don't wait. Expose the "guilty party"!

Lamp

S: The lamp is related to light.

V: If a bright light is burning in the lamp: a happy event is waiting for you—a project is proceeding without a hitch. Turning on a lamp: a relationship with a loved one is getting closer and more intimate, because you have made the person very happy. If it is a candle lamp that gives off soot: a misdeed has serious consequences. If the candle goes out: an intimate relationship is breaking up. Breaking a lamp: your own carelessness will cause you harm.

D: The lamp is a sign that you would like to better understand (or "see through") people or circumstances. Paying careful attention will make this possible. See **Lantern, Light.**

Lance, Spear

S: The lance—one of the oldest weapons of man—is also a phallic symbol.

V: Seeing a lance means a fight—instigated by others—is about to break out. If you are handling a lance: because of your actions, you will be the one to start a fight. See **Dagger, Rapier.**

D: As a phallic symbol, the lance also refers to sexual appetites. See **Weapon.**

Land

V: Reaching land from the ocean or a lake: your plans and projects are now on a solid footing and will be completed successfully. Walking on land: the state of the land is an indication of how your life will unfold. Walking across a healthy **Meadow** means you are getting ahead in life. Walking over a field: hard work is the only way to have a good "harvest." An empty field: disappointment and failure—because others have already harvested the crop. See **Earth, Field.**

Landlord

V: Speaking to your landlord: you are spending much more money than your bank account can handle. See **Coffee.**

D: You are either partying too much, or you should do more of it. An honest answer can only come from you!

Lantern, Traffic Light

V: According to ancient folklore, a lighted lantern stands for an impending, sorrow-filled event. A blinking traffic light is always a warning to be careful. If you or someone else is turning the traffic light off: the danger has passed, expect improvement in the present situation. If the light in the lantern is burning brightly: you have gained great insights, or you are about to reveal a secret. If the light in the lantern is flickering or going out: don't get involved in other people's business; you are probably misreading the situation. See **Light.**

D: The image of a traffic light is always a sign of a budding love affair—particularly when the traffic light is **Red.** A softly burning lantern reflects deep insight and inner wisdom. See **Lamp.**

Lap

V: A man dreaming about a woman's lap: strong sexual cravings that need to be brought under control. Sitting in someone's lap: you have a great need for tenderness.

Lark

V: Hearing a lark sing: your private life and professional work are going well. A lark high in sky: life will get easier. See **Bird, Heaven.**

D: A lark indicates lofty intellectual goals; it also means you have a better understanding of your past and present situation—and a better idea of your future!

Larva

V: Seeing a larva: you are not happy right now—everything is still hidden. See **Caterpillar.**

D: Nothing on the outside gives any indication that you are going through a period of profound change (from caterpillar to butterfly). Give yourself time and let the process work!

Last Will and Testament

V: If you are writing your will, you will reach a ripe, old age. Seeing a will: you are about to inherit something.

D: The will is a sign that you have completed an important stage in your life.

Laughter

V: Hearing laughter: you are afraid that others will mock you. Watching a former friend laugh: a past, somewhat embarrassing experience is surfacing because you are not yet over it. If you are the one laughing: you are trying to cover up a burden or worry from others or yourself.

D: Liberating, uproarious laughter is releasing all your tensions, suggesting that it's better to laugh about yourself than to take everything so seriously.

Laundry

V: Dreaming about clean laundry is a sign of good health

and a prosperous future. Dirty laundry: your relationship is in doubt—you are acting carelessly. Seeing laundry on a line outside: it is time to come clean. Seeing a laundromat: clean up your act and your attitude.

D: Either other people are getting you in trouble or your own outdated, "crusty" attitude is creating trouble and disappointments. See **Soap, Washing.**

Laurel, Laurel Tree

S: The laurel tree is a "God Tree"—a symbol of everlasting life and youth.

V: Looking at a laurels or a laurel tree: you are being honored. Wearing a laurel wreath on your head: you are too ambitious and crave admiration—these traits need to be controlled. Picking laurel: you are making a fool of yourself.

D: You either want more recognition or you expect to be rewarded or honored. Beware, if this is the case, you could make a fool of yourself.

Lava

D: Repressed (unconscious) feelings and emotions are going to erupt soon. See **Crater, Heat, Mountain, Volcano.**

Lawn

V: Seeing a green lawn: unexpected encounters; also you might win back someone's love. Walking on a lawn: your relationship with your relatives is improving—and possibly your personal affairs as well. Mowing a lawn: you will be able to deal with the loss or even the death of a friend or acquaintance. Sitting or lying on a lawn: you are in excellent shape and feel very energetic.

D: Usually, the lawn is a sign of erotic needs and the condition of the lawn is a metaphor for the state of the relationship with your partner. Is the lawn green? Is it neglected and overgrown? What does your relationship look like these days? See **Grass, Meadow.**

Lawyer

V: Dealing with a lawyer in a dream means troubles or arguments with bureaucrats. Maybe you have been unfair to someone? Now is the time to make up. Visiting a lawyer: you need to clear up a legal matter. If the lawyer is wearing a black robe: the chances for a change in your present situation are slim. See **Notary Public.**

Leaf, Piece of Paper

V: Dreaming about a white, empty piece of paper means new possibilities and new opportunities; an empty piece of paper promises future possibilities already in the making. Receiving an empty piece of paper from another person: you are under the influence of somebody else (whether negative or positive depends on the rest of the dream images). If you are looking at pages in a book, it means you are thirsty for knowledge, This is good for studying, and also for finalizing contracts. See **Paper** and the chapter on **"Letters in Dreams."** Looking at many green leaves: expect a happy event; you are entertaining new ideas and establishing interesting goals. Wilted leaves: worries and defeat. Watching falling leaves: misfortune or loss in your family. See **Branch, Leaves, Tree.**

D: Green leaves symbolize emotional and intellectual growth; wilted leaves stand for what has passed. You have lost your footing and feel tossed about like "a leaf in the wind."

Learning, Reading

D: Dreaming about learning and reading are both signs of your intellect, ideas, and expectations, as well as a healthy self-criticism. Your life experiences will serve you well in the future.

Leather

V: Buying or selling leather: you are firmly grounded in reality and have a clear mind. Making something out of leather: a secret wish will come true, because you have worked hard for it.

D: Leather is a symbol of your determination and patience. But since it is an animal product, it also indicates your more "animalistic instincts," urges, appetites, and the like. See **Cow, Pig.**

Leaves

V: Looking at green leaves: you enjoy emotional balance and are continuing to grow in all areas of your life. Wilted or decaying leaves: your chances for success are zero right now; you are forced to pull out of a job with a loss. Collecting leaves means you are getting or inheriting money. See **Leaf.**

D: Green leaves are a warning: enjoy your good fortune right now—because leaves wilt and die quickly!

Lecture

V: If you are giving a lecture: you are too vain and self-satisfied—expect no sympathy. Losing your concentration during a speech: learn to speak freely—stage fright is not necessary.

Left

V: Left is a symbol of the feminine. Making a left turn means that the women in your life will "show the way." It also means that you will gain greater insight.

D: *Left:* be cautious because it is the dark and mysterious side. The "road to the left" is always dangerous, because left stands for the unconscious, destructive, and irrational within us. Dreaming of being paralyzed on the left side says you are operating too much from intellect and reason and that you should try to strengthen your emotional, intuitive side. See **Right.**

Legs

S: Legs are a symbol of a steadfast person and of the "road of life." It is important whether you are dreaming about the **Right** or the **Left** leg.

V: Running on healthy legs means success in life. Swollen legs are a sign of difficulties and stagnation. Breaking a leg: be prepared for financial losses or being reprimanded at the job. A leg being amputated means inhibition and frustration in a present situation; either you are "stuck" or asked to wait and be patient. Dreaming about running: you are very ambitious, in a hurry to reach your goal, or running away from something!

D: Legs symbolize everything that has to do with the road and your life's journey. Are you well grounded? Will your legs carry you the distance? Do you need "crutches"? Are you limping? Are you insured? Looking at a woman's legs expresses sexual needs; hairy legs are a sign of masculinity or unexpected surprises. Unshapely or thin legs: completing a project is going to be difficult. See **Foot.**

Lemon

V: Eating a lemon: expect trouble in an official matter. Looking at a squeezed lemon: people are taking advantage of you and you can do nothing about it.

D: Are you mad? At yourself or at others? No matter how sour the lemon is, the juice is very good for you. Maybe your anger is justified and emotionally healthy, because you are venting it. Does your body need more vitamin C?

Lemonade

V: Drinking lemonade is a sign of shallowness—you

would like to "sweeten" your life and have as much fun as possible. See **Coca-Cola.**

Lentil

V: Dreaming about lentils usually suggests getting ready for arguments and fights.

Leopard

S: The leopard is an ancient symbol of pride, war, and hunting.

D: The leopard stands for a strong sexual drive that is about to take over your life. Establish some control; change your spots! See **Animals, Predator.**

Leper

V: Seeing a leper means worries, restlessness, or danger in the near future. Becoming a leper: you are unable to see your true self. You feel separated from the people around you or not accepted by them; everything in life seems negative.

D: "Emotional garbage" is pushing up from the unconscious and is symbolized in the face of the dreamer. Lepers have always been shunned by society and forced to live in isolation. Seeing yourself as a leper: the harmony in your life, your spirit, is broken. Pay attention to other images in the dream.

Letter

V: Writing a letter is a symbol of being too much involved in your own affairs. Receiving a letter means that the future looks very promising for your financial situation.

D: A letter in a dream symbolizes the intuition or insights you have concerning another person, or that you have gained more self-knowledge.

Letter Carrier

V: Meeting a letter carrier on the road: someone is sending you money unexpectedly. Seeing a letter carrier: you are gaining new insight into your personality and character. This newfound self-knowledge brings new hope.

Letters (as in the alphabet)

D: Individual letters are discussed in the chapter **"Letters in Dreams."** Letters are a symbol of order. A dream about letters in "marching-formation" is an urgent message to get your life in order!

Library, Librarian

D: According to C. G. Jung, a library represents not only the place where you "store" the experiences, knowledge, and wisdom acquired during a lifetime, but also the "collective unconscious." The library may also stand for your well-developed memory and the ability to be in constant contact with the collective unconscious. (If this is true in your case, be proud of it!)

Lice

V: Dreaming about lice usually means changing something for the worse. It might also refer to "a human parasite," a freeloader who is looking for an advantage at your expense. See **Bug.**

D: Lice are a symbol of emotional unrest, deep-seated insecurities, and negative thinking.

Light

S: "God is light and in him there is no darkness" (1. John 1.5). Light brings order to chaos.

V: A light always symbolizes a signpost, a guiding force. You are either on the right path or it will soon dawn on you what path you want to travel. Candlelight is a suggestion to look inside, to be more reflective and reverent. Seeing a light in the distance: happiness and good times ahead.

D: The light is a sign that you are raising your consciousness through awareness. Light will bring clarity and understanding to your life.

Lighthouse

V: Seeing a lighthouse by day: your chances for the future are getting better because you can see things more clearly. It also is a good sign of a happy homecoming. If the lighthouse is flashing: pay attention to the advice of a friend—it might save you from a bad experience.

D: The lighthouse is usually a warning of impending danger. It might also be your unconscious pointing you in the right direction when you are "in the dark." See **Light.**

Lightning

S: Lightning is a symbol of the powerful and swift fires of the heavens.

V: Dreaming about lightning always points to unpleasant things to come, maybe on the job. Getting hit by lightning means an impending illness or annoying issues; it can also be a timely warning, allowing you to prevent the above. Seeing a quick bolt of lightning, followed by **Thunder** might indicate sudden, unusual events on the job, or good fortune. Feeling the pain of being struck by lightning: bad news or unexpected hardships will "hit you like lightning." Seeing a lightning storm means good fortune and new chances. See **Weather**. Lightning striking your **House**: expect financial losses, sometimes health problems. See **Fire**.

D: Lightning symbolizes a sudden discharge of inner tension. It also can be a sign of "lightning-quick insights" (sudden recognition of certain connections, or the solution to a problem). Sometimes it might also be a sudden fear of punishment or the revenge of another person.

Lilac

V: Seeing a lilac bush: you need affection and tenderness. The fragrance of lilac indicates budding love and romantic feelings. A wilted lilac bush: a wonderful love affair is ending in disappointment. Picking lilacs means someone is admiring you.

D: This fragrant flower is a sign of budding love; it is also a symbol of romance and the need for affection and tenderness.

Lily

S: The lily is a symbol of purity, innocence, and virginity.

V: Looking at a lily: "just do it"—your chances of success are excellent! Holding a lily in your hands: you are loved and respected by others. Throwing a lily away: you have misused your power—and punishment will be swift.

D: The lily is a sign that the time is right for you to increase your self-knowledge, which will allow you to gain emotional balance. A dream about lilies usually means you are looking for peace, serenity, and rest—you will have all three.

Limping

V: Watching a person limp or limping yourself: your business affairs will take a turn for the worse.

D: Limping indicates hard times and the difficulty you have managing your life. Present problems are clearly of your own making. Are you making things more difficult than they have to be? Are you the one who is putting obstacles in your own path? Do you want to force others to help you? Who is it that you are "limping" after? See **Foot, Legs.**

Lion

V: Seeing a lion: a certain friend sometimes looks dangerous. Being attacked by a lion: a warning of danger. Defeating the lion: you are eliminating an opponent. Looking at a caged lion: a powerful enemy has no way of attacking you right now, because you are protected. See **Animal, Predator, Tiger.**

D: The lion is a symbol of dignity and intensity. It has enormous energy, determination, and aggression toward others. The dream means you might be afraid of these characteristics (in yourself as well as others) and it is a warning to better control your emotions.

Lips

V: Dreaming about red lips means luck in love and friendships. Pale lips mean you have to give up something you love, or that your love for another person is fading. Looking at lips grimly pressed together: other people's envy and hate is hurting you.

D: Lips in dreams usually stand for erotic desires, but can also be a reference to love, sympathy, and friendship in your private life. See **Mouth.**

Listening, Eavesdropping

V + D: Listening or eavesdropping behind a closed door: don't be so nosy—you are only harming yourself. Instead, listen to yourself and what *you* think.

Liver

V: Eating liver: pay more attention to your health—you might become ill. Buying or looking at liver: your health is going to improve. Looking at spoiled liver: illness is about to strike. Be particularly careful with alcohol and medication.

D: The liver is often a sign of impending illness; sometimes it is a warning of physical, emotional, or mental "poison" you have either inflicted on yourself or others have inflicted on you. You are weak right now. In case of emotional poison, get rid of the "garbage," and do a thorough cleansing!

Livestock, Livestock Dealer, Livestock Auction

V: Seeing an animal herd: be happy, your finances will improve. Selling animals at a livestock auction: you thought you were particularly smart, but others will outbid you by a mile! Negotiating with a livestock dealer: watch out—you are being "taken for ride"! See **Cow, Stall.**

D: An animal represents instinctive urges. The livestock dealer and the auction point to sly and foxy people. Either someone wants to "put something over" on you or vice versa. The other symbols in the dream are important. See **Animals.**

Lizard

D: The lizard is a symbol of dissension in your life, including arguments or secret hostilities. Find out whether—in this situation—you are the perpetrator or the victim.

Locomotive

V: In men's dreams, a locomotive is a sign of pursuing goals with all available strength and power. The locomotive releasing steam suggests that you are doing the same right now. In women's dreams, the locomotive indicates a great trip in the making. Seeing a locomotive under steam: you are making too much of something; you are overly ambitious.

D: The locomotive in a dream stands for the emotional energy that is driving you forward in life. See **Train.**

Log

V: Splitting a log: you are trying to straighten out a "blockhead," and bring him to his senses. Stubbing your toe on a log: boorish, uncouth people have insulted you. Carrying a log on your back: you are taking on an unnecessary **Burden**, one that will do nobody any good.

D: The log stands for an unnecessary burden or irritating responsibility you have assumed and for which you will not be rewarded. It can also be a warning to defend yourself against the rudeness of others.

Loneliness, Abandonment

D: Feeling lonely: a sign of your isolation. Has someone abandoned you? Were you unable to count on another person? Examine the rest of the dream symbols so you can act quickly. See **Hermit, Orphan.**

Loss

V: Losing something: a reminder that you have missed something. Losing money: you will gain something in other areas of your life.

Lottery, Lottery Ticket

V: Drawing a ticket means things will soon take a turn for the worse. Looking at the numbers of a lottery ticket: consider buying a lottery ticket and use the numbers in the dream if you can remember them. Dreaming about playing the lottery: you are too optimistic and what you hope for is unrealistic. Participating in picking numbers means disappointments.

Love, Love Letter

V: Dreaming about being in love with someone: you can almost count on being disappointed. If someone else is in love with you: a person will be of great service to you. See **Admiration.** Dreams about love do not always have a sexual meaning; they might be a symbol of your desire for love or a sign of unfulfilled love (particularly if you feel very alone at the moment). Dreaming about getting a love letter: bad news. Writing a love letter: you are in love right now.

D: Dreaming about love usually means that you are looking for warmth, affection, and tenderness!

Lover

V: Dreaming about a lover means you have broken out of a present relationship but scorn faithfulness. Old traditions also say that a dream about a lover might be a sign of impending illness.

D: Dreaming about a lover means you are looking for a love partner with perfect attributes—something you probably will never find. You are trying to compensate for unfulfilled expectations and disappointment in personal relationships. You are looking for idealized and unrealizable love. Be sensible, lower your expectations!

Low Tide

S: Low tide and high tide are symbols of the rhythm of life, its ups and downs, birth and death.

V: Being on the ocean and watching low tide: your fate will be as full of changes as the tides of the ocean. Seeing the ocean at low tide: life is stagnating, nothing is moving, nothing new is happening, but keep the faith; everything will change again for the better soon. Watching high tide: the fortunes of your life have a tendency to change and are unreliable. See **High Tide, Water.**

D: Low tide is an expression of dissatisfaction and resignation; life is boring! But don't fret—nothing lasts forever!

Lowly, Humble

D: Dreaming about being lowly or humble usually refers to vulgarity, questionable morals or ethics, crude behavior (your own or someone else's), or an emotional low. The rest of the dream symbols are very important. See **Shrinking.**

Luggage

V: Carrying heavy luggage is a sign that you carry a lot of emotional baggage and unnecessary problems, problems of your own making. What is it that you are lugging around?

Lung

V: Dreaming about having strong, healthy lungs means a strenuous task is ahead. If your lungs are weak: you are unable to deal with a task assigned to you.

D: The dream may be suggesting either a physical examination (particularly of the bronchial tubes and lungs), or that a difficult job lies ahead. Take a deep breath—it's the only way to succeed in whatever you have been asked to do.

S = Symbol V = Vision D = Depth psychology

Machine Gun

V: Seeing or hearing a machine gun: someone around you feels guilty—and rightfully so—for what he/she has done. Firing a machine gun represents repressed aggression or the sign of a bad conscience. The dream is a way of relieving tension.

D: See **Pistol, Rifle, Weapon.**

Machine

V: Watching a machine in action: life will continue to go smoothly and without a hitch. If the machine is idle: obstacles and difficulties. Working with a machine: a complicated matter is keeping you busy.

D: A machine is an expression of both the conscious and the unconscious strength that powers you forward in life. It also symbolizes what is "routine" in your life—often at the expense of spontaneity. Are you functioning like a machine?

Madonna

V: Looking at a madonna (maybe in a picture): your sorrows or an illness will soon be over.

D: The madonna (not the rock star) represents motherhood, gentleness, and a rich emotional life. Your connection to a higher power is positive. Your faith is strong and promises help and/or solace.

Maggot

V: Looking at meat crawling with maggots: be careful, certain people want to live off your success and are shamelessly exploiting your knowledge and skills.

D: A maggot usually stands for your own negative behavior; it might also be a sign that you are trying to change your behavior.

Magic, Magician

V: Watching a magician at work means an unexpected event ahead. But don't believe everything that you are told! You are the magician—even if in real life you can't "cast a spell" or reach your goal by "magic."

D: Either you overestimate your skills, believing you can perform magic, or you are hoping that magically you will get out of a difficult situation. Are you trying a bit of trickery?

Magnet

V: Seeing a magnet means you will soon make an important connection or start an important relationship. Dreaming of pulling people or objects toward you: you are about to lose something expensive, or you will lose or alienate someone you love. Being pulled by a magnet: you are about to "lose your heart" to someone.

D: The magnet is a sign of how charismatic you are, and how much sympathy you have for people. Do you attract people easily? Does someone or something else draw you like a magnet?

Magnifying Glass

V: Looking at a magnifying glass: a small incident will have huge consequences. Looking through a magnifying glass: you are making a mountain out of a molehill; or you are looking for something that does not exist.

D: The magnifying glass is usually a warning about making too much of little things, believing that they are bigger than they really are. Don't exaggerate so much. In other cases, it may indicate that you are not taking something seriously enough—look more closely.

Mail, Mailman, Postcard

V: The postman in a dream usually has pleasant information. A postman bringing money: you are spending money on useless things. Seeing a package: you are about to receive a gift. Writing a postcard: you need to take care of an unpleasant matter.

Receiving a postcard: in a certain situation you are guided more by false hopes than reality. See **Package.**

D: Mail represents your attitudes, opinions, and thoughts that can influence others. See **Letter**. A postcard can also refer to an irritating obligation that should be fulfilled as soon as possible.

Makeup

V: Seeing makeup: don't try to make something negative look better than it is or hush it up. Also, don't be impressed by appearances—they are deceptive. Seeing people wearing makeup: beware of false friends. If you are wearing makeup: you want people to think you are better than you really are, but you are only deceiving yourself. See **Powder, Wig.**

D: The best motto always is to live the "unvarnished truth." Do you want to hide something? Are you easily deceived by what people "seem" to be, by people whose intentions are not honest? These are questions that only you can answer. See **Mask.**

Man

V: Seeing an old man: it's difficult right now, but relax;

you'll get good advice and, if you follow it, your problems will be over. A fat man in a woman's dream: a certain man is worshiping the ground you walk on. Seeing a young man; discomfort and stress in the near future. Men seeing a man without a head: you are acting without thinking and need to change that quickly. Women dreaming about men means they have secret sexual desires. A man dreaming about women means he is in conflict with himself—it is time for some soul-searching.

D: In women's dreams a man usually stands for her secret, erotic, and sexual desires. In men's dreams, a woman stands for how he sees and judges himself.

Manure

V: Looking at manure (a pile of it) means great success in business affairs. The bigger the manure pile, the greater your wealth. Spreading manure: pending actions will have great results. Stepping in a manure pile means good luck. Take advandage of the opportunities that are coming your way. Toiling in manure: success and wealth through hard work. See **Excrement, Mud.**

D: Manure/garbage can create something new. Past experiences make it possible for you to grow in a positive way and develop your personality.

Manuscript

V: Seeing a manuscript means you are unsure what to do, but it would be a mistake to postpone a certain task much longer.

Map

V: You are either about to go on a trip; or the dream wants to point you in the "right direction." Do you recognize a specific region? See **Four Corners of the Compass, East, North, South, West.**

D: A map reveals your life's journey; use the map to determine your route—you might avoid unnecessary detours! The map also may represent your intellectual strength that will guide you on your journey through life. See **Compass.**

Marble

V: Working on a piece of marble: you are wasting your time—and energy—on a hopeless matter; people around you are "cold." Looking at a marble sculpture: your property seems secure and your friendships solid. Looking at a marble pillar: in some areas you are too rigid and insist on holding to a point of view even when you know you are wrong.

D: Marble represents hopeless ideas and fantasies that have no chance of being realized! It is also a sign of your own "coldness." Try to have a softer heart!

Market

V: If you are at the market: you are involved with people and nurture the contact you have with them, but make sure that people do not take advantage of you. Shopping at the market: delicate and uncertain situations ahead. Selling things at a market: business is unstable right now, or a change at work is ahead. See **Shopping.**

D: The market is always a symbol of your positive attitude toward people and a good business sense. Also, never measure your worth by what you own. Particularly in men's dreams, the market may indicate strong sexual needs and becomes a code word for a place where men buy sexual pleasures. See **Businessman, Fair.**

Marmalade, Preserves

D: The image of marmalade refers to your past efforts and work in "preserving" the "fruits of your labor," so they will nourish you in the future. See **Fruit.**

Marriage

D: If you are single, dreaming about marriage often means you secretly wish to be married. It might also be a reference to marital problems, either in the present or from a former marriage. The best of all possibilities would be that the dream reflects harmony between your conscious and unconscious.

Mars

D: As a positive image, the planet Mars, ruling the warrior, is a symbol of courage, willpower, assertiveness, and physical strength. In a negative form, Mars symbolizes war, male aggressiveness, hot temper, and destructive energies. See **Planets, Signs of the Zodiac.**

Martyr

D: For whom or what are you being the martyr? Do you expect someone else to sacrifice feelings, ideals, opinions, or habits for your benefit? Neither scenario can be considered very healthy. See **Victim.**

Mask

S: A mask refers to a cynical attitude in the "theater of Life."

V: Looking at a mask: you are either trying to hide your true self or the dream is a warning of false friends or an intrigue. Don't be fooled by others and don't fool yourself! Seeing a person with a mask: a good friend is shamelessly deceiving you. Watching a masked ball or being at one: you like to play with the feelings of other people (consciously or unconsciously). The dream might also be warning about other people who are playing with your affections.

D: The mask is a sign that you are afraid of the truth or emotional "unmasking." Are you unsure about the intentions of other people or maybe your own? See **Makeup.**

Mason

V: Looking at a mason: you need to have more patience in a present situation. Working as a mason: you are "building" your own luck. Be proud—good luck will be with you a long time.

D: The mason is a wonderful symbol: you will build your life on a solid foundation if you take one thing at a time and don't make hasty decisions.

Mass

V: If you are participating in a mass at church: your life is going well and advancement at your job is practically guaranteed.

D: Your participation in a mass means that now you will be guided more by your spirit.

Massage, Massage Therapist

V: Getting a massage is either an expression of sexual desire or an indication of possible health problems. Giving someone a massage: you need to correct something or put something right.

D: The massage is a suggestion either to be less rigid or to let go of emotional tension. If you live alone, the dream means that you are in need of human touch and/or contact.

Mast (of a Sailboat)

V: Looking at a mast: you have accomplished an enormous task and should be proud of yourself. You can start on a new project now. If the mast is without sails: you still have hard work ahead before reaching the goal you have set for yourself. A mast under sail means everything is going well. See **Ship, Tree.**

D: A mast is either a phallic symbol (and therefore about sexual desire) or a sign of a strong personality. You are walking with your head held high on a straight and narrow path. You won't bend for anything.

Mat

V: A braided mat: you have created a solid foundation and have no need to worry. Lying on a straw mat: stop spending so much money, because your budget is shrinking. Looking at a green mat: circumstances are going to change for the better.

Matches

V: Playing with matches: you like to play with the emotions of other people, but one day people might turn the tables on you! See **Fire.**

Mathematics

V: Dreaming about a mathematical formula means you are facing a very tricky assignment—but rest assured you will make it.

Mattress

V: Dreaming about a mattress: you need to work harder and show more ambition. Lying on a mattress: insecurity and indecision could cause you a great deal of grief. See **Bed.**

Meadow

V: Seeing a green meadow: let joy and happiness rule the day—you deserve it! The grass in the meadow has dried up or been cut: don't waste your time with things old and obsolete. Seeing an unfenced pasture: the space you live in has become too restricted. See **Hay.**

D: The meadow is usually a symbol of your need for rest and relaxation. Do you really need a break or simply hate to work hard? Are there **Animals** in the pasture? Is the grass green? See **Grass,** and the chapter **"Colors in Dreams."**

Meal

V: Dreaming about eating a rich meal: you lack empathy and concern for others—it is important to change this at all costs. Dreaming about a big meal while fasting (in real life) should not surprise you—your unconscious is looking for food. Wanting to eat but facing an empty table: you don't have enough energy. Sharing a good meal with others: your kindness has made you very popular. See **Eating.**

D: Eating is a symbol that your soul is being nurtured. The dream is suggesting that you can obtain vital energies through spiritual nourishment. There is also something very sensual about a good meal.

Meat

V: Seeing or eating meat points to erotic cravings and material gluttony. Eating the flesh of another person: you are shunned by society. Rotten meat means bad luck. Throwing meat to a dog: somebody dislikes you.

D: Meat often points to your likes and dislikes. It also deals with your material, physical (including sexual) needs.

Medal

V: Receiving a medal: you are not aware of it, but you are overly ambitious and arrogant. Giving a medal to someone else: your career will get a boost.

D: Your need for recognition, reward, or authority has become almost pathological; make some drastic changes and do it quickly. Too much pride and ambition will chase away good friends and partners. See **Tassel.**

Medicine

V: Taking good-tasting medicine: you are hoping to get a large sum of money—but that isn't going to happen. Taking bitter medicine is a reminder that success may not come easily, because "nothing is for nothing." Giving medicine to another: you will help someone with advice and action.

D: Medicine is either a wonderful symbol stating that your body's capacity for healing has been activated, or it is a hint that you may soon have to swallow "a bitter pill," depending of the rest of the images in the dream.

Meditation

D: You would like very much to explore and gain insight into your unconscious. Why don't you act on it? Try meditating—it will do you a world of good!

Meeting

V: Being in a meeting: you have neglected your interests, and the consequences are unpleasant. Holding a meeting: unpleasant discussions among your friends.

D: See **Club.**

Melon

V: Seeing or eating a melon means a wonderful get-together with the person you love.

Melting Pot

D: The melting pot is the place where hopes and desires, rational thinking and passions together make up your personality. The dream is a challenge to resolve contradictions in your personality. If the pace of the dream is moderate, it means that you are maturing at a steady pace, but if it is hectic and explosive, growing up for you is wrought with tension.

Mentally Ill Person

V: Seeing a mentally ill person in a dream: it would be wise to get your life back to a more orderly state—it might prevent serious harm.

D: Mentally ill people in a dream are a sign that your thoughts and actions don't make sense. Use your head! You have a good mind! Seeing yourself as mentally ill: stay away from people with too much imagination, people that love to build "castles in the air." See **Fool.**

Merchandise, Warehouse

V: Looking at a lot of merchandise: your business is doing well. Piling up merchandise: admit your miserliness and greed and get it under control! Spending time in a warehouse: you are having a hard time making decisions.

D: See **Shopping.**

Mercury

D: Mercury is the god Hermes—the "winged messenger." He is also the patron of thieves and shopkeepers. This planet stands for your financial situation or talents. Mercury is also responsible for communication, buying, selling, financial negotiations, and travels. See **Planets, Signs of the Zodiac.**

Mercury (Quicksilver)

V: Seeing mercury is a sign of restlessness. Be more focused and steady in all your endeavors, otherwise your life will change constantly, depriving you of rest and quiet.

D: Mercury is a symbol of your fate that is forever in flux. Are you as restless as a drop of mercury? Is your life hectic and people around you irritable? Try to do something about it—mercury is a poison!

Mermaid

V: Men who dream about mermaids need to be careful: they are being seduced by a woman they know and things could get dangerous.

D: The mermaid is a symbol of female sensuality that has

yet to be lived, particularly in women's dreams. It might, however, also indicate a strong but unconscious love you feel for someone, particularly in men's dreams.

Merry, Jolly, Happy

D: Dreaming about being happy and exhilarated: you can at last "laugh" about something. On the other hand, are you hiding a serious matter behind a "happy face"? That could bring real sadness. Pay attention to the rest of the dream symbols.

Merry-Go-Round

V: Seeing a merry-go-round: a warning that you are about to do something foolish. Acting without thinking might get you in real trouble.

D: A merry-go-round is a warning not to be foolish and careless. It also might refer to an actual ear problem (possibly impaired balance). If these dreams appear frequently, see a specialist. See **Dizziness.**

Message

V: Receiving a message: expect to get news. Receiving bad news: good news in real life. Receiving good news: bad news in real life.

D: Receiving a message: thinking things through first will clear up uncertain or problematic situations. See **Letter, Telephone.**

Messenger

V: Seeing one or more messengers: you will get good news in a few days. If the messenger has a letter for you: the news will probably be unpleasant and your hopes dashed. If the messenger is bringing a gift or a package: a very nice surprise.

Microphone

V: Dreaming about a microphone is like a question: are you still not ready to tell what is bothering you? Are you trying to get people's attention? Are you demanding admiration? See **Magnifying Glass.**

Midget

V: Seeing a midget: develop more confidence—there is no reason to diminish yourself. Have you met a person who—compared to you—seems to be a **Giant**? See **Small.**

D: Are you suffering from feelings of inferiority or have others not satisfied your ego?

Midwife

V: Seeing a midwife: a long-held secret is going to be revealed. Speaking to a midwife: celebrating a baptism or you will watch the birth of a child. Being examined by a midwife: you have a bad conscience and want help and relief.

D: The midwife stands for needing help in the **Birth** of a new idea.

Military

V: Watching a military parade: beware, the immediate future will be hectic; you might also experience terror or a dangerous situation. See **General, Soldier, Uniform, Weapon.**

D: Dreaming about the military might indicate a hidden desire to be sexually exploited (sexual fantasies). If the dream returns frequently, it might be a sign of masochistic tendencies or even perversion. See **Officer.** Look for other important images in the dream. What else took place in the dream?

Milk

S: Milk is a symbol of physical and spiritual nourishment.

V: If you're looking at or drinking milk: congratulations, you have a clear conscience. You are at peace with yourself and the world, and are willing to help anybody who is in trouble at any time. Looking at a pitcher full of milk: expect a visit from a dear friend. See **Butter, Cream, Cottage Cheese.**

D: Dreaming about milk is a message: nurture the new aspects of your personality that you have just discovered. Milk is also a symbol for motherliness, empathy, and generosity. Milk provides life-giving energy and vitality.

Milking

V: Milking a cow: everything you are about to undertake will turn out well. If you are attempting to milk a cow but there is no milk in the udder: a project you are determined to do won't work out, because you don't have the energy to carry it through. See **Cow.**

D: Take your luck into your own hands!

Mill, Mill Wheel, Mill Stone

V: Dreaming about a mill: your income will improve, your projects are making good progress, and your future will be a happy one. Watching the wheel turning at a mill: you will win something. If the wheel is not moving: a specific project is coming to a stand-still. A broken wheel stands for old problems, illnesses, or the death of a person close to you. Having a mill stone around your neck: try to resolve a difficult situation as soon as possible. See **Burden, Log, Luggage.**

D: The mill is a symbol of your need for safety and your fear of not accomplishing your goals, or—even worse—of being ground into dust by the "wheel of the mill." The dream might also suggest dealing with old attitudes and convictions (grind them up), or that emotional conflicts are turning around and around in you head like the wheel of the mill.

Million, Millionaire

V: Looking at a million dollars: someone is about to disappoint or deceive you. Dreaming about being a millionaire means social isolation and loss of money. See **Money, Wealth.**

Mine

V: Entering a mine in a dream means good look and increased prosperity. Working in a mine (shoveling coal, etc.) means a loss of energy: you have taken on too much; step back and listen to your inner voice. See **Tomb.**

D: Just like a miner who is finding and recovering treasures from deep inside the earth, so you are growing spiritually and finding and bringing to the light your inner treasures. See **Cave.**

Mineral Water

V: Drinking mineral water: a pleasant event ahead. Drinking carbonated water means more exciting events to come. See **Excitement, Water.**

D: You are either in the midst of an exciting but harmless erotic adventure or you are hoping for one.

Mink

Seeing or wearing a mink coat indicates strong sexual urges, materialism, and a good deal of ambition. All three desires need to be reined in! See **Fur.**

Mirror

S: The mirror is a symbol of vanity but also self-knowledge.

V: Seeing a mirror: try to become more self-aware. Looking into a mirror: the opinion you have of yourself differs totally from that of the people around you. Seeing yourself in the mirror: somebody is making you aware of a mistake; or you notice a mistake in the nick of time. Seeing a large mirror: fame or success. A broken mirror: quarrels with other people.

D: The mirror is a sign of your efforts to gain more clarity. But beware: a mirror shows the reverse of the way things are in reality. See **Picture.**

Miscarriage

V: Dreaming about a miscarriage means a new project, a new enterprise—the old way of doing things is unprofitable. A pregnant woman's dream about a miscarriage might indicate guilt feelings. Watching a miscarriage: someone will let you down or abuse your trust, and all your hopes will turn to ashes.

D: Dreaming about a miscarriage means either failure in a close relationship, or that efforts to mature have been abandoned. Too many anxieties, guilt feelings, and insecurities stifle your true personality.

Misfortune

V: Being involved in a calamity means you are afraid of being punished for something you have said or thought. Being an observer of somebody's misfortune: you don't feel confident and secure enough to meet the demands of everyday life. See **Accident.**

Mistake, Error

V: Making a mistake—or recognizing that you have made a mistake: don't let others bamboozle you.

D: Dreaming about a mistake reveals a fear of being disappointed or lied to. This dream is a warning: you are either being lied to and deceived—or you are lying and deceiving yourself!

Mold

V: Mold is a sign that an emotional illness may overtake your whole personality—unless you seek professional help soon.

Mole

V: Looking at a mole: you are about to give up in a certain matter—but see it through! Watching a mole digging: beware—someone is trying to get your job. Killing a mole: you are either the victim of an error, or you have made one yourself.

D: The mole could be a sign that you are about to harm someone. The dream is telling you to be open and honest. It also suggests that you feel misunderstood and your efforts are not recognized. Are you feeling like a mole? Do you like to dig around in other people's affairs? Would you like to hide in a hole like a mole?

Money

V: . Money has erotic meanings and stands for a woman's "stockpile of feminine, erotic power and attraction." In a man's dream, money is a symbol for vigor and sexual performance. Looking at a lot of money: you want to improve your station in life. Finding money on the street: you have too many debts and it's bothering your conscience. The postman is bringing you money: don't always rely on others and don't wait for help from your relatives or friends.

D: Money is the measure of the actual or hoped for strength you need. Dreams about money are about your energy reserves, possible accomplishments, and personal worth. Money is also a symbol of sexual energy, influence, power—and last but not least—financial security. Do you dream about money often? Giving so much weight to material things may be robbing you of happiness. See **Bank, Wealth.**

Monk

V: Having frequent dreams about a monk might be a sign that someone will help you deal with the troubles in your life. From a spiritual point of view, a monk might represent your inner guide. If a man dreams about a monk: don't take sexual energies quite so seriously; use them instead to mobilize your intellectual power.

D: Worldly matters no longer interest you; you are striving for wisdom and faith or are in search of a spiritual guide. See **Cloister, Guru, Nun.**

Monkey

V: The monkey is a symbol of an embarrassing encounter. Or you may be worried about your bad habits. If the monkey is playing with you and making faces, you are surrounded by superficial and instinct-driven people, or you may be examining your own "animalistic tendencies." Several monkeys: your enemies don't want to show their "real faces." If a monkey is climbing, your chances for romance will improve.

D: The monkey is considered our animalistic shadow, a distorted image of ourselves. We are afraid of the "lecherous monkey" in us, because it is only looking for physical gratification. Sometimes the monkey may be a warning against false, manipulative friends.

Monster

D: Monsters appearing in a dream reflect a fear of dying or hate directed toward oneself. Unresolved events or emotional experiences hiding beneath the surface have too much influence over you. Failing to learn how to control these energies may lead to serious problems. Seek professional help if monsters appear in your dreams frequently. See **Demons, Mysterious Creatures.**

Monument

V: Building a monument: your efforts will soon be rewarded. Looking at a monument of yourself: you have a tendency to overestimate your talents. Arrogance, unrealistic expectations, and grandiose plans could cause people to ridicule you. Seeing someone else as a monument is a sign of envy. Seeing a monument of a person you know means profiting from the success others have achieved.

D: The monument represents people who have been recognized for a special achievement; or it may remind you of an important event.

Moon

S: The moon is a symbol of dependence, femininity, change and growth, biological rhythms, and the passing of time. In a man's dream, the moon always represents female buttocks.

V: Dreaming about a rising (waxing) moon: your personal affairs are going well. Waning moon: you would do well to wait, because right now everything you try to do will fail. A full moon: your love for another person is becoming intense, and beautiful experiences await you. A half moon: Good things are unlikely to happen in your love life at this time. Seeing the reflection of the moon on the water: if the water is calm, expect a successful trip, or receiving something from somebody who is taking a trip. If the water is choppy, misfortune, troubles, or bad luck because of a trip someone else is taking.

D: The moon is a symbol of femininity and eroticism; also of a woman's buttocks—particularly in men's dreams. The moon reflects the dreamer's feelings, yearnings, mood swings, romantic love, and erotic urges and hopes. Dreaming about a new moon: your feelings "are hidden in the dark." This is a warning: don't always be so logical and rational. See **Planets.**

Morning

V: Morning is a symbol of youth, noon a symbol of maturity, afternoon a symbol of the autumn of life, and evening the beginning of the end.

D: Morning is the symbol of youthful energy and vitality (even if you are over 70 years old!). The morning is reminding you of the many possibilities of the day.

Mosaic

V: Looking at a mosaic: you are in the midst of a very difficult situation. Creating a mosaic: your actions are making a complicated affair even more difficult.

D: The mosaic of your life is a picture of the many different thoughts, ideas, and experiences you have had. Does the mosaic present a picture of harmony and contentment? Do you see only parts of it? Examine the rest of the dream symbols!

Mosquitoes

S: Mosquitoes, flies, and snakes are representations of the devil.

V: If mosquitoes are buzzing about your head: you are too generous and others are taking advantage of you; also you might have a troublesome visitor. Getting bitten by a mosquito: the friends you selected turned out to be bad company. Things will get unpleasant, but your regrets are too late. The people you invited will bring much strife into your house.

D: See **Flies, Insects.**

Moss

V: Looking at moss: chances are good that you will receive money, maybe even a great deal of money. Sitting on a mound of moss: everything, including your health, is in the best shape ever. See **Grass.**

D: Dreaming about moss: you need not worry about money; however, your emphasis on material things needs to be changed, because it hampers your freedom and keeps other parts of your personality hidden.

Moth

V: A man dreaming about a moth flying about: be more careful in your choice of female friendships. Wearing moth-eaten garments: your present situation is precarious. Only determination will bring about positive changes. See **Clothes.**

D: See **Insects, Vermin.**

Mother

V: Dreaming about your mother means either a bad conscience or the need for emotional support and a sign of good things to come. But the dream can also be a warning: stop—you are on the wrong path. Watching a happy mother caring for her child: you are going to be part of a joyous, happy occasion and might even profit from it. If the mother is anxiously looking after the child: someone's misfortune is going to affect you. Dreaming about your deceased mother: you have done your grief-work; the dream could also be a warning about taking thoughtless actions you might later regret.

D: If you rarely dream about your own mother, that is, in the eyes of psychologists, a sign that your emotional connection to your mother is good. If you dream about your mother frequently, you may fear that you will never become emotionally independent. Unresolved childhood issues are another reason for frequent dreams about your mother. If the dream is positive: you are at peace with yourself and the feminine and unconscious aspects of your personality. See **Father.**

Mother's Lap

D: Dreaming about being on your mother's lap: you don't

want to take responsibility for yourself. Is life, with all its responsibilities, tasks, and problems too much for you right now? Did you—psychologically—go back to the early stages of childhood in order to work through experiences from the past? Would you like to "give birth" to something new in your life? Try to find the appropriate answer for the present situation, taking into consideration the rest of the dream symbols.

Motorboat

V: Dreaming about a motorboat means a fun-filled pleasure-trip in the near future. See **Boat, Ship.**

Mount Olympus, Olympic Games

D: Seeing Mount Olympus means you are hoping for spiritual insights or "help from above." At best, the dream indicates your trust in a higher power. Dreaming about the Olympic games refers to the daily competition you face.

Mountains

S: Mountains symbolize the place where heaven and earth meet. They also stand for personal progress.

V: Seeing mountains in the distance: be prepared for misunderstandings in the near future. Climbing a mountain successfully: you are not afraid of emotional hurdles of any kind. However, if your climb is difficult, it might mean that you might have set your goals too high. Seeing a volcano: danger or unpleasant events are imminent. Coming down from a mountain: you have overcome difficulties, gained new insights—now get your just reward. Seeing a **Castle**, or several castles on a mountain: financial gains. Seeing **Ruins** at the top of a mountain: a warning about the loss of vitality.

D: Mountains symbolize situations in your life that might cause ruin. Mountains may also have great spiritual meaning if you feel you have been lifted above the dark or seamy side of life. A mountain symbolizes obstacles that need to be met head on. Reaching the summit of a mountain: you have gained new insight.

Mourning Clothes

V: Wearing black mourning clothes: you have a tendency to be depressed, pessimistic, and melancholic. Wearing white mourning clothes: you are on a spiritual journey and will be taking another step toward maturity.

Mouse, Mouse Trap

S: The mouse is a symbol of avarice and gluttony.

V: Seeing a mouse: difficulties and worries. Hearing a mouse "whistling": a sign of impending danger—but you are going to avoid harm just in time. Catching a mouse: misfortune, but it could have been a lot worse. Looking at a mouse trap: beware, you are too naive to notice that someone is setting a trap!

D: The mouse is a sign that circumstances have robbed you of your strength. Unpleasant images are sneaking silently about and depleting your energies. A mouse trap is a sign that others are setting a trap for you or that you are setting one for others. What is "nagging" at you? Is your basic outlook one of fear? Would you rather crawl into a hole?

Mouth

V: Seeing a person with a large mouth is an admonition: don't "talk so big" or so much! The dream also is a reminder that it is in silence that we discover our innate abilities. See **Lisp.**

D: The mouth is one the most important human "tools," used for eating (taking in something new and sensuous) and also for spitting out, getting rid of something "indigestible" or bad. The mouth is for speaking (communicating with others, making contact, expressing feelings), but also is for kissing (sexual/sensual needs). What did your mouth "do" in the dream?

Movies

V: If you're standing in front of a movie theater: others are keeping secrets and it's bothering you. Being inside a movie theater: you are in the dark and undecided about a certain matter.

D: Is it possible that a movie of your life is playing? The dream might also be an indication of your insecurity or that others want to lead you "up a garden path." Who is trying to fool you? Are you fooling yourself? What movie is playing in the theater (drama, comedy, western, etc.)?

Moving

V: Dreaming of moving out of your home means changes in your personal life are imminent. You are changing your habits, present situation, or your attitude toward life.

Mud

V: Wading through mud: things will move painfully slowly in the next few days, the mood is bleak and troubles abound. Getting stuck in mud: you are in a difficult situation and need some peace and quiet to figure out how to get things moving again. Most of all, you need to stand on solid ground again. Looking at mud: you are in the company of questionable people. See **Manure, Quagmire, Swamp.**

D: Many treasures could be hidden in the "mud of the unconscious." Dig them up, even if it means getting your hands dirty. Mud points to negative things from the past which—if you dig them up—could provide insight and wisdom. Maybe you are afraid of fears and cravings you think are "dirty"? Beware, though, that the more you repress these emotions, the more power and influence they have over you. Taking a mud bath: healing from emotional illness. Mud dreams are very important. Pay close attention to other symbols in the dream. Do you feel "dirty"? Are you and your partner "slinging mud" at each other? Or are you "stuck in the mud"? Since mud consist of part **Water** and part **Earth**, make sure you explore both of these topics as well. See **Dirt.**

Mud Pile

V: Seeing or stepping on a mud pile means good luck—take advantage of the chances that are coming your way. See **Excrement, Manure.** Toiling in the mud: success and wealth through hard work.

D: Dreaming about mud is a sign of good luck!

Mug

V: Drinking from a mug means continued good health. If you are ill (in real life), the mug is a message that you will get better soon and enjoy newfound vitality. A mug falling to the floor and breaking: illness or bad luck. Receiving a mug as a gift: an inheritance or an honorary post.

D: A mug in a dream always stands for good health and luck; it is a symbol, if in good condition, for the "chalice of life." See **Chalice, Cup, Goblet.**

Mummy

V: Looking at a mummy: a long-forgotten event from the past is coming up again.

D: You need to change some of your personal habits, bringing them more in line with your new life. But it seems you would rather "preserve" (mummify) them—which will make life more difficult for you or lead to conflicts with others. Face the changes in your life head-on, and do it as soon as possible. See **Cadaver, Canned Food, Cans, Skeleton.**

Mums

V: Seeing white mums in a dream means somebody in your immediate circle has died or will die. However, colorful mums mean success and joy. Red mums: you will be lucky in love. Blue mums: superior intellect and clear decisions. Deep-yellow mums: your well-developed intuitive sense makes a correct decision possible. Light-yellow mums: betrayal, disappointment, even intrigue and jealousy.

D: See **Flowers** and the chapter on "**Colors in Dreams.**"

Murder, Murderer, Being Murdered, Hanging, Stabbing, Suffocating, Drowning

V: Dreaming about being murdered: difficulties in the near future. Murdering someone else: watch out and don't be careless, you could be the one who gets hurt. See **Aggression.** If you are hanging yourself: it is a message from your unconscious that your personality is unfolding and still "up in the air," but this stage will soon be completed. See **Hanging.** A stabbing refers to an immature, aggressive sexuality (See **Dagger**) and the desire for a quick resolution to conflicts or problems. Suffocating refers to situations you have not yet accepted. See **Asthma.** Drowning either serves as a warning or indicates that you are about to drown under the weight of present events, responsibilities, and dangers. See **Execution, Gallows, Murder.** Being an eyewitness to a murder: the disagreements that people around you have are none of your business—leave them alone. Murder-dreams imply that you will live to a ripe old age. Dreaming about being murdered: are you refusing to accept the harsh reality—that a phase in your life is coming to an end? If you are participating in a murder: you are shamelessly exploiting someone's bad luck for your own ends.

D: While you feel you should be ashamed of what you have done, you have pushed your guilt feelings underground and now are facing the consequences. Sometimes the dream also means that you want (or need to) end a phase in your life. The murderer represents hidden fears coming to the fore, which weaken or threaten to destroy your personal growth. Do something about it and do it quickly. Dreaming about murdering someone: you are struggling with problems and would like nothing better than to get rid of someone (unconscious aggression). Clear the air as soon as possible! Dreams about murder mean that an insight or opportunity for advancement has been "murdered." Usually you yourself are the murderer and are being murdered. Additional dream symbols will be highly informative.See **Aggression, Anger.**

Mushroom

V: Collecting mushrooms: be satisfied with a small profit and don't chase high-flying plans. Good fortune can only be found away from the clamor of the world. Mushrooms sprouting out of the ground: an ongoing string of pleasant surprises. Eating mushrooms: you are getting ahead without difficulties.

D: In erotic dreams, the mushroom (a phallic symbol) expresses your sexual needs. In other dreams it warns against giving in to temptation: it could mean disaster; some mushrooms are poisonous.

Music, Musical Instrument

V: Dreaming about hearing music means being happy and celebrating with the people who are close to you. Listening to annoying music: meeting unpleasant people or finding tension among your friends. Making beautiful music: growing personal and domestic happiness. Jarring sounds: conflict and arguments in the family. See **Orchestra.**

D: Listening or hearing beautiful music: inner peace and harmony. If the music is annoying, of course, it means the opposite. The dream might also be an expression of your musical talent. Do you play an instrument? If so, what kind? See **Dance.**

Muzzle

V: Looking at or wearing a muzzle: keep your extraordinary habit of gossiping under better control in the future.

Mysterious Creatures

V: Dreaming about mysterious, frightening creatures, or monsters: you have been shaken to the depths of your soul. Hidden emotions deep in your unconscious are taking shape, troubling you. Sometimes the reason for nightmares is actual physical stress. Did the creatures resemble real animals? See **Animals.**

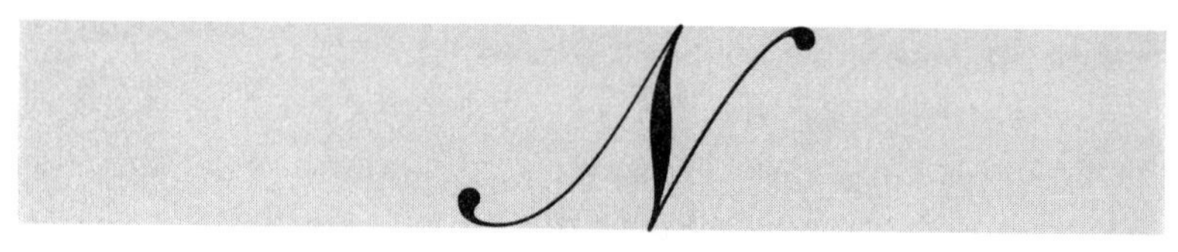

S = Symbol V = Vision D = Depth psychology

Nail, Toenail

V: Finding a nail: your wealth will continue if you are more careful with your money. Putting a nail in a wall: you will learn that telling the truth is to your advantage; you also should expose an opponent. Particularly long fingernails are a warning about speculating on a risky venture. See **Fingernails.**

D: A (carpenter's) nail is a symbol of the strength that holds your relationships together. Dreaming about finger or toenails: you want to hold onto a person or possession—but he/she/it will slip through your fingers anyway. For the outcome, look at the dream symbols.

Nakedness

V: Did you walk the streets naked or did other people see you are naked? Let go of your shame! The dream is a memory of the fun you had as a child—and that your parents considered being naked a taboo. Every now and then our psyche needs to relive the excitement of past feelings: like your father holding both your hands and swinging you through the air, or your early childhood feeling of freedom when free of clothes. If you frequently dream about walking the streets naked, this means feelings of inferiority have prevented you from achieving your personal goals in the past. Taking off your clothes: you want more independence and freedom. Seeing naked children in a dream: your family is about to have a new member (your own or the family of your friends). Seeing a person of the opposite sex naked: your secret or burning passion for someone will be reciprocated.

D: Dreaming about being naked means you are afraid of being "found out"—you are emotionally upset right now and don't want others to know. The dream is a challenge to be emotionally vulnerable, to take a chance and admit your weaknesses. The dream might also express erotic needs that are either being met right now or that you think are foolish.

Name, Nameless

V: Hearing your name or writing it on paper means receiving a pleasant message, but it is also a warning about making hasty promises or taking on responsibilities you have not thought through. Seeing your name written somewhere: you will be known to the public soon.

D: Dreaming about your name is an appeal for more introspection and, at the same time, a warning about the danger of losing your individuality. Occasionally, the dream refers to your vanity and ambitions. Being "nameless" in a dream also warns about an immature personality. If others have no name, it means you are not taking them very seriously. See **Soul.**

Native People

D: A native person may represent emotions and instincts that have remained free and unfettered by civilization, often secret sexual desires that you are unable to live out. Accept these hidden desires in the same way you accept the more "noble" ones!

Navel

V: Seeing a navel: relatives of yours are in danger. See **Stomach.**

D: Dreaming about a navel: you are too self-absorbed; you are not the center of the world! This is also a sign of emotional and psychological dependence on your mother, a close relative, or a friend!

Neck

V: Looking at a swollen neck: good chances for a win and business success. Looking at a long, thin neck: misfortunes are spoiling your fun. An injured neck or cut-off neck is a warning about dangers ahead. Wearing a shawl around the neck also is a warning—about possible throat, nose, and ear infections.

D: The neck stands for the connection between the head and the body (from the intellect to the material). Looking at a neck is often a warning: "Don't risk your neck." Sometimes it suggests taking care of all three—mind, body, and spirit. Do you sometimes feel "strangled" by others or by the demands of life? Are you "out of breath"? What is sticking in your throat?

Necklace

V: Looking at a pink or red necklace (coral, ruby, rose-quartz, etc.): a very happy love-relationship, or you will fall in love. A pearl necklace or a necklace with dark precious stones: tears and grief, but also an emotional cleansing. Wearing a very expensive necklace with precious stones indicates an inheritance from a distant relative, or a financial reward.

D: A necklace, as an erotic symbol, indicates unmet sexual needs. It may also indicate your desire for more power, property, authority (more influence on others). Or is there simply too much "hanging around your neck" (too many responsibilities, chores, worries, obligations). See **Jewelry, Precious Stones.**

Needle

V: Getting pricked by a needle: arguments and nitpicking

ahead. It also could mean losing a friend. Seeing a needle: some people have hostile intentions. See **Stabbing.**

D: The needle is often a symbol of emotional pain, unpleasant events. Who has hurt you? What or who has "stabbed" your heart? Has someone hurt you with "sharp words"? On occasion, the needle is a phallic symbol. See **Sewing.**

Neighbor

V: Seeing a neighbor: somebody is gossiping about you. Speaking to a neighbor: a confrontation is about to take place.

D: In most cases, a male neighbor represents your masculine energies and a female neighbor your feminine energies. Most of the time the dream represents the actual relationship you have with your neighbors. The rest of the dream symbols will tell you if this relationship is positive or negative.

Neptune

D: Neptune, the god of the oceans, represents your very core, your unconscious emotions, fantasies, dreams, and also your addictions or unrealistic expectations. Do you often look at the world "through rose-colored glasses"? Do you daydream? Are you are a very spiritual person? Do you entertain many illusions? Only an honest analysis can answer these questions.

Nest

V: A woman looking at a **Bird**'s nest either wants more freedom or does not feel safe. Seeing a nest means a friendship is breaking up—maybe you have been too miserly? Looking at an empty nest: you want a cozy home of your own. For singles who live with their parents: they will soon move out. Others want a love relationship, but that is not going to happen. Seeing a nest with a bird or bird eggs in it means you can continue to count on your good luck.

D: Seeing a nest with eggs inside: if you have been through a great deal of emotional suffering, you are about to put your troubles behind you. See **Egg.** But the nest also symbolizes your longing for emotional warmth, family, security, and also refers to the relationship you have with your mother (a warm nest). The dream also suggests childhood problems. Start building your own nest now (provide for your own emotional safety)! See **Chick, House.**

Net

S: The net is a symbol of apprehension, confinement, and anxiety.

V: Dreaming about fishing with a net: you want to accomplish something, but believe that success is only a matter of luck. Getting tangled in a net: you have been tempted to do something that was unfair to someone else. In a woman's dream, the net suggests an unconscious wish to be "caught in a man's net." In a man's dream, it also stands for the desire for a relationship. Have you cast your net? Who or what do you want to catch?

D: A net represents erotic and or sexual needs, the desire for emotional connections, sexual loyalty (getting caught in the net of love), or "finding a good catch." Be honest, which of the above applies to you?

New House, Building

V: Seeing or walking into a new house: be more respectful and attentive to other people and the world around you.

New Year

V: If you're at a New Year's celebration: the new year will bring sorrow and worry. If the party was a serious affair, the new year will be happy and exciting. Dreaming about being unhappy on New Year's Day: the coming year will see a long-held wish fulfilled.

Newspaper

V: Reading a newspaper means you will receive interesting news—but who should you believe (everybody is saying something different)? Seeing a newspaper (without reading it): you pay little attention to what is going on around you—but be less cavalier, more observant. Seeing your name in the paper: watch out—someone is determined to wreck your reputation. See **Leaf, Name, Paper.**

D: A newspaper represents things we don't know. However, information in newspapers is not always clear; it presents different opinions. Are you uncertain right now about who to believe? Newspapers reveal and expose things: are you afraid that someone is revealing your personal secret?

Night

V: Wandering around in the night: a warning about "invisible" dangers. The night might also represent an uncertain future. A starlit night means you're on the right path. See **Darkness.**

D: Night is always a period of transition, with the promise that morning will always follow. It also symbolizes dangers lurking in our unconscious. See **Evening, Morning, Noon.**

Night Watchman

V: Seeing a night watchman: take better care of your property; if you lend something to someone you will never see it again. If you are the night watchman: your domestic tranquility is in danger.

D: The night watchman represents your insecurities and helplessness. You want to place your responsibilities in the hands of a guardian or trusted person. But the dream could mean also that you refuse to let anyone interfere in your affairs.

Nightclub

V + D: Seeing or being in a nightclub: you are traveling in bad company and spend too much money on things you don't need. The dream might also be a warning about falling prey to temptations that you will later regret. Be careful!

Nightingale

V: Secing or hearing a nightingale is a good omen for your private and professional life. Seeing a nightingale in a cage: someone would love to "clip your wings," control, or even "own" you.

D: See **Bird.**

Nightshirt, Nightgown

V: Seeing someone in a nightshirt: you insist on trying to hide your true character. Is the nightshirt clean or dirty, beautiful or torn? See **Clothes.**

D: The nightshirt or nightgown indicates hidden erotic desires and needs. It could also point to your own character and that of the people wearing the gown.

Noble

V: You see yourself acting very nobly in a dream: you are still too vain and too arrogant. Being in distinguished company: develop more skepticism—you are too easily impressed by appearances—look behind the "curtain"!

Noon

V: Dreaming that it is noon: a worry-free future—everything will proceed as planned. Dreaming of evening means something is coming to an end. Eating lunch: your worries are almost over.

D: Noon means your maturity, awareness, and intellect are at their peak. See **Evening, Morning.**

North

D: Dreaming about the North: lack of compassion, an intellectual impasse, and depression. North is always a place from which people search for light and it holds the promise that **Morning** will soon dawn. See **Light, Four Corners of the Compass.**

Nose, Nostril

V: If your nose in the dream is bigger than in real life: you have an excellent chance of becoming influential and wealthy. But the dream is also a warning: don't stick your nose where it doesn't belong. If the nose is smaller: be happy with the fortunes you already enjoy. Someone else pulling at your nose: take care of your own affairs. Pulling someone else's nose: you obviously haven't found the right partner yet. Being unable to breath through your nose: difficulties in a certain matter. A man dreaming about his nose: he wishes he were a better lover. In a woman's dream, the large nose of a man indicates that her sexual desires are very strong.

D: Think of what the dream wants to tell you: Who is it that you can't stand? Who or what "stinks to high heaven"? Are you constantly putting your nose where it does not belong? Do you always "follow your nose"? Do you have a particularly "good nose" for things and opportunities? Nostrils represent part of your personality. Did you see the **Right** or the **Left** nostril?

In a man's dream, an exaggerated helmet (See **Armor,**

Knight) is an indication of the dreamer's need for safety. He is either afraid of other men's malice or concerned about his own masculinity.

Nosebleed

V: If you dream about a nosebleed, you believe the world is shunning you, or you are depressed or feel restricted by something. You are warned about losing money.

D: See **Blood, Nose, Scar.**

Notary Public

V: Dreaming about a notary public means official business in the near future; it also might refer to a big family affair or even an impending inheritance. See **Lawyer.**

Notebook

V: Reading in a notebook: you are remembering something very important that you had forgotten. Losing a notebook: a well-kept secret will be revealed. Writing in a notebook: someone is fulfilling a responsibility that was promised—even if you had lost faith that the person would ever do so.

D: The notebook is a warning about being forgetful and untidy, and about keeping things more under control. Start writing important appointments and chores on your calendar!

Notes (as in a letter or musical notes)

Writing a note in a dream indicates false friends.

D: See **Music.**

Novel

V: Reading a novel: you have too many illusions and a rather poor sense of reality. Get more actively involved in real life.

D: Who is telling you stories—or who are you telling them to? See **Book, Learning, Writing.**

Number

S: Ever since the times of Pythagoras and Plato, numbers have played a vital role in explaining the order of the Universe.

D: Dreaming about a specific number: the dream number might prove to be *the* lucky number you need to win the lottery. See the chapter **"Numbers in Dreams."**

Number One

See the chapter **"Numbers in Dreams."**

Nun

V: A man dreaming about a nun: cravings and emotions are stirring in the dark recesses of the unconscious and are about to surface. Trying to repress them won't be possible in the long run. The dream is a call for more self-knowledge. For others, dreaming about a nun is a warning of impending danger, perhaps even a death. See **Monk, Sister.**

D: The nun is a symbol of spirituality or having spiritual experiences. Sometimes, the nun is a warning about your own insincerity or that of others.

Nurse

V: In a man's dream, the nurse represents the demand that a woman pay attention to him. It is also means marital dissatisfaction.

D: The nurse is the anima of the man, who is still searching for his woman-ideal. Particularly in a man's dream, it shows the longing for a woman's love and caring.

Nursing (as in suckling)

D: If you are being suckled at your mother's breast: you

are either undergoing quite immature emotions, or an old memory is surfacing. In addition, this dream could be a sign of dependence (on your mother or others), which is becoming an issue. See **Baby.**

Nut, Nutcracker

V: Eating nuts means good fortune and recognition. Cracking nuts but not eating them means hard work but slow success. If cracking nuts is difficult: you will need every ounce of strength to reach your goal. Looking at nuts: a noble character is hidden behind a rough exterior. Eating a bitter nut: bad luck, but you don't need to take the coming events too seriously! Cracking an empty nut shell: someone is going to disappoint you very deeply. See **Almonds.**

D: A nut may be a reference to your character or the truth about a certain matter. Sometimes it also indicates stupidity, your own or that of others. It may be a symbol for a difficult task—"a tough nut to crack"—or one that can't be accomplished without assistance.

Nutrition, Food

D: The food you are eating in the dream indicates what is important to you. Is it love, ideals, or your beliefs? Is it wealth and confidence? How well or how badly the food tastes and is digested reveals the life experiences of the dream. Dreaming about eating a lot of food: your extreme needs and desires—need to be reined in soon. See **Eating, Meal.**

Nymph

V: Dreaming about a nymph promises "lucky in love" relationships. Being surrounded by nymphs: who will be the lucky person to receive your love? Two people are in the running and the choice will be hard. The nymphs disappear: your heart is heavy because of a sad experience in your love relationship.

D: Nymphs primarily represent emotions, but may also indicate a desire to have an affair. See **Elf.**

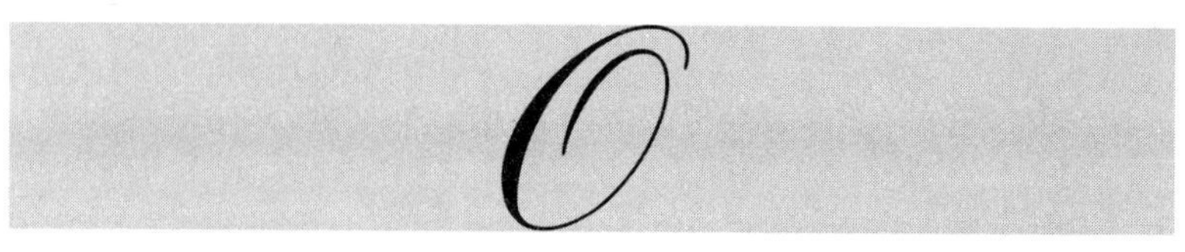

S = Symbol V = Vision D = Depth psychology

Oak Tree

S: The oak tree is a symbol of immortality.

V: Seeing a magnificent oak tree full of leaves means a long life and good health. An oak tree without leaves: loneliness or separation from a friend or relative. Seeing many oak trees with green leaves: every personal and professional project is going to work out well. Sitting in the shadow of an oak tree: a good friend is going to protect you.

D: The "king of the trees" is a symbol of good health, vitality, power, and being firmly rooted in the ground. Sometimes it also indicates a need for protection. Are you yourself "as strong as an oak tree"? Do you wish you had a strong person on your side?

Oasis

V: Being at an oasis means your hopes and dreams have not come true and life has not been kind to you, but don't give up in your efforts to make things better. Maybe your life is like a desert and you went to find that oasis? Seeing an oasis means you can relax now or go on vacation. Leaving an oasis means a difficult road ahead.

D: The oasis means you have left little room for feelings and emotions; you've been too busy pursuing intellectual and money matters. Try changing that. See **Desert.**

Oath

D: Dreaming of taking an oath suggests that it is time to be more open; it is the only way to solve present problems. Committing perjury means you like to solve your problems using unethical means.

Oats

V: Looking at a field of oats means finances are improving—if you act carefully. Carrying oats: reckless decisions will cause problems. Threshing oats: a good omen for success and satisfaction on the job.

D: Oats represent adolescent passion and foolish, youthful appetites—start growing up. Grownup dreams about oats indicate immaturity—you are still "sowing your oats." See **Grain.**

Ocean

V: Looking at a wide expanse of ocean, or being on an ocean liner: you will go on a long journey; the dream also reveals your need for more space and freedom in your life.

D: See **Sea, Ship, Water.**

Offering, Victim

V: If you are asked to make an offering: people are either asking too much of you or you are overextending yourself. If you willingly sacrifice something: you will be rewarded for a selfless act.

D: You have either sacrificed some essential part of yourself to one thing or another or you are a perpetrator who is recklessly sacrificing the needs of others to your own advantage and goals. Frequent dreams of being a victim raises a question: have you chosen to be a victim, unforgiving of the "injustices" done to you? Psychology believes that victim and perpetrator are mutually dependent upon each other—one cannot do without the other. See **Martyr.**

Officer

V: In a woman's dream: she wants to make her love relationship "official." The dream also means that she wants to bring order into her life. See **Military, Soldier, Uniform.**

D: The officer represents your need to bring or keep your impulsive urges under control. Do you need to think more before you act—or are you already thinking too much? The rest of the dream symbols will tell the story.

Oil

S: Oil is a symbol of the spirit of God and the strength flowing from it.

V: Looking at oil: everything is going smoothly (is "well oiled"). Burning oil: an unexpected windfall. Drinking oil: you are enjoying the best of health. Spilling oil: dealing with a string of unpleasant experiences. Oiling something: a reminder that courtesy will always get you further in life. Buying oil: you can expect to make a profit.

D: Oil can be a symbol of many things, among them being anointed with oil as a sign of maturity. Sometimes oil suggests avoiding friction and arguments—"pour oil on troubled waters!" Pouring oil onto the fire would mean emotions are "ignited." Pouring oil: are you hoping to foil your enemies' attack by having them "slip and fall"? Only you know the truth!

Old Man, Old Woman

V: Seeing an elderly man you don't know: practice more levelheadedness and examine your actions and your life. Sometimes, the old man wants to warn of evil-minded people in your immediate environment. Seeing an old woman: anxiety, limitations, or worries. Seeing yourself as an old person: you might receive great honors; or be smart and keep your distance from certain events in the near future.

D: The old man is seen as a symbol of maturity in all

aspects of life. This dream is always significant and should be examined carefully. Old men or old women represent either wisdom or malice, and are a warning to take a closer look at your (bad) habits. See **Youth.**

Olive

S: At the end of the Great Flood, a dove comes back to Noah with an olive branch. The olive and the olive branch (and the dove) are symbols of peace.

V: Looking at olives: a present conflict is coming to a peaceful conclusion. Eating an olive: a personal or love relationship will collide with "reality" and might end in a separation and/or divorce.

D: While olives may also represent erotic desires, they usually stand for the need for peace, kindness, and love for others. See **Oil.**

Olive Tree

V: Seeing an olive tree: conflicts in your family will end in peace and harmony.

Onion

V: Seeing an onion: tears and sorrow. Peeling an onion: slowly mysteries are being uncovered. Eating cooked onions: have courage—a small unpleasant affair is resolved.

D: The onion is a sign that after a period of depression things are beginning to improve. Tears are there to wash the pain from the soul. As an aside: in ancient Egypt, onions and garlic were worshiped like gods.

Opera

V: The opera is the "stage of your life." Sometimes it is a warning against exaggeration, deceit, or making a drama out of a minor event or thing. See **Stage.**

Opera Glasses

D: Do you feel you are constantly being observed? Are you too self-involved? Would you like to get a better view or a clearer picture of your situation? See **Binoculars, Magnifying Glass, Microscope.**

Operetta

V: Listening to an operetta: celebrating something in good company. Performing in an operetta: you are still building too many "castles in the air."

D: The operetta is a sign that you are looking at the bright side of life most of the time. See **Opera.**

Opium

V: Smoking opium: your ideas about life are quite unrealistic; such self-deception has dangerous consequences. Watching others smoke opium: you are hanging out with dubious, reckless characters. Walking into an opium den: you will become involved in a very risky project or adventure.

D: The use of opium always indicates a "flight from reality." Or it might be that you're trying to hide your mistakes and weaknesses behind unrealistic ideals. Neither possibility will get you very far; they will only weaken your character. See **Smoking.**

Orange

S: Similar to **Apple.** The orange is also considered a symbol of love, temptation, and worldly and sensual pleasures. Also see **Fruit, Grapes,** and **Tomato.**

V: Seeing an orange in a dream: a pleasant romance is on its way; you are also changing for the better. Peeling an orange: many difficult hurdles need to be overcome before you reach your goal. Seeing many ripe oranges in a tree: a promise of positive things to come in your love life. The orange represents your erotic needs and desires. See **Fruit.** Sometimes it is also a sign of the beginning stage of jaundice. Eating an orange: your love is reciprocated and you will soon be fit again!

D: The orange is primarily an expression of your erotic needs; the orange color refers to your spirit and sunny disposition. See **Fruit** and the chapter **"Color in Dreams."**

Orchard

V: Sitting in an orchard: you receive a large sum of money—maybe even an inheritance. Looking at an orchard: you can't decide who to choose, because you're not sure who you love most.

D: See **Fruit, Garden.**

Orchestra

V: Watching an orchestra: you will soon see a great performance. Playing in the orchestra or being the conductor: you will either join a club or organize one. See **Music.**

D: You have combined all the contradictions, feelings, thoughts, and desires of your personality into a harmonious whole—an incredible achievement!

Orchid

V: Receiving an orchid as a gift: somebody is going to flatter you. See **Flowers.**

Organ

V: Hearing the sound of an organ: expect an invitation to a great party (maybe even a wedding). Playing the organ: you want more time for yourself so that you can pursue your interest in peace and quiet. See **Music, Piano.**

D: You are a very serious person and strive to bring into balance all aspects of your personality. You will succeed if the organ music in the dream is harmonious!

Orgy

V: Watching others at an orgy: protect yourself from base and expensive pleasures. Taking part in an orgy: your reputation is rapidly deteriorating.

D: The dream is a challenge: stop repressing your urges and passions. Face them squarely or your sexual energies may explode into a real orgy some day. Pay attention to the rest of the dream symbols, they will provide helpful advice.

Orphan

D: Dreaming about being an orphan: you feel unloved, rejected, and lonely. You don't quite know where you belong or whom to trust. You are looking for safety and security. The rest of the dream is important; you might find a solution. See **Abandonment, Child, Loneliness, Parents.**

Outer Office

V: Sitting in an outer office: whatever you have planned, have courage and keep on going—don't second-guess yourself.

D: Providing you haven't set your goals too high, you will succeed. See **Secretary.**

Owl

S: The owl seems to be serious, thoughtful, and wise—plus it can see in the dark.

V: Dreaming about an owl often indicates that your judgment of a personal situation was correct. It is also a sign that a rather murky matter can be seen more clearly. If you see an owl, do not dismiss well-meaning advice from others—you will learn a valuable lesson from it. If the owl is making sounds: bad luck and frustration. Listening to an owl screeching means sadness and grief—less often it is a message that someone is going to die. Catching or seeing an owl in a cage:

be wary of weird people and bad (scary) company. See **Bird, Eagle-Owl.**

Ox

S: The ox is a symbol of kindness, calmness, and strength.

V: Seeing an ox at work in the field: you will meet a very influential person and the relationship will be useful to you. Seeing an ox pulling a cart means hard work and a handsome payoff. Hearing the bellowing of the ox: be careful, there is danger afoot. Being attacked by an ox: an influential person becomes hostile. Watching an ox being slaughtered: beware of an impending illness; watch for physical symptoms. This dream also urges you to be less selfish and think more of others.

D: The ox represents clumsiness and being earthbound, and sometimes also being naive. For older people, the dream is a sign of diminishing sexuality. Are you working like an ox? Acting like one? Do you think of yourself as a "dumb ox"?

S = SYMBOL   V = VISION   D = DEPTH PSYCHOLOGY

Package

V: Receiving a package: expect a surprise from which you will profit. Receiving an empty package: you are in for a disappointment. If the package contains gold or other valuable items: expect to receive a great deal of money, or you are going to be honored.

D: The package stands for life experiences with which you have yet to come to terms. Sometimes you are "packing" up sexual desires you have not admitted to yourself yet. The only thing to do is unpack and take a close look. See **Box.**

Packing

V: Packing your belongings: expect life-changing events with worries, a shift in attitude, or possibly a separation. Watching a stranger packing: expect a visit.

D: Internal and external influences are about to change your daily routine. Whether these influences are from your surroundings or self-initiated can be determined by the rest of the dream symbols.

Pain

V: Dreaming about physical pain usually indicates "emotional" pain in real life. Try to get to the bottom of it. Sometimes the dream indicates that you have inflicted pain on someone else.

D: Pain is either a sign of emotions stressed to the limit, or that someone has hurt you. Where in the body is the pain? Look up that entry to determine its meaning. See **Body, Injury, Wound.**

Painter

V: Seeing a painter being lucky with the opposite sex: you want to make a change in your life and your relationship. Watching a painter at work: good fortune.

D: The painter means you want things in your life to change. You would like to start over and give your life and love relationship more "color." See **Painting** and the chapter on **"Colors in Dreams."**

Painting (a House or Wall)

When dreaming about painting a house or a wall, the color of the paint is important. White paint: you are feeling threatened or pursued by another person. Brightly colored paint (particularly red): soon you will have reason to rejoice.

Black paint: a warning of impending illness. (See the chapter on "**Colors in Dreams**.")

Painting (Art)

V: If you have had a portrait made of yourself: you need admiration too much, try for less grandiosity—people don't believe you anyhow. Dreaming that you are painting: take your artistic talents seriously and use them. There might also be a new love affair in the making. The colors in the dream are very important—see the chapter **"Colors in Dreams."** Seeing a beautiful painting in your dream means that happiness is on the way. What else do you see in the picture? What are the colors? See **Colors, Picture.**

D: Dreaming about painting means self-realization and self-fulfillment. Are you "painting" your future? What does it look like? "Is the "handwriting on the wall"? Do you paint over things you don't like? What does "as pretty as a picture" mean to you? See **Colors, Picture.**

Pair of Pliers

V: Seeing a large pair of pliers: Someone or something is going to maneuver you into a very difficult situation.

D: Pliers usually represent a present moral dilemma. Who or what is tightening the vise? What kind of trouble are you in? What do you need to do to get out of it?

Palace

V: Seeing a palace: you feel very superior, underestimating the qualities of other people; over the long run, this attitude is dangerous. Dreaming of owning your own palace: come back to reality soon or expect to be rudely awakened. See **Castle.**

D: Do you crave recognition? Your palace is a "golden cage": external and material things are keeping you from growing (you feel "caged"). If you are in a difficult financial situation, you may get a bit of relief.

Palette

V: Looking at a palette with many colors: nurture your creative talents. What creative talents do you have that are clamoring for attention?

D: See **Painting** and the chapter on **"Colors in Dreams."**

Palisades

T + D: Seeing palisades in a dream: your future is wrought

with tension, obstacles, and problems that you can overcome only by being very cautious. See **Wall.**

Palm

S: The palm is a symbol of victory, resurrection, rebirth, and immortality. A palm branch means resurrection after sorrow and death.

V: Looking at a palm tree: you are entertaining romantic illusions. The dream is a warning about losing touch with reality. Pay more attention to what is real. A palm tree outside: a long-held desire is coming true. A potted, indoor palm tree: something is not going according to your wishes; you are dissatisfied.

D: Particularly in a woman's dream, the palm is a sign of her erotic needs and her longing for a very masculine partner.

Palm Reading

V + D: Looking at a palm with strong, very distinct lines: you have too many ambitions! Try to be more selective. A delicate and elegant hand with fine palm lines means you are oversensitive. Be more energetic and show more enthusiasm.

Panther

V: Seeing a panther: beware of false friends. Killing a panther: you are getting over false accusations. Being attacked by a panther: cunning intrigue and slander may harm you.

D: See **Animals, Leopard, Predator, Tiger.**

Pants

V: Putting on a pair of pants: you would like to be in charge of your family and your surroundings (this is the case for men's and women's dreams). It may also indicate that you resent the power others have over you. Taking off a pair of pants: you seem to be leading a very superficial life.

Losing your pants: other people are mocking you. See **Clothes.**

D: Pants in a dream are a sign of your need for protection; or are you afraid that others will expose you? See **Shirt**. Are you paying too much attention to your appearance? Have you been "caught with your pants down"? Are you afraid of getting caught *without* your pants on? and if so, why?

Paper

V: Looking at printed paper: you trust others. Torn paper: the conflict you have provoked is your own fault. Be very careful if you get involved in legal matters right now. Plain paper: an important document will suddenly play a large role. Writing or drawing on a piece of paper: you are preoccupied with a personal situation. Printed paper: you are asked to do a lot of unnecessary and unimportant paper work.

D: A plain piece of paper represents either immaturity and lack of experience, or is a sign that you are open to new thoughts and opinions. Paper with print: expect to receive new instructions or spiritual insights that will be useful to you. See **Leaf, Newspaper, Writing.**

Paprika

V: Red paprika means quarrels and resentments. See **Vegetables** and the chapter on **"Colors in Dreams."**

Parade

V: Looking at a parade: stop living beyond your means. You would like to be more than you really are, or you are using your appearance to inflate your self-esteem.

D: The parade in a dream is always a challenge to be more self-disciplined, because that is the only way to solve your difficulties.

Paradise

V: Seeing paradise: you hope for "heavenly" rewards; joyful days are ahead. If you are in paradise: a never-ending paradise on earth does not exist; let go of your illusions.

D: A pleasant dream about paradise: you live in harmony with yourself and the world around you—or you hope to. Sensitivity and virtue will bring the peace you desire! Dreaming about two people in paradise: if the dream is pleasant, you just might find a little paradise on earth—a wonderful time with your partner, full of love and harmony. If you are in the midst of a conflict, you only want a little piece of paradise to see you through a difficult time. Ethical and moral people have the best chance of finding a true "paradise on earth."

Paralysis, Paralyzed

V: Watching a paralyzed person means difficult times ahead. Projects are being delayed. You are paralyzed: your plans are (or going to be) interfered with. Be patient and careful! See **Illness, Invalid.**

D: A dream about paralysis indicates that you are wrestling with problems or conflicts of your own making. Sometimes you are paralyzed by a hidden, unconscious fear over which you have no control. Are you sometimes paralyzed in your reactions? What is it that paralyzes you? Try to overcome this paralysis as soon as possible.

Parasol

V: The open parasol promises a visit from a good friend.

Parents

V: A man dreaming about his parents is hoping for support because he is in a hopeless situation. Seeing your already deceased parents: a good sign—you are finished grieving.

This dream also promises unexpected help in a dire situation. Seeing your parents dead while they are still alive: an expression of your own fear. It often implies that your mother and father will have a long life. Talking to your parents: happiness and lots of fun.

D: Dreams about parents are a sign of maturity and letting go of the standards, rules, and problems with which your parents raised you. The dream also may refer to your need for more guidance, security, and emotional warmth. Important here is the actual relationship you have with your parents!

Park

V: Walking in a park: don't worry about the future; also, you will take a pleasant vacation. Seeing a park: you long for peace and quiet, or some form of recreation.

D: Your nerves are really in need of a break, it is the only way to regain your emotional balance. Take a vacation, you need a change of scene!

Parrot

V: Seeing or hearing a parrot: curb your need to talk and you can avoid other people gossiping about you. A tattletale friend is about to divulge a well-kept secret.

D: Don't accept everything others would have you believe—develop your own opinions, make your own judgments.

Parsley

Seeing parsley is a good omen: you have a happy family and good health. See **Herbs, Spices.**

Partridge

V: Seeing a partridge: you are much too shy—start being more assertive. Let others know and respect your talents and qualities. Catching a partridge: someone will disappoint you. Seeing a flock of partridges take flight (in men's dreams): a warning about seductive women who are not very serious. Shooting a partridge: your lover or partner is very jealous. See **Chicken.**

Pass (Mountain), Passport, Passport Control

V: Looking at a mountain pass: real-life problems can be handled successfully with patience and concentration. Going over a pass: you now get to see the "other side of the coin"—either that of a person or an issue. Looking at your passport: a trip is imminent. Losing your passport: you are losing respect. Looking at a strange passport: a problem with the authorities; or you are worried about someone else's trip. Going through customs: your movements are restricted by "higher-ups."

D: The mountain pass warns against problems in your path but you are able to handle them. Unless you are actually dealing with the authorities or want to take a trip, the passport dream points to issues similar to those of your **Name**.

Passageway

V: If you find yourself in a long, dark passageway: you will confront an unpleasant surprise and search for a solution. Men who find themselves in a passageway are looking for sexual experiences. If they see an open door, they get their way.

D: The passageway is a symbol of the female and strong erotic needs (in men's dreams). In women's dreams, it indicates the direction their lives should take. If the passageway is dark, long, and without doors, your search for direction will take a little longer. See **House, Tunnel.**

Pasta

V: Looking at pasta: somebody is boring you, or your life right now is pretty dull! Buying or cooking pasta: dull people are coming to visit. Eating pasta: you are annoyed about a visit you have to make—which also turns out to be very boring. Dreaming about Italian pasta: see **Italy.**

D: Dreaming about pasta is usually a sign of unfulfilled sexual needs—or maybe you're fasting or on a diet and you're actually just hungry!

Pastor, Minister

V: Seeing a pastor: your constant "preaching"—or telling people what to do all the time—is making you increasingly unpopular. Being the pastor: even if it is difficult, have the courage to admit or confess to something you have done. Speaking with a pastor: you are feeling guilty about something—come clean and reduce the pressure.

D: See **Church, Preacher, Priest.**

Pasture, Willow Tree

V: Seeing animals in a green pasture: your life is going well—you will prosper. Seeing a willow tree: You need to remain steadfast now, but "bend like a willow tree" at the right time. Seeing a weeping willow: a friend is very sad and pours her heart out to you. Pussy willows: your life is peaceful; be satisfied (humble).

D: Why are you so "flexible" and accommodating? Are you hiding feelings of inferiority? Do you have so little confidence in yourself? Don't you trust yourself? Do you always take the easy way out? Your "adaptability" is too extreme. You need to change that! See **Reed.**

Patent

V: Receiving a patent: you have a good idea and need to put it into action. Seeing an unfamiliar patent: you have reacted much too late in a certain matter.

D: The dream usually means that you have a good idea

that you should act on. Pay attention to the rest of the symbols in the dream.

Path

V: Seeing a wide path: you love to circumvent difficulties, preferring an easy life. A narrow path or walking along a path: don't be deterred from the life path you have chosen. Seeing a path in front of you: you want to keep your happiness hidden from friends. Getting lost: you are on the wrong path. Standing at a crossroads: it is important that you stay on the path you believe intuitively is right for you.

D: A path in a dream is an indication of your attitude, ideals, and/or hopes that determine the direction of your life. It is not only a sign of your desire for self-fulfillment, but also for all, still dormant, possibilities.

Pavilion

V: Looking at a pavilion: a secret love affair is in the making. Is the pavilion in a **Park**?

D: See **Castle, Palace.**

Pawnshop

V: Walking into a pawnshop means financial difficulties lie ahead. Be frugal and watch your expenses. Working in or owning a pawnshop: you're getting drawn into other people's problems.

Payment

V: You have to make a payment: now is the time to take care of old debts and bring order into your life. See the chapter **"Numbers in Dreams."**

Peach

V: Like all fruit, the peach is a sign of erotic desires and needs. Seeing a peach: a love affair you thought was over is going to revive. Shaking peaches off a tree: you are impatient in your love relationship, you "can't wait." Eating a peach: your partner is taking your relationship more seriously than you would like. A rotten peach: an unpleasant discovery and a disappointment in your relationship. Seeing a ripe peach: your love relationship is maturing—your happiness is solid. See **Fruit.**

D: The peach is always a sign that erotic tendencies and sexual needs are clamoring for attention.

Peacock

S: A peacock, with a fanned-out tail, is a symbol of the sun—but also of vanity.

V: Seeing a peacock with a fanned-out tail: being brash and overconfident might impress some people; most, however, think it laughable. You would make a much better impression on people if you were less vain and arrogant. Screeching peacocks: a tempting invitation or project—but extreme caution is in order! In a man's dream, the peacock means meeting a woman who is hiding ambition and ego behind her charm.

D: This dream also is an indication of too much vanity. Even if you do just normal bragging to impress others, or attempt to amaze people with your intellectual faculties, someday you are going to make a fool of yourself—give it up!

Pear, Pear Tree

V: Eating one or several pears: you are participating in a fun event or starting a beautiful romance. Seeing a pear tree with many pears: a very good omen for all personal affairs. Seeing a pear tree in bloom: expect good news that will affect your life in the future. Harvesting pears: you can look forward to many successful business transactions. See **Fruit.**

D: The pear—like the apple—is a sexual symbol. But it is also a symbol of positive contacts and a sign that your relationships are solidly based.

Pearl

S: The pearl stands for enlightenment and spiritual rebirth.

V: Pearls in women's dreams don't always mean tears. They also express the desire to create something of value. A housewife who lives a restricted life often dreams about pearls, or that she was given pearls as a gift. Wearing pearls: old emotional scars are resurfacing and need to be addressed. Giving pearls as a gift: you won't get thanks for your willingness to help.

D: See **Clam, Mussel, Oyster, Jewels, Jewelry.**

Penguin

D: The penguin is a sign that outwardly you are always correct. But in everyday life you are still a captive of your emotional world. Try to change that!

Peony

S: The peony—the "rose without thorns" is a symbol of the Virgin Mary.

V: A peony in bloom promises happiness in love. Receiving a peony as a gift: you have a secret admirer. Giving a peony as a gift: don't be timid in your love relationship, have courage! Throwing the flower away or if the flower is wilted: a love affair is deteriorating. See **Flower.**

D: A beautiful peony always means good luck in matters of love. A peony that has broken off: conflicts in your relationship. A wilted peony: the relationship is deteriorating.

Pepper

D: This potent spice is either a sign of your passionate longings or a suggestion to get more "spice" in your life. See **Salt, Spice.**

Perfume

V: Using perfume on yourself: you are trying to deceive others. Giving perfume as a gift: your attempts to find favor with another person are going to be successful. In a man's dream, smelling perfume: you are influenced by a female whose thoughts and actions will have negative effects on you. See **Makeup.**

D: Perfume is a symbol of your attempts to gloss over your mistakes and failures (selling something negative by making it fragrant). People around you will soon smell a rat. See **Smell.**

Perjury

V: Seeing other people committing perjury: through no fault of your own you are dealing with a disaster and looking for help. You are committing perjury: the dilemma you are facing is of your own making. See **Oath.**

D: Your present difficulty can be remedied easily if you are completely open. Committing perjury: you would like to solve a problem, but by not quite legal means.

Person, Human Being

V: Looking at a beautiful person: a special treat is in store for you. Seeing an ugly person: something ugly is going to happen. Dreaming about other people might mean that you ought to be less self-involved. Try to find company or make friends.

D: Seeing people in dreams means you should pay more attention to others and be less self-absorbed.

Perspiration, Perspiring

D: If the dream is a reflection of what is happening in real life, ask yourself why you are sweating. Usually the reason for perspiration is strong emotions, often extreme fear. Are you "sweating out" something negative in a "psycho-sauna"? If the answer is yes, take care of it and you will feel better.

Pheasant

V: The pheasant is a positive symbol and means good luck and happiness—you just don't know it yet. Eating a pheasant: your health is good and stable. Catching or shooting a pheasant means luck in love.

Photograph

D: A photo stands for unconscious memories that—even though you may have already dealt with them—are coming alive again. See **Picture.**

Physician

S: The physician in a dream is not only a symbol of your own self-healing powers, but he or she can also take on the role of an advisor, or father, an authority figure, or a guiding presence.

V: A physician-dream is a warning of some kind or expresses an exaggerated fear of illness. It might also suggest that your illness needs treatment. Speaking to a physician: a good sign that the illness can be cured. But no matter what, do pay more attention to your health. Being the physician: a sign of profound self-knowledge or a desire for a better social position.

D: If the physician is an old man: you are unable to cope with something and are searching for advice or for help. The dream image of the physician is always a symbol of the powerful healing capacity of the soul. It is often the image of a wise man and strong father.

Piano

V: Buying a piano means you are spending more money than you have right now. Playing the piano: you are wasting your time with frivolous things. However, this is not true for musical people who are using their talent. In the case of very creative people, a dream depicting a piano and a rose is a challenge to be more creative. For all others it means emotional issues are making their appearances. The kind of melody coming from the piano is important: is it heavy, sad, or a lighter tune? A fully open rose means love is blossoming. If you have no particular person right now, music or dance may become your "great new love"!

D: The piano is a sign that feelings denied thus far are about to break through. Try to determine what kind of music you are hearing and if you or someone else is playing the piano.

Piccolo

V: Playing a piccolo: you are worried about a close friend.

Pickax

V: Working with a pickax in the garden: a good sign for the successful outcome of your plans. Looking at a pickax: misfortunes are forcing you to "dig deeper."

D: This garden tool is a symbol of caring for the "garden of your soul." The dream is an invitation to do just that right now. The state of the garden in your dream is important. See **Garden, Spade.**

Pickpocket

D: The pickpocket is warning you against being careless with your "inner reserves," and suggesting that you make sure others won't rob you of them. See **Thief, Robbery.**

Picture, Photo

V: Seeing several people in a photo: you are thinking of them often. Seeing yourself in a photo: you are too preoccupied with yourself; you see things only from your side; on one hand, that's a sign of egotism; on the other, it's a sign of success and happiness. Dreaming about a picture (or several) falling off the wall: bad luck or at least something unpleasant, often a separation or a death. A picture of a relative or friend falling off the wall for no reason: illness or even the death of that person. Seeing pictures of your deceased parents or friends: freedom from an unpleasant situation soon. The picture of a child, a woman, or friend: you will soon receive some new information.

D: Seeing a picture of people that are part of your immediate world often is a challenge to try to get to know them better. Sometimes we see pictures of people in a dream before we have even met them. Seeing one's own picture/photo in a dream is a symbol of what we know and what we think about ourselves.

Pie

V: Eating a pie: don't overindulge right now, your health is not in the best shape. Seeing one pie: enjoy a small pleasure. Making a pie: you are being good to yourself—do it more often!

D: A pie is a more refined form of **Bread, Nutrition.** Making your own pie: See **Baker, Cook.**

Pig

S: The domestic pig is a symbol of fertility, the wild pig of the demonic.

V: Seeing a pig: good luck in everything you do—including playing the lottery. Feeding pigs: good luck and success. Eating pork: being more restrained in certain matters could translate into monetary success. Looking at a pig pen: you are in unsavory company and should walk away quickly.

D: The pig is usually a sign of what you think of yourself ("I acted like a pig") or others ("that person is a pig"). It is a sign of a very materialistic attitude and greed. However, it could also reflect the "good luck" you had recently in a very tricky situation, and the dream is promising more of the same.

Pile (as in Stake)

V: Looking at a pile: try to be more accommodating and a long-held desire will be fulfilled. Driving a pile into the ground: you are now able to lay the foundation for a secure future and happiness!

D: You are creating a solid basis for the future. The dream is also a sign that your intentions are solid and convincing. See **House.**

Pilgrimage

V: Dreaming about participating in a pilgrimage: your strategies and goals are good. but you need patience and perseverance to be successful.

D: This dream is either a symbol of deeply held religious convictions or a promise that you will reach your goal. See **Worship.**

Pillar

S: A pillar is a symbol of the tree of life, as well as the axis of the universe. It gives support to a structure and provides stability.

V: Seeing one or more pillars in your dream: you are very popular because people can depend on you. Also, when you are in trouble, you can always depend on support and help from others. Seeing a broken pillar: a friend is abandoning you when you need help the most. If you are hoisting a pillar: you have accomplished something entirely by yourself, which is attracting people who will support you in the future. See **Pole.**

D: If the dream is not a sign of hidden sexual desires, the pillar is either a testament to the solid and strong foundation on which you have built your life, or it indicates the support you will receive in a difficult situation. If the pillar is falling, you will face conflicts and no support from others. The dream may also ask if you are as rigid as "a pillar of salt"? And if so why? See **Salt.**

Pillow

V: If you are buying a pillow, you will have peace and quiet and be allowed to be lazy. Lying on a pillow means help in a difficult situation.

D: Pillows mean that peaceful and relaxing times are imminent, let your gentler side come to the fore.

Pills

V: Taking pills: the next few days will be unpleasant, but the aggravation is small and you will manage. If you have made a mistake in the past, now is the time to "swallow the bitter pill."

D: What kind of "bitter pill" experience did you have to swallow? Did it help you to come to terms with past events? Did it help you to digest past experiences, transforming them into something positive? The pill in the dream can support emotional healing if you can let go of your prejudices!

Pin, Pinprick

V: Getting a pinprick: becoming involved in a very unpleasant situation; nothing will go as planned. You need to be especially careful in the company of women. Seeing a pin: someone is "needling" you. Pinning something together: a new relationship won't last—your hopes will be dashed. See **Needle.**

D: Getting a pinprick: you were forced to act by outside factors, or someone has hurt you. A pin warns you against "prickly" people. All you can do is walk away and get a "thicker skin."

Pine Tree, Pinecone

V: Seeing a pine tree: you are going to meet an upright, honest person. Seeing a pine forest: you have started something that will bring you security; you are in excellent health. Seeing a pinecone: good fortune. Finding a pinecone on the ground: a so-called coincidence will play a major role in your life. See **Forest.**

D: The pine tree (as a phallic symbol) may express sexual desires; but it might also indicate the need for more peace and quiet or a vacation. Pinecones sometimes announce an unexpected, positive, "accidental" surprise.

Pipe

V: Seeing a pipe: an old friend is coming to visit. Seeing someone smoking a pipe: slow down—you need more comfort, contentment, and less stress in your life!

D: A pipe is a sign of self-assured masculinity, inner peace, and serenity. In a woman's dream, it is a sign that she is looking for a partner. See **Smoke, Smoking.**

Pistol

V: Seeing a pistol: you have a bad conscience; animosity is brewing. Shooting a pistol: you are certain who your enemy is—but be more careful in the choice of your weapon! If you are pulling the trigger but the bullet is stuck in the barrel: you are defenseless and powerless in a very unpleasant situation.

D: See **Shooting, Weapon.**

Pitch (as in tar)

V: Working with pitch: coming events are leading you straight to success. Looking at pitch: somebody whose opinion you value is told that you have "blackened" your reputation. Seeing someone with pitch on his/her clothes: the person is taking the credit that should really go to you.

D: Pitch usually stands for failure and bad luck. It could also mean that other people are envious or begrudge your success. Are you having a "streak of bad luck"? Does everything look "pitch-black"? If so, try to do something about it soon! See **Soot.**

Planets

D: Planets in a dream are symbols of your unconscious. Each planet stands for a specific area of your life and your personality. Dreaming about a specific planet means that its characteristics are important at this time.

Sun: Self-confidence, life goals, will power, masculine energy.

Moon: Emotions, sensitivity, desire for contact, feminine energies.

Mercury: Reason, intellect, communication, learning, information, negotiations, traveling, selling, buying.

Venus: Esthetics, harmony, art, assimilation, love, sensuality, pleasure, female libido.

Mars: Vitality, courage, will power, drive, determination, male libido.

Jupiter: Self-worth, judgment, kindness, tolerance, wisdom, and religious foundation.

Saturn: Physical strength, order, limits, security, peace, concentration, responsibilities.

Uranus: Intuition, creative intelligence, originality, change, discoveries and explorations, reforming.

Neptune: Universal love, idealism, support, social engagement.

Pluto: Death and rebirth, metamorphosis, transformation, collective strength and energy, destruction, power (powerlessness).

Plant

V: Seeing plants: favorable connections are possible—maybe even a wedding. Watering plants: a happy family and social advancement. See **Bush, Flower, Meadow, Tree.** Looking at a creeping plant: you are afraid, uncertain, and full of self-doubt. A vine refers to instability and fears that interfere with your life.

D: Dreaming about a creeping vine means that you are insecure and fearful, and these feelings are getting in your way.

Plate

V: Seeing a plate: you will receive a dinner invitation. A plate full of food: you can count on the successful completion of your plans and project. An empty plate: misfortune. Breaking a plate: difficult days and worries are ahead. A silver plate means that you will take part in a formal, sophisticated event or receive an invitation to one.

D: A plate represents your responsibilities and your desires and needs. What do you have on your plate? Is the plate full or empty? Are you eating from the plate? See **Cup.**

Plateau

V: Looking at a plateau: the present unrest in your life will soon be replaced by a time of tranquility and satisfaction. Looking at an open space in the middle of a forest is a sign of a well-balanced, quiet life. If you are looking at a plateau from up high: you will achieve much in your life, even if nothing points to it right now.

D: Are you somehow dissatisfied with your life at the moment? Are you bored? Remember, a plateau may also be a sign that you can look to the future without worries and obstacles.

Playing a Ball Game

V: Playing handball—or any other ball game: you always catch the luck that life is throwing your way and just in time (if—in your dream—you do catch the ball!). See **Ball, Hand.**

Playing Card

V: A playing card stands for reckless optimism. You are "betting everything on one card." Be careful! Watching others play cards: a rather unpleasant situation ahead. Playing cards with others: you want to avoid a fight, because someone with bad intentions is trying to harm you. See **Games.**

Pledge

V: Making a pledge: you have thoughtlessly entered into a harmful relationship or made a foolish commitment. Accepting a pledge: you can count on a good friend. If your property is attached: a loss or a separation is imminent. If you are impounding something: your good-natured actions are shamelessly exploited.

Plow, Plowing

V: Seeing or working a plow: you have not been productive enough in the past. Increasing your efforts, being persistent, and having patience—in spite of the hurdles in your way—is the way to reach your goals. A broken plow: you want to start something new, but your plans will probably fail. Seeing someone else plowing: you are looking at a task and wonder if you should take it on. It could be profitable.

D: The plow is a challenge to "plow under" past experiences, injuries, insults, old behavior, and attitudes. This gives you a chance to change the old into something new for the future; the "soil" on which you grow and build a new life will be healthier. See **Earth.**

Plundering

D: If, in real life, you are in financial straits, plundering in a dream is understandable. Your unconscious is looking for some kind of satisfaction. In all other cases, it is a sign of a materialistic attitude and an egotistical ruthlessness.

Pluto

D: This planet—the ruler of the unconscious—stands for death and rebirth, destruction and rebuilding. "Die and be born again" is a constant process. Pluto supports emotional-psychic changes and metamorphosis. Its enormous motive power is the driving force for far-reaching changes. See **Planets, Signs of the Zodiac.**

Pocket Watch

V: Seeing a pocket watch in your dream: you have either overslept or you have no sense of time. Pay more attention to your appointment calendar—and keep your appointments! See **Clock.**

Pocket, Purse

V: Dreaming about having a hole in your pants, dress, or coat pocket: you are not careful enough with your things. If you lose your purse: you will be faced with a very embarrassing situation. Finding a purse: a joyful surprise is on its way.

D: The pocket contains experiences and memories. It is

also a place where you store your emotional and physical reserves. If there is still room in the purse: you are open to new insights as well as sexual adventures.

Pocketknife

V: A closed pocketknife: you are a discreet and unassuming person. An open pocketknife: you are seething with anger, aggression, and rage—and out for revenge, something you are not yet able to acknowledge. See **Knife.**

Pointer, Hand of a Clock

D: The hands of a clock are interesting because of the numbers at which they point. See **Clock** and the chapter **"Numbers in Dreams."**

Poison

V: You are taking poison: you are forced to admit your participation in an unpleasant incident, a mistake, or a weakness. Poisoning someone else: you are about to lie to another person. Being poisoned: don't aggravate other people—you will make enemies that way. Seeing several poisonous plants: dishonest people bother you.

D: Poison in a dream is either a warning about your own deception, or you are suffering from the misdeeds of others. It could be that negative thoughts and influences are "poisoning" your life. Is your environment poisonous? Do you want to solve your problems by force? Do you hate others—or the way your life is going? Both hates will make you miserable and "poison" your life.

Polecat, Ferret, Skunk

V: Seeing a polecat is a warning: pay more attention to your physical body. If you have problems or troubles, don't delay in seeing your physician. Sometimes the polecat is also a warning about a dishonest person who wants to steal something from you (but you would have to literally "smell" the deceit!).

Police, Police Officer

S: The police officer in a dream represents the dreamer's father.

V: Aside from the above, a police officer symbolizes constraint and control. Men dreaming about the police feel constrained and controlled. Seeing a policeman: *do not* get involved in other people's arguments—you could be seriously harmed. Calling the police: a situation that might have resolved itself is now getting out of hand. Getting arrested: it is high time for you to change your behavior—you were out of control and your actions were ethically and morally suspect. Seeing police officers: what you are about to do is highly improper. Talking to the police: you want to settle a score with someone—however, do it person-to-person, without an audience. Seeing a female police officer: the dream will be emotional in nature.

D: The police officer is a symbol for the internal conflicts you have with conventional rules. On the other hand, the police officer wants to make sure that you at least obey the minor moral laws, and thus is the symbol of your conscience. An unpleasant encounter with a policeman: a bad conscience or guilt feelings. If the police come as "friends and helpers": you are at peace with conventional norms, laws, and values.

Pollen

D: Seeing pollen on a flower means your ideas or conclusions will "fertilize" your personal growth. See **Seeds.**

Pond

V: Swimming in a pond: stay away from mysterious company; people may not be quite what they seem. Seeing a pond with clear water: you will find a new friend.

D: The pond is a place where secret hopes and passions reside. You are not yet ready to admit them to yourself because they are like "forbidden fruit"! Look at the rest of the symbols in the dream. See **Lake, Water.**

Poodle

V: Seeing a poodle is a sign that you need more information and experience if you want to be successful in life. Getting bitten by a poodle: you are about to do something foolish—even stupid.

D: See **Animals, Dog.**

Pope

V: Seeing the pope: you will receive recognition or a reward for your efforts; past mistakes are forgiven. If you are the pope: be more self-critical and practice more humility, because the difficult decisions you have to make will have far-reaching consequences.

D: Are you looking for forgiveness for mistakes and failures that made you feel guilty? Maybe the dream is a symbol of your spiritual and religious beliefs?

Poplar Tree

V: Seeing a poplar tree: unlike the palm tree, the poplar promises happiness and a peaceful old age—you are on the right path! Seeing a crooked or stunted poplar tree: let go of deceptive opinions and negative attitudes! Failing to do so means you will always chase after the wrong goals.

D: A straight poplar tree is a good sign and means that you are on the right path. A crooked poplar tree: you need to make changes!

Poppy

V: Looking at red poppies in bloom: you are feeling passionately about a certain person, but it could be unwise, because the love affair is going to end in sorrow. Seeing a large field of poppies in bloom means you love sexual experimentation; but beware—things can easily go wrong. Eating poppy seeds: you overestimate yourself and your abilities.

Porcelain

V: Seeing porcelain: an exaggerated wish for wealth and luxury! Porcelain shards: it is not only in folklore that broken crockery brings good luck; it does it in dreams, too. Breaking china or porcelain: you have made a mistake that you can't undo. It is time to learn from your mistakes. See **China, Fragments.**

Porcupine

S: The porcupine is a symbol of miserliness and food cravings; also—because of its quills—it represents wrath.

V: The porcupine serves as a warning: don't be so naive. It could also mean that you either planned to do a good deed for another person and were rebuffed, or you have painted yourself into a corner. Killing a porcupine: you got rid of a "prickly" person. Watching a porcupine catch a mouse: a very materialistic or stingy person is taking advantage of you. Getting pricked by a quill: someone is trying to ruin your reputation or harm you.

D: The porcupine reflects your need for safety and security. It could also indicate actual mistrust on your part, which could influence your relationships. Have you "painted yourself into a corner"? Are you "being prickly"?

Postcard

V: Receiving a postcard: be prepared for a disappointment in matters of love. If the postcard depicts faraway places: get ready—you may go on a long journey. The dream may also be a sign that you want to take a trip and/or are in need of more diversion. What is depicted on the postcard? Search for and examine other symbols in the dream.

D: See **Picture.**

Poster

V: Seeing a poster: expect interesting news. If your name is on the poster: you have behaved badly in a certain matter and others will expose you.

D: The poster usually announces news, sometimes even excitement. See **Advertising, Newspaper.**

Pot (Overflowing)

A pot overflowing is a warning of obstacles in the way of your advancement.

Potatoes

V: Eating potatoes: be careful with your money—your budget is shrinking. Digging potatoes: you will have to work long and hard to reach your goals. Peeling potatoes: your household budget needs adjustment—you need to spend less.

D: A pleasant dream about potatoes: you have maturity and inner strength. Unpleasant dreams involving potatoes: financial or emotional worries; you may soon have to make do with less.

Potbelly

V: Being potbellied: life may be easier to take when you have an extra layer of fat for protection, but in this case it means you are too egotistical. Don't overdo it! See **Bacon, Ham, Pig.**

Powder, Face

V: Using face powder: your conscience is not quite clear. Spilling powder: you want to make up for something but without success. See **Makeup.**

D: See **Face.**

Power

V: Dreaming about being a powerful person: step back, get a better perspective and look calmly at your characteristics and mistakes.

D: Even if the dream is not implying that you are too domineering, still take a closer look at yourself, examine your mistakes, and make the necessary correction.

Prayer, Prayer Book

V: Dreaming about praying: while the future will be blessed, you are in need of advice from an objective counselor or support from your family and/or friends. Your humility will make it possible for a wish to come true. If you see or read a prayer book, it means comfort in your present sad situation. Seeing someone else praying: you have good friends who will always be on your side in times of need. Receiving a prayer book as a gift means that a very good person will help you. Losing a prayer book means losing a loyal friend. Throwing a prayer book away: you will be the cause of emotional conflicts. See **Worship.**

D: Prayers stand for humility and the faith you have in finding help in a dire situation. Sometimes it also means that a wish will be fulfilled. Praying in front of a cross is an expression of anxiety, fearing for one's existence. The soul is looking for God's help; ask for it! The prayer book is a symbol of your need for comfort and better insight.

Preacher, Sermon

V: If you are listening to a sermon: you are not inclined to listen to the advice of others—even if it is good advice. Listening to a preacher: you will have disagreements with someone. See **Pastor,**

Priest

D: This dream symbol is an indication that you have high intellectual and moral expectations of yourself and others.

Precious Stones

S: Looking at a precious stone: you are tempted by material things. Receiving a gift of a precious stone: your wealth will increase. If you are wearing precious stones: you are arrogant and egotistical. Seeing or finding precious stones always indicates that something valuable is going to happen. Finding a blue precious stone means new ideas, an inspiration, or a new field of knowledge. A red precious stone means a new romance. Finding a yellow stone, means a new opportunity due to a many-layered connection. A violet stone means pay more attention to the spiritual part of your life. It might lead to valuable insights or bring help "from above." See **Jewelry, Jewels, Gems,** and the chapter **"Colors in Dreams."**

D: Dreams about precious stones indicate that the dreamer likes external, material things, and lacks spiritual depth.

Precipice

V: Women often dream of **Falling** into the abyss. Falling off a precipice means that somewhere the "bottom is falling out." People who meditate or have out-of-body experiences have a similar sensation when their soul returns to their body. Suddenly falling off a precipice: something unexpected and positive is going happen.

D: The dream is a symbol that you are in emotional distress right now and are searching the depths of your soul to find the reason. Don't stop searching—it is the only way to get back on solid ground. It may also be a sign of your difficulty "letting go." See **Abyss, Cliff, Slope.**

Predator

V: A predator animal in women's dreams is always a sign of unconscious sexual urges. A large, beautiful predator refers to sexual "hunger" (beware!). Small wild animals indicate that you are still unsure about male sexuality. Fear of and fleeing from a predatory animal: you are "fleeing" from your own sexuality. See **Lion, Tiger.**

D: Make sure that your "wild" passions and appetites are under control. See **Animals.** A wild cat means deceit (either your own or that of someone else). See **Cat.**

Pregnancy

V: Seeing a pregnant woman: creative ideas and plans will begin to take shape. If you dream that you are pregnant: it is time to put your ideas into action. See **Birth.**

D: If you are pregnant, the dream is a sign of anticipation and the fears you have about the pregnancy. For all others, it is a symbol of new feelings, ideas, talents, or behavior (either your own or others) that want attention.

Pressure, Pressing

V: Feeling pressure in your throat is an expression of deep fear; take a look at the other symbols in the dream.

Priest

V: A priest is always a reminder to face life's tasks and responsibilities.

D: See **Pastor, Preacher.**

Primrose

V: Seeing a primrose: a happy love relationship. Receiving a bouquet of primroses: somebody is in love with you—you just don't know it yet. Picking primroses: with patience your longing for love will be answered.

D: See **Flower.**

Prince, Princess

V: A prince is a promise of happiness. Speaking to a prince: a wish will come true. Seeing or speaking with a princess: a woman is very fond of you and could be helpful. See **Emperor, King.**

D: A prince stands for masculinity, knowledge, and intellect: you are either looking for such a man, or you could nurture these qualities in yourself. Dreaming about a princess: you might be repressing, maybe unconsciously, your feminine side, your compassion, and your feelings in general. If you are a man, are you looking for a female partner who is "better" than so-called ordinary women—maybe in appearance, heritage, upbringing, education?

Prison, Prisoner

V: If you dream you are in prison: if you are married, it means you are dissatisfied. You feel locked up in your relationship or removed from real life. Visiting someone in prison means either a very bad conscience or deep regret over past actions. If you are released from prison: a new phase in your life is beginning. Seeing a prison: somebody is offering you something "uninviting."

D: Dreams about prison are usually a sign of fear about an emotionally intense relationship. Maybe your personal growth is hindered and you want to do something about it quickly (like "breaking out")! If you are the one imprisoned, it might be an indication that you have guilt feelings—justified or not.

Prophet, Prophecy

S: The prophet is the instrument, voice, and interpreter of divine revelation.

V: Seeing a prophet: he/she may reveal a secret; or you will soon find out what you want to know. The prophet's pronouncements or predictions are very important, because they convey valuable information that could influence future life-changing decisions. See **Astrology, Fortune-teller.**

D: If you get negative information, it may indicate your fears and lack of self worth. Should this dream recur frequently, psychotherapy might be in order. Positive prophecies could become reality. It is not clear if the prophet has clairvoyant qualities, or if the dream-behavior is programmed by hidden expectations. Whatever the case, keeping these prophecies in mind makes it even more likely that they will come true.

Prostitute

V: Seeing a prostitute: be careful, you are keeping bad company. This dream always is a warning that the company you keep might have serious consequences.

D: A prostitute can indicate many things. These dreams may, for example, point to uncontrolled lust, sexual fantasy or bondage, or may be an expression of guilt because someone's love has been misused for selfish purposes. A prostitute may also stand for everyday "sell-outs," like being nice to well-connected people that you really don't like, or doing something strictly for the money even though it is against your better judgment. Human life is full of all kinds of prostitution. How do you stack up?

Protection

V+ D: Looking for protection in a dream: improve your self-confidence so that you can stand on your own two feet.

Psychic, Fortune-teller

V: Seeing or visiting a fortune-teller: you are looking for security and contact in the wrong places—be more confident. Speaking to a fortune-teller: good advice isn't easy to find—but some of what the person is prophesying will come true.

D: You are desperately in need of advice in a present situation. See **Astrology.**

Psychologist, Psychoanalysis

D: Both images clearly show your desire to understand yourself better. Dreaming of undergoing psychoanalysis: you are starting to make the connection between your actions and what is going on inside. The psychologist is a sign that you are able to work through inner conflicts on your own. See **Guru**. Are you afraid (usually without reason) that you are "going to lose it," to go insane? If this dream recurs frequently, see an appropriate therapist and explore the reason for the dream.

Puddle

V: Stepping into a puddle: be careful, you are about to risk your good reputation. Don't take part in a "dirty" business—it could be nothing but bad luck.

Pulling

V: Pulling a wagon or a large object: your reward will be in direct proportion to the amount of effort you put into your work. If someone is pulling you: either comply with a request or decide not to act.

D: What are you pulling in the dream? If you are pulling hard: you will try hard to remove the obstacles in your path. If other people do the pulling: you would like to profit from the work other people do.

Pulpit

S: The pulpit is a preacher's special place.

V: Seeing a pulpit or standing in one: you will appear in public and give a speech, or people are attacking you and you have to defend yourself. Standing in a pulpit also means that you want to influence and instruct others.

D: You are either prone to be a know-it-all who, with your "teachings," gains power over others, or you are suffering because of a person with these character traits. Your motto should be: "Everybody is entitled to his own opinions—no matter how wrong they are." Follow that advice or face lots of conflict.

Pulse

D: A fast-beating pulse: you need more energy and strength in order to deal with a present situation. A normal pulse indicates that your life is going smoothly at this time. See **Heart, Vein.**

Pump, Pumping

V: Looking at a pump: dealing with worries on the job will require every ounce of strength you have. Are you hesitating in a certain matter? Have courage and "just do it." Pumping until water begins to flow: if you work diligently right now you can count on winning. See **Water.**

D: The pump is a reminder that you need to pump more

energy into a present project, one you have been avoiding far too long. Have courage—you can do it!

Pumpkin

S: The pumpkin is a symbol of rapid growth and a rapid demise.

V: Looking at a pumpkin means dashed hopes—particularly if you have counted on help from others. Use your own strength and things will turn out okay. Receiving a pumpkin as a gift: a mentor is going to support you in the near future. See **Fruit.**

D: The pumpkin is usually a symbol of your sexual appetites and desires.

Puppet

D: Puppets usually represent dependence—on other people, substances, sex, etc. Sometimes they indicate the negative influences and control that you feel others have over you. Do you feel like a marionette? Are you known to pull "strings" to manipulate others? In either case, you need to make some changes! See **Thread.**

Pursuit, Chase

V: If you are chasing someone: you can't make up for an old mistake. If you are being chased: someone who has wronged you wants to make amends. In a man's dream, being chased means he has not yet come to terms with the sexual prohibitions of his childhood. Unconsciously he still believes that sexuality is disgusting and is afraid of being punished.

D: Are you treating others unfairly? Are you hounded by guilt feelings? Or do you feel that prejudice or condemnation by other people is hounding you? Only you know if you are the perpetrator or the victim.

Pyramid

V: Seeing one or more pyramids: you want to go to faraway places, or get a better understanding of the laws that govern the universe. On the other hand, the dream also suggests the desire to seriously study the humanities—wonderful discoveries might be in store for you.

D: The foundation of the pyramid represents the body, the sides of the pyramid your spiritual desires, and the peak stands for a harmonious integration of the human with the "higher mind" (God). A pyramid is flowing energy that connects the physical to the spiritual. For that reason the dream gives you insight into your spiritual maturity. The more powerful the pyramid, the more spiritually mature you have already become. If the pyramid is partly hidden in the dark, let no stone go unturned until you bring the shadow side of your character into the light of day!

Pyre, Stakes

V: Seeing a pyre: work diligently to overcome past experiences so you can look forward to a happy future. Do you believe you should be "burned at the stake" for something you did? The dream is a warning about a dangerous love affair which could have disastrous consequences. Pay attention to this dream! Building a pyre yourself: you are breaking with your own convictions and have to take the consequences.

D: The pyre is always a symbol of purification: everything stale and old needs to be burned. The dream might also indicate that your moral beliefs or compassion are going "up in flames" because of your behavior or your refusal to help someone in need. Remember your convictions and act accordingly. See **Blaze, Fire.**

S = Symbol V = Vision D = Depth psychology

Quagmire

V: You are walking through a quagmire: you are working extremely hard, but the rewards for your efforts are small. See **Mud, Swamp.**

D: Emotional barriers interfere with your independence and self-development. Take this dream very seriously and find out how you can get out of the swamp. The source of the quagmire is often either emotional confusion or your relationship!

Quartz

V: Quartz is a symbol of the solid core of your character. See **Crystal, Mountain, Rock Crystal.**

Queen

V: The queen in a game of cards has several different meanings: Queen of Hearts promises good luck in matters of love; Queen of Diamonds suggests changes in general, or a change of address; Queen of Spades stands for sadness and grief; and Queen of Clubs warns of financial problems (caused by a woman).

Quince

V: Eating a quince: you will soon meet your partner for

life, just be patient. Shaking a quince tree: losing your temper is costing you the person you love. If you change course and proceed gently, you can still reach your goal. Picking quinces off the ground: your partner "has been around." Seeing a rotten quince: a certain person is not worthy of your love.

D: In ancient Greece, a bride had to eat a quince, reminding her that married life is made up of the sweet and the bitter. This fruit, too, represents your erotic or sexual needs and desires. See **Fruit.**

S = Symbol V = Vision D = Depth psychology

Rabbit

V: Seeing a white rabbit: a pleasant experience in the near future. Seeing a black rabbit: news of a death . Catching a rabbit: you will meet a younger person. Raising/breeding rabbits is a sign of long life and virility. Watching a rabbit being killed: you are sacrificing your own ideals and positive qualities for the good of other people—but in the long run you will be unhappy. See **Hare.**

D: This animal represents sexual desires and fertility, as well as feelings of inferiority, insecurity, or anxieties hiding in your unconscious. What is making you so timid? Why do you withdraw? Is it because you think you are not good enough? Who is the human predator threatening or chasing you? Analyze this dream carefully!

Racetrack, Racing

V: Dreaming about the racetrack: be prepared for a lot of excitement in the coming weeks; it also suggests being careful: someone else might be faster than you. Watching a horse race: if you use your strength judiciously, you will overcome the hurdles facing you. Participating in a horse race: you are going to miss an opportunity. See **Horse, Riding.**

D: A racetrack means you are confident that speed is all you need to prevail in life or win a competition. Or are you running away from your mistakes, failures, or feelings of inferiority? Why don't you stop for a moment and think about which of the above describes your situation best and then act accordingly!

Radio

V: Seeing or buying a radio: you are looking for diversion. Listening to beautiful music on the radio: a secret pleasure that you can enjoy with all your heart. Listening to someone on the radio: someone will let you in on a secret.

D: The radio means you are looking for social contact or some news. Through the radio, many telepathically talented people receive news "from above" (so, in your dream, don't turn your radio off!).

Radish

V: Dreaming about radishes: small pleasures ahead. Eating radishes: you are angry about someone's sharp and critical remarks.

D: The radish could indicate a love affair about which you are still uncertain—is it only an erotic adventure? The dream also might indicate that you are angry about spiteful remarks by other people—or the reverse: you may be making spiteful remarks about others.

Raid

V: Watching a raid: a warning of imminent danger, unless you stop your foolishness. Getting involved in a raid: through no fault of your own you will become involved in an embarrassing or critical situation.

D: You are either innocently involved in an unpleasant situation; or someone is going to betray you if you continue to be reckless. Keep your eyes and ears open so that you can escape in time.

Rain, Raincoat

V: A warm rain shower is a symbol of fertility, success at work, and happy relationships. A cold rain means others are going to treat you badly. Getting soaked in a rain shower: you won't find your luck where you think. Watching a rain shower with the sun already shining: while you are still in tears, Lady Luck is already smiling on you. In a man's dream, rain is a sign of his unmet need for relaxation.

D: Rain is a sign of an emotional release you should not try to prevent—don't be afraid, you won't lose control. See **Water**. The raincoat means you are letting negative influences "roll off your back." Maybe you will experience a "cloudburst" of good fortune soon. See **Cloudburst.**

Rainbow

S: The colorful arc of a rainbow symbolizes the bridge between heaven and earth.

V: Seeing a rainbow: a warning that your good fortune could be an illusion. In spiritual terms, however, the rainbow is positive: you are at peace with God and the world. It is often a sign that an important reconciliation will be possible.

D: The rainbow is a symbol of inner peace and harmony of body, soul, and spirit.

Raisins

V: Eating raisins means conflicts with a neighbor; it is also a warning about how you spend your money. Looking at stale raisins: forgotten things from the past burden your mind. Seeing raisins in a cake: very favorable opportunities are waiting for you. Picking raisins out of a cake: you will have to face a side of life that is not very comfortable.

D: Raisins (and dried fruit): something from the past, something you have lost, or something that has died is coming up again. Maybe you only want the raisins, not the rest of the cake—thereby avoiding unpleasant experiences?

Ram

S: The ram is a symbol of male fertility.

V: Seeing a ram with horns: don't be intimidated—insist on being respected in a certain matter and you will succeed. If you are the ram with horns: you are too rigid. Killing a ram means material and/or financial losses, which are entirely the result of your own bungling.

D: See **Animals.**

Rape

V: Sometimes a dream about rape is a sign that the dreamer is looking for aggressive sex. In general, however, a dream about rape means that others are ignoring your feelings and wishes—or you are ignoring theirs. See **Aggression, Intercourse, Sexuality.**

Rapier

S: Unlike Freud, who insisted that the rapier is a phallic symbol, we believe today that the rapier stands for "separation," for cutting something. See **Scissors.**

V: Dreaming about a rapier may have a sexual connotation, but the image can also stand for an immediate separation (or fear of separation). Being attacked by a rapier stands for a drastic event. Fighting with a rapier: success in the struggle to combat evil gossip, if you can keep present emotions under control.

D: The dream image of a rapier means you will soon be required to make an emotional decision. The rapier might also be a symbol of aggressive sexuality. Woman may see such a dream as a sign of danger, since women generally have an aversion to violent sex.

Raspberries

V: Looking at red raspberries is a good omen: your present social and family situation will remain stable. White raspberries are also a good sign: you will either be very lucky in love or receive satisfaction from something else. Black raspberries might mean a broken heart, because your partner or husband is unfaithful. Looking at raspberries on the bush: you will meet good-hearted people. Drinking raspberry juice: you want diversions that make you feel good.

Rat

V: Seeing a rat means unpleasant experiences with other people. Being bitten by a rat warns you about a "friend" who is determined to wreck your reputation. Seeing a caged rat: your friend is very dishonest. Catching or killing a rat: trouble in your love relationship or in a friendship. Rats leaving a sinking ship: you are about to find out that you have miscalculated a situation at your job. See **Animals, Mouse.**

D: A rat is a sign that negative influences are undermining your vitality. Dreams about rats and mice always mean that grief and worries are "gnawing" on you. Are you sometimes repulsed or sickened by other people or yourself?

Raven

S: The raven is smart and cunning, but usually a harbinger of bad luck.

V: Seeing a raven: hostility and misfortune are on the way. Sometimes the dream refers to possible theft. Chasing a raven away: you might escape danger—if you keep your eyes and ears open! Watching ravens taking flight: misfortune will be avoided just in time.

D: The raven is the messenger of death; or a symbol of repressed, dark appetites. Is your mood often "very dark"? Are you expecting failure? Are you afraid of death and dying—or the unknown? Are you seeing everything right now "as black as pitch"? See the chapter **"Colors in Dreams."**

Ravine

V: Looking at a ravine: careless actions on your part can harm other people. Falling into a ravine: your careless actions could cause a disaster—be satisfied with what you have rather than risk an uncertain future. Seeing someone in the ravine: a good friend is in need of help.

D: A deep ravine always is a warning about taking the wrong path or being careless—both will cause problems. See **Abyss.**

Rebel

V: Seeing a rebel means: you expect something from another person but are disappointed. Being involved with rebels: you are creating a great deal of trouble with your boss or a person in authority.

D: Are you rebelling against your boss or other high officials? A rebel represents difficulties you have with other people; but it is also a sign of other people opposing your actions and goals.

Receipt

V: Being handed a receipt: it is urgent that you take care of an important matter—take this dream to heart and be careful in all financial matters. You are being accused of something and now must pay for your mistake. Making out a receipt: there will be a considerable strain on your wallet. See **Bill.**

D: Dreaming of paying a bill and being handed a receipt: debt relief is in sight. The dream is also a warning about thoughtless decisions for which you will "pay" later.

Recipe

V: Receiving a recipe: it's time to examine your character. Stop making excuses or lying to yourself about your weaknesses. See **Pills.**

D: What is the recipe about? Sometimes it refers to your attempt to find "the right recipe for living," or "the golden mean" in a conflict, or the right "ingredients" to deal with emotional contradictions and desires. The dream is often full of very helpful advice!

Recruit

V: Seeing recruits: your freedom might be restricted, but you have enough strength to break down the barriers. You have not yet been able to cope emotionally with a humiliation.

D: Your efforts at self-realization will be restricted by external circumstances, or you will be asked to exercise more self-restraint. Sometimes (when you have taken self-discipline too far) the recruit is telling you to loosen the reins a bit. You will know which scenario most likely applies to you. See **Parade, Soldier.**

Recuperation

D: If you are dreaming about recuperating: difficult times are over; but stay low for a while so "things" can mature in their own good time.

Red

V: Seeing red flames means either a job is going well or love is burning bright. Looking at someone with red hair is a warning about an impassioned character or violent temper. It also means that you are suspicious of a person who means well.

D: See the chapter **"Colors in Dreams."**

Reed

V: Looking at reeds: pursue your dreams with more determination. Too much hesitation and too many delaying tactics won't get you far. There are many obstacles to overcome before you reach open waters.

D: You are able to bend like a reed in a storm (you know how to adapt), which is a sign of wisdom, determination, and intellectual curiosity. You are humble and are bending your will to a higher power. Your down-to-earth faith is the source of your confidence and vitality!

Regulation, Rule

D: Dreaming about rules and regulations: your unconscious wants to give you advice. Can you "read" the regulations? What are they telling you? Check past experiences and what they taught you!

Relatives

V: Seeing or talking to a relative: someone you know will disappoint or betray you.

D: This dream often reflects the actual feelings you have for your relatives. Sometimes the dream points to your own character traits that are not totally integrated yet. See **Aunt, Uncle.**

Remorse

V + D: You are feeling remorse about something: follow the honest, well-meaning advice somebody is giving you and you'll find the right solution for an unpleasant situation.

Rendezvous

V: If you have planned a rendezvous: be careful, you might ruin your good reputation. It's not worth it.

Rescue, Rescuing

V: Rescuing a person: you need to tackle a public duty and do it soon—not only for the recognition you will receive. Being rescued: you need strong, male support in order to overcome a crisis.

D: You are either very afraid, or the dream is a warning about a real danger that you need to try to avoid.

Restaurant

V: Sitting in a restaurant: be honest, aren't your favorite habits getting just a bit out of hand? What drives you out of the house? Seeing a restaurant: you will get together again with a good friend. Eating in a restaurant: you want more social contact, entertainment, and "food for the soul." See **Café.**

D: The dream indicates your need for company. You want more human contact and diversion. Do you need a break?

Resurrection

V: Dreaming that a person who has died some time ago has come back to life: something very oppressive is being lifted from your shoulders. Experiencing the dream in a religious context: a new chapter in life is about to begin, a change for the better—professional or personal success. Dreaming about being resurrected: immense changes await you—bad luck changes into good luck.

D: Resurrection signals your desire for something more lofty—more spiritual. In most cases, you have successfully completed an important step in your development and undergone inner renewal. This is a wonderful dream symbol!

Revenge

D: You find yourself in a very difficult situation and blame others, which is usually a mistake. You are thinking of revenge, hoping to get off the hook. Not a good plan!

Revolution

V: Watching a revolution: unexpected, disruptive events will interfere with your life. Sometimes this is also a visionary dream that you might have prior to actual political unrest. Participating in a revolution: you are instigating a fight that will bring turmoil into your life. See **Rebel.**

D: Due to external circumstances, you will face far-reaching changes in your life. Additional information can be gleaned from the rest of the dream.

Revolver

V: Holding a revolver: be particularly careful to avoid becoming "unfit for battle." Seeing a revolver: you are using strong-arm tactics to get your own way. Pointing the gun at someone: you will end up with "the short end of the stick." Having a gun pointed at you: you may be harmed by sudden events or a violent person and experience losses.

D: Are you trying to accomplish something by force? Are you in danger of failing? Sometimes the dream is a warning to be careful around people who could hurt you. See **Pistol.**

Rheumatism

D: Suffering from rheumatism: you are hiding emotional bitterness and disappointments from the outside world. Work through your anger and you will regain your emotional equilibrium.

Rhinoceros

V: The rhinoceros is a warning: use good sense and don't rush headlong toward your goal. In a man's dream, the rhinoceros means that he would like to have more sexual stamina.

D: While this animal is a symbol for external power and might, its insides do not match its imposing appearance. Does this also apply to you? Do you feel inferior to people who are as imposing as the rhinoceros? Either way, ambition or feelings of inferiority could be a problem in sexual relationships and need to be addressed.

Ribbons

V: Seeing ribbons in a dream: you might soon learn from or meet new friends. Dragging endless ribbons around: you have too many financial responsibilities or debts. The color of the ribbons also plays a role (see the chapter on "**Colors in Dreams**"). A ribbon blowing in the wind means good luck and success!

D: Ribbons are symbols of many things: "tying the knot," "my hands are tied." Have you already "tied the knot"—or would you like to? Do you have friendly ties to someone? Are you all tied up?

Rice

V: Eating rice means good health for some time to come, and whatever you are doing, success will come easily. Seeing rice: expect an increase in your income.

D: Either you are really hungry or your soul "hungers" for excitement and new experiences. See **Grain, Wheat.**

Rider

S: The New Testament in "The Revelation of John" speaks of four riders: the rider on a white horse is the symbol of Christ himself; the rider on a fiery-red horse represents war; the rider on a black horse with a scale in his hand means hunger; and the rider on a greenish horse symbolizes pestilence.

V: Seeing a rider on a horse: your prestige is growing and your climb up the career ladder is going well. Riding a horse in full gallop: you are chasing a questionable goal and need to be more realistic. If young girls see a rider on a horse: a love affair is in the making.

D: See **Horse, Horseback Riding, Riding.**

Ridicule

V: Dreaming about ridiculing others: you are not taking yourself too seriously.

Riding

V: Riding on a **Horse**: you are too vain and ambitious. Riding a **Donkey**: you are making fun of others unfairly. Riding on a **Camel**: you are pursuing your goals with patience and poise. Riding on an **Elephant**: you can look forward to a pleasant adventure. Riding on a **Cow**: you don't quite know where you want to go or what you want to do.

D: Riding might indicate your sexual desires, or a conscious effort to guide and control those desires.

Rifle

V: In a man's dream, a rifle is a symbol for energy, strength, power, and the need to impress others. Women dreaming about rifles are afraid of aggressive sexuality and would do well to develop more courage. Shooting a rifle means you are trying in vain to accomplish something through force. Others holding a rifle points to a feelings of inferiority, being less than others. See **Shooting, Weapon.**

D: A rifle is a symbol of aggressive male sexuality, a tendency to use force in general. Fear of being attacked may be the reason for a rifle dream. It may also indicate your attitude toward life—"I'd rather fight than run!"

Right (as in side, turn, etc.)

V: The right side—things placed on the right—always represents male energies. A woman dreaming she has a ring on her right hand means she is ready to make a lasting commitment. The right side is the good and positive side; turning to the right, making a right-hand turn means the right path has been chosen.

D: Right is the symbol of conscious intentions, actions, energies, creativity, and ambition. Do you feel you have the "right" to something, are right about something, are standing on the "right side"? See **Left.**

Rigid, Rigidity

V: Why are you so rigid in your opinions and principles? Being stubborn won't save you in the event that you are wrong. This toughness needs to be softened!

Ring

S: The ring represents a bond or vow to share your destiny with another person or a community—a beginning without end.

V: In a woman's dream, a ring on a finger or slipping a ring on a finger is a sign that she can't let go of an old relationship. Dreaming about a ring that won't come off: letting go of a relationship is even more difficult than you had anticipated. Finding a ring: things in your love relationship are going well. A broken ring: a separation is unavoidable. Losing a ring: your lover or spouse is unfaithful or you are temporarily separated. Seeing two rings: either a budding love relationship or marriage. Pulling a ring off your finger: your affair will have nasty consequences.

D: The ring represents the relationship you have with the person who gave you the ring or to whom you gave the ring. See **Circle.**

Ritual

D: Watching rituals: try to be less formal in your everyday dealings and don't use empty phrases. See **Ceremony.**

River

S: The river indicates that "everything is moving along well." The river is a symbol of universal hope, fertility, death, and renewal.

V: Dreaming about a big river where the water is very clear: a good sign, everything in your life is moving along without interference. If the water in the river is murky: people around you are hostile and you may need to fight back. If the river is flowing over its banks: others are gossiping about you—your plans are going to "drown." Falling into the river: bad luck. Swimming in the river: you may have to deal with a dangerous adversary, but you will succeed. Swimming against the current is a symbol of internal contradictions that need attention and resolution. Swimming across the river means you are leaving the past behind—positive changes are beginning to take place. See **Brook.**

D: The river is considered the energy reservoir of your soul. You are not making enough use of these energies—or you may not even be aware of them (see **Stream**). The condition of the river represents your emotional energy and strength. These energies may carry you where you have no intention of going and they can also destroy! See **Water.**

Road

V: A straight road: you are still trying to live your life as easily as possible. If the road goes uphill: your life will reach new heights. Going downhill: don't continue what you are doing right now; you will only lose by it. A rocky road: there are obstacles to overcome—but don't give up; you will make it. A winding, zigzagging road: you will have to make compromises, even if it is difficult. See **Hike, Path, Street.**

Road Sign

V: Dreaming about seeing a road sign: you need to carefully evaluate your plans, take your life into your own hands, and leave nothing to chance; you are on the wrong path.

D: The dream is strongly suggesting that you make a decision—it will determine your future. To what direction is the road sign pointing? See **Four Corners of the Compass, Path.** Is it pointing to the **Left** or the **Right**? If it is pointing straight ahead, keep on going the way you had planned from the start!

Robbery, Robber

V: If you are being robbed: you will have to face losses, but you are not altogether innocent in what is happening to you. Be especially careful right now. Being robbed while on a trip: don't overdo it when exercising. If you are the robber: you are about to get involved in a dangerous situation. Catching a robber in the act: be prepared to deal with a loss. Watching a robbery or being involved in one: hidden aggression; you are after something that is not yours. See **Burglary, Thief.**

D: The robber is part of your character, symbolizing primitive and dangerous impulses to which you should pay attention. The dream is also a warning about losses to come—be very careful for the next couple of weeks. Sometimes the dream also warns you about a friend you trusted and who disappointed you.

Robin

V + T: A robin indicates tender feelings and brings love and joyful news. See **Bird.**

Rock

S: A rock is a symbol of rigidity but also strength. Rocks serve as a warning: don't set your sights too high.

V: If you are rock climbing: hard work at your job will pay off handsomely. Falling off a boulder: you are overextended and exhausted. Pay more attention to your health. Looking up at a tall rock: an extraordinary project or task will come your way. Climbing down from a rock with great effort: relatives or friends are withdrawing from you, or your hopes are dashed.

D: A rock in a dream means you have to overcome something, but must do so gently. It is also a challenge: be steadfast, like "the rock of Gibraltar." Sometimes the rock refers to a tombstone or marker, or it may be a phallic symbol. See **Altar, Mountain.**

Rock Crystal

V: Seeing a rock crystal in a dream or owning one has great symbolic meaning because it wants to guide you on your journey through life. If the dream is pleasant, everything is going in the right direction. The rock crystal symbolizes serenity, concentration, and noble goals. See **Crystals, Jewels, Mountain.**

Rocket

V: Watching a rocket launch: sudden changes will offer great and unexpected advantages. A rocket soaring into the sky: you have very good ideas that you need to put into action.

D: The rocket suggests that you are about to "overshoot your goal." On the positive side, the rocket is a symbol of ambitious, lofty goals. See **Cannon.**

Rod, Cane

S: The rod is a symbol of the power of invisible things.

V: Walking with a cane or seeing one: you have a good

sense of yourself and should continue on your path—even if you have been uncertain at times. Leaning on a cane: you thought you could trust another person, but are now faced with the opposite situation. Getting hit with a cane: you are either learning a painful lesson or want revenge. A broken cane: a quarrel with a person close to you.

D: The rod, as a phallic symbol, usually refers to sexual needs and desires. See **Crutch.**

Rollerblading, Inline Skating

V: Watching someone rollerblading: you are too slow lately—others have passed you by. If you are rollerblading: you are working on an important project and would like to get it over with—don't be in a hurry, that won't work. Looking at rollerblades: you must act fast.

D: Depending upon the rest of the images, the dream could have either meaning—slow down or get moving because others might overtake you.

Roof

V: Standing on a roof: professional success is in sight. Falling off a roof means setbacks and bad news. Climbing on a roof: problems in the coming week, but you are going to solve them. A shingle falling from the roof: your effort are for naught—you are wasting your time. Standing underneath a rain gutter: unhappiness in matters of love. Looking at a damaged roof: bad news. Putting shingles on a roof: prospects are good for the future, expect to be more secure. If a roof is on fire: pay attention, you might be getting sick!

D: Standing on a roof means that deep-seated passions are clamoring for attention. You are in danger of "losing your footing." The roof stands for good sense and the future. See **House.**

Room

V: Looking at a room: something in your life is going to change. If it is a room that you live in: you might be moving soon. If the room is empty: to improve your lifestyle, you have to work for it. See **House.**

D: The room is part of your house—your personality. It's important what you did in the room and what the room looked like.

Roots

V: Looking at roots: you have talents that you have ignored so far. Or you finally understand the connection that exists between certain events. Digging out roots: you are getting to the "bottom" of things and will be astonished about what you find. Having a tooth pulled: somebody is hurting you deliberately. See **Tooth.**

D: The root is a symbol of your personality and represents your basic needs. It also points to the relationship you have to things and people who have become indispensable to you. Occasionally, it also shows your need to get to the essence of a thing or person.

Rope, Tightrope

V: Seeing a rope; you will soon make a commitment to a relationship. Untangling a rope: you are very tolerant and compassionate, and this makes a great impression on others. Climbing a rope: because of your courage and determination you will reach your goal. Seeing a tightrope: you are letting yourself be dragged into a very risky adventure. Also, someone might be setting a trap for you. If you are the tightrope acrobat: your serenity is threatened by others. You have lost the ground under your feet! Crashing to the ground: severe emotional conflicts are ahead. See **String.**

D: The rope represents your dependence on other people or things. Maybe you are asking others to pull with/or for you. The acrobat on a tightrope (if the walk is successful) represents inner balance or (if the crossing is not successful) the lack of it. If the rope is strung very tight: be more tolerant toward others.

Rosary

S: The rosary consists of consecutive beads that are like budding roses.

V: Seeing a rosary: you need to be courageous and steadfast so that feelings of sorrow and pain won't crush you.

D: The rose represents the life experiences that you can use to reach spiritual wholeness; for very religious people, the dream may mean that they want to be closer to God.

Rose

V: Dreaming about red roses: you are in love and that love will be returned. White roses: someone is secretly in love with you, but too shy to tell you. Yellow roses: jealousy and alienation in your love relationship. Wilted roses: your love for another person is dying. Getting pricked by a thorn: you will face obstacles on your path and feel hurt in your love relationship. Picking roses: you want to take someone by storm (or be taken by storm). Picking yellow roses: bouts of jealousy will be a burden on your relationship. Young girls dreaming about a wreath of red roses: a wedding is not far off. See **Flowers.**

D: The rose is a symbol of blossoming as well as wilting love, but it also shows the grace of your soul and may express your longing for a "pure," platonic relationship—the highest form of love.

Rosemary

V: Seeing rosemary: this little plant means separation or sadness in general.

D: See **Herbs.**

Roulette

V + T: Watching others play roulette means you are being tempted. Playing roulette: great fortunes are ahead. If you are winning: be prepared for losses in the near future. See **Wheel of Fortune.**

Rowing

V + D: Rowing in a dream means you will have to work hard to reach your goal, but patience, effort, and a steady hand will make things possible. See **Boat.**

Rubble

V: Looking at a heap of rubble: something entirely unexpected is going happen and new opportunities will open up. Seeing or transporting rubble: your financial situation is finally improving and your future looks much brighter than you had hoped. Seeing a house in ruins: now is the right time to start rebuilding. See **House.**

D: See **Dirt, Garbage.**

Ruins, Ruin, Ruined

V: In men's dreams, ruins indicate a craving for pleasure or too much ambition. Ruins are a warning about being more modest—otherwise, your health will be "in ruins." Seeing a ruin: you are still holding on to something from the past, or neglecting something important in your life. Spending time in a ruin: something rather strange will take place—be careful. Seeing a burned-out ruin: right now you, too, are in need of some "reconstruction"; are you "burned out" from too many passion and cravings? See **Fire.**

D: A ruin might refer to past experiences that you have not processed yet. But in general, it reflects a fear of old age and illness, or of losing strength. Sometimes the dream is a warning of impending material losses (being "ruined").

Running

V: Running in your dream and making good progress: everything you do is going to be successful. Running and getting nowhere: you are sabotaging your own efforts or someone else is. See **Walking.**

D: Are you running after someone (or something)? Are you running away from something, someone, or yourself? Maybe your own fear or your own feelings? How does running make you feel: satisfied and happy? Or do you feel you're being chased?

Rust

V: Seeing a rusted object: you are not active enough on the job and don't pay enough attention to the importance of human contact; it could also mean you are a clumsy lover. Seeing rusted iron: make every effort to keep your reputation intact.

D: Rust symbolizes aging, but also illustrates the destructive influence of bad experiences. The dream might also be a reference to the transitory nature of life. Or is it perhaps about a blemish on your character?

S = Symbol V = Vision D = Depth psychology

Saddle

V: Sitting in a saddle: you are going places in your life, because you are "in the saddle." Falling out of a saddle: expect to lose your good reputation. Seeing a saddle: you will receive a valuable gift—but there is a responsibility attached to it.

D: You are now prepared to accept an unpleasant obligation, but don't force your will on other people or misuse them for your own selfish reasons. You can use unconscious energies in the pursuit of higher goals. See **Horse, Riding.**

Sailboat

See **Boat.**

Sailing Vessel

V: See **Air, Ship, Water.**

Sailor

V: Seeing a sailor means traveling or an extraordinary event.

D: The sailor might represent change or new experiences.

Salad, Lettuce

V: If you are eating salad: your body needs vitamins in order to deal with an oncoming cold. Seeing a big bowl of green salad: prepare well for an upcoming test; it is the best way to avoid humiliation. Looking at lettuce gone to seed: sexual needs call for attention.

D: Lettuce is a symbol of something alive, of food for the soul. Lettuce gone to seed refers to sexual needs or is a hint to keep physical appetites better under control. See **Vegetable.**

Sale, Selling

D: Did you sell yourself? Have you "sold" important principles or ideals for material gain? If so, your spiritual health is suffering because of it. See **Prostitute.**

Salt, Salt Shaker

V: If you are salting food: don't get involved in the affairs of other people. Someone handing you the salt: family life is harmonious and the household is in good shape. Spilling salt: sorrow and grief or a fight with your marriage partner. Seeing a salt shaker: you will regret something in the near future because someone is in a "pickle" because of you—or is it the other way around? See **Sugar.**

D: Salt is a symbol of the stuff that life is made off, as well as your energies and vitality. Have you turned into "a pillar of salt"? Is everything stagnating because you are looking only to the past? Salt is also a symbol of hospitality—the "salt of the earth." How important are your friends?

Salve, Ointment

V: Dreaming about a salve: physical or emotional ailments will heal soon. Buying a salve: be patient—things are going to get better. Using ointment on yourself: other people need your help; or don't give other people trouble. Using ointment on someone else: recovery is in sight. See **Oil.**

D: If you went through painful experiences recently, the dream means that your wounds will heal soon!

Sanatorium

V: Being a patient in a sanatorium: try to find out why things are at a standstill right now—difficulties and problems can be overcome! Looking at a sanatorium: you need a break and some space between yourself, people, and events. Working in a sanatorium: your knowledge and willingness to help will be rewarded.

D: The sight of a sanatorium is assuring you that setbacks and failure are going to be overcome faster than you had hoped. See **Hospital, Illness.**

Sand

V: Looking at sand in a dream: you are wasting time and energy on a matter that will not be successful. Lying in the sand: your situation is getting worse. A sandstorm is a sign that the success you have enjoyed so far may be coming to an end.

D: Sand is a symbol of instability in your life. Have you been building "sand castles?" The dream might also be a signal that a present relationship is unproductive.

Sandals

V: Seeing or wearing sandals: you want to make one of two statements: I am different from the rest of society, or I am light-hearted and have a great need to be free. See **Foot, Shoes.**

Satan

See **Devil.**

Saturn

D: This planet indicates that many responsibilities need your attention, and hard work is ahead. Obstacles, standing in the way of your success, may dampen your enjoyment of life. You are plagued by what you perceive as emotional or physical shortcomings. Saturn also separates us from people and things that stand in the way of personal growth. See **Four Corners of the Compass, Planets.**

Sausage

V: Seeing or eating sausage: while you will start a new relationship, in the long run it won't be satisfying. See **Butcher, Ham, Meat.**

D: The sausage as a phallic symbol indicates sexual needs or a very materialistic attitude.

Saw, Wood Shavings

V: Seeing or working with a saw: someone is out to humiliate or irritate you. Hearing someone use a saw: you are in need of a break—your nerves are irritated. Watching someone use a saw: somebody has disappeared and now you have to face the damage by yourself. Seeing a dull saw: you are working with inferior tools and won't succeed. Seeing wood shavings: your work is creating useless "garbage." See **File.**

D: The saw is a sign that you are overly critical and at times too cynical. Working with a saw: you need to solve conflicts and problems on your own. The dream might also suggest you let go of a relationship. Sometimes the saw indicates sexual desires that call for attention.

Scaffold (as in gallows)

V: Standing on a scaffold: Don't worry—only your qualities are being tested here; with honest efforts you will overcome a difficult situation.

D: See **Execution, Gallows.**

Scaffolding

V: Standing at a scaffolding: reexamine your social "contracts," your bank account, and your expenses. Don't make risky decisions, and work out plans to save money—you have clearly miscalculated your situation. Working on a scaffolding: your courage is a good foundation for making your dreams come true. If a scaffolding is falling down, or you're falling off, a warning is necessary—you're too daring! Standing under a scaffolding: you are making too many compromises—or too many excuses. Taking down a scaffolding: your tendency to "cover all bases" is extreme—be more trusting!

D: A scaffolding is usually a symbol for help that is available to you in a difficult situation. It will help you to "move up the ladder."

Scales

V: Standing on a scale: you must have made a mistake. Weighing something: you need to make a decision and ought to deal with others more fairly.

D: The scale is a symbol of your sense of justice, which is either too strong or too weak. It could also be a sign of indecision in a certain matter. Examine closely which it is and act accordingly!

Scandal

V + D: Dreaming about a scandal: things will soon take a turn for the better.

Scar

V: Seeing a scar on your body: you are still dealing with a recent painful conflict you had with another person. Should you meet a person shortly after this dream, be careful. The relationship will eventually disappoint you.

D: A scar is a reminder of a painful experience from the past, even if the "wound" has already healed. Who or what left you scarred?

Scare, Being Scared

V: Experiencing a scare: expect to receive a pleasant announcement. Frequent dreams of being scared mean your nerves are shot and you need a vacation.

D: Scares and fearful emotions have made you vulnerable and insecure. The dream is a sign that you need to come to terms with the reasons for them. Pay attention to the rest of the symbols in the dream.

Scarecrow

See **Bird.**

Scenery/Landscape

V: Dreaming about a sunny landscape or beautiful scenery: many of your wishes will come true; you can look forward to happy times. If the scenery is dark and cloudy: conflicts with the world around you. What else do you see—**Meadows, Mountains, Valley, Water?**

School, Student

V: Dreaming about being back in school as an adult: pay attention to things from your childhood and your past; in addition: life wants to teach you a lesson, to make you understand that we are all "students." Looking at a school building: you continue making the same mistakes—it is time to learn from past experiences. Seeing a student: somebody wants to play a trick on you.

D: Are you revisiting experiences that you haven't come to terms with yet? If that is not the case, the dream is showing you the "school of life" and challenging you to learn from past experiences. Maybe you are going to be "tested" in the near future.

Scissors

V: Looking at a pair of scissors: when two people fight and you get in the middle, guess who gets hurt! Both will turn on you! The dream also indicates an impending separation caused by a woman. In a man's dream, cutting with scissors means a relationship with a woman is ending.

D: In men's dreams, scissors often have to do with a fear of castration or impotence. Generally speaking, scissors mean losing a loved one, but it might also be a call to end a relationship at last. Scissors also stand for irony, sarcasm, and harsh criticism that you yourself are guilty of, or that others use toward you. In scissors dreams, other symbols have great meaning.

Scorpion

S: The scorpion is a mortal enemy of people; it is a symbol of demonic, life-, and health-threatening powers.

V: Seeing a scorpion: you have secret enemies—try to confront them. Getting bitten by a scorpion: one of your enemies is giving you a great deal of trouble.

D: This animal represents biting sarcasm, cynicism, aggression, and bitterness. Either you are the perpetrator or the victim. If you are the victim, someone or something will negatively influence your life.

Screen (Folding)

V: Seeing a folding screen: you are hiding something from yourself or someone is hiding something from you.

Screw, Vise

V: Looking at screws: hold on to everything you own. Losing a screw: a very profitable relationship is coming to an end. Watching others work on a vise: it is likely that you'll find yourself in a very tight spot. Working on a vise yourself: you are able to extricate yourself from a difficult situation. Working a screw into something: you have a well-rounded personality and your relationships are getting stronger. A loose screw: a relationship is coming to an end.

D: Seeing a screw: you want to strengthen and protect what you have already accomplished, making sure that your future is secure. The vise is an obvious sign that you are in a very tight situation right now. Get out of it, let go!

Sea

V: If the sea is calm and the sky is clear: peaceful days are ahead. If the seas are stormy and the waves high: you feel threatened and are afraid of "stormy" times. You are swimming: friendly, if invisible, energies are carrying you right now. Falling into the water: a tragic event. Drowning: a harmful situation has been avoided, because you are discovering the substance of your being. Emerging from the sea: a new beginning, one that is in harmony with your very essence. A man dreaming of standing on a beach means he wants to be free and independent.

D: The sea is a symbol of the collective unconscious; you can trust it to carry you. It may also be a symbol of your feminine, motherly side—all life originated in the sea. Unconscious thoughts, feelings, perceptions, and hopes are at home here and are now beginning to surface and become conscious. This is the sea on which the boat of your life is sailing. See **Archetypes, River, Ship, Water.**

Seal

D: Since these animals live in the water, they represent energies rising from your unconscious—try to make use of them! If you dream about seals frequently, it may be because you are concerned about their fate and identify with them. What the seal is doing and the rest of the dream images will provide further insight. See **Water.**

Seal, Sealing Wax

V: Seeing the seal (on a document): you are looking at a "done deal." Seeing a sealed document: you are looking for security and it will be provided. Sealing a letter: you are determined—and will go to any lengths—to keep a secret. Seeing sealing wax: you are excited about a new contract.

D: Seeing something already sealed means that you need to accept a decision—resisting it would be futile. Have you sealed something or received something from someone else that was sealed?

Secretary

V: A secretary in a man's dream usually expresses his desire for an erotic relationship with his real secretary. In other dreams, the secretary represents an area in your life that, while important, plays a secondary role. To find out more about the dream, observe what the secretary is doing.

Secretary of . . . (State, etc.)

V: Dreaming about a member of the cabinet means being faced with decisions for which you would rather not take responsibility. Seek professional advice!

Secrets

V: If somebody is telling you a secret: it's a good sign, promising a new relationship or a new friend. Betraying a secret, however, will bring shame and misfortune.

D: Dreaming about secrets refers to something you know but won't admit, because you are still in denial. This dream is a clear indication of self-deception. Lift the veil of secrecy—the sooner the better!

Seeds

V: If you are sowing something in your dream: whatever

you start right now is sure to bring success—particularly at work.

D: Seeds are a sign that you are gaining new insights and that the chances for personal growth are excellent. See **Germ.**

Self-Image

D: Seeing a picture of yourself: you believe that your actions, words, and conduct define who you are. Seeing a portrait of yourself: you haven't been honest with yourself lately and are overimpressed with your own opinions and talents. See **Picture.**

Sentence

V: Dreaming about being sentenced: you need to take care of a few unpleasant matters. Someone is sentenced to death or sent to prison: you are involved in a questionable matter that could cost you your reputation. You are pronouncing sentence: someone is right and you are wrong.

D: A dream about sentencing means that you are settling a score with yourself (if you are the defendant) or with the outside world (if you are the judge). Maybe you are revisiting an old argument. Or one part of you is in conflict with and is sitting in judgment over another part of you? Sometimes people work through an actual legal argument in their dreams. Were you the defendant in the dream or the prosecutor? The rest of the dream symbols should provide additional insight.

Serpent

S: The serpent is a symbol of self-renewal and profound wisdom, and also of the dragon.

V: Seeing a serpent: be careful dealing with other people—somebody has it in for you—a healthy mistrust would be prudent. If you are bitten by a serpent: avoid disagreements and don't get involved in the affairs of others—both could have potentially harmful consequences. Are you trapped in an unhappy relationship? In a young girl's dream, serpents frequently indicate a fear of the power of male sexuality. In the dream of a mature woman, the dream might indicate fear of a rival. In a man's dream, seeing a serpent could mean that a woman wants to seduce him. It could also be a warning that a conniving woman is after him, or about false friends or deceitful people. In general, however, the serpent is a phallic symbol and being bitten by a serpent indicates repressed desires for sex and erotic pleasures, which will soon be more powerful than ever. Seeing a white serpent: you will receive either a wise or a secret message. If a serpent is shedding its skin: you have grown beyond your limitations, because you have shed your timeworn existence and personality. Looking at the serpent of the caduceus (the symbol of physicians): your emotional conflicts will be healed. See **Viper.**

D: The serpent symbolizes psychic energy. For women, it is a symbol of a fear of, as well as a desire for, male sexuality, though it can also be used as a weapon against the opposite sex. As a phallic symbol, the serpent might refer to temptation, seduction, and unbridled urges. A white, yellow, or golden serpent means spiritual insight and experience; a red serpent stands for strong sexual needs; an orange-colored serpent refers to a combination of idealism, emotions, and sexuality; a blue serpent stands for religiosity; a violet serpent is a symbol of intellectual power; a green serpent promises emotional energies and budding hopes. In any case, the serpent awakens unconscious energies that influence your feelings, urges, and instincts, bringing them into awareness where they will shape your personality. The serpent can and will greatly increase your self-knowledge. It is a very important dream symbol!

Servant

D: Dreaming about a servant means you are much too

subservient and humble toward others. The dream stands for your conscious and unconscious feelings of inferiority. The servant is also a warning to beware of false friends who are out to take advantage of you.

Sewing

V: Dreaming about sewing means prosperity through hard work. If a man is sewing something and is pricked by the needle, more likely than not a wedding is in the near future. See **Needle.**

D: If you are sewing two pieces of fabric together: you want to "join" another person; or you want to minimize the contradictions of your strength and weaknesses. See **Zipper.**

Sexuality

D: Dreaming about sex may be a sign of repressed or hidden erotic desires, but it often reflects problems you have with your sexual performance or that of your partner. The rest of the dream symbols are very important. See **Intercourse, Rape.**

Shadow, Shade

V: Seeing your own shadow: detach from negative friends—troubles and grief are at your door. Sitting in the shade: be careful—someone is about to cheat you. Seeing the shadows of objects: you are worrying for no reason—the danger you see exists only in your imagination!

D: The shadow represents your present uncertain situation. You are ambivalent. But the shadow is also a symbol of your unconscious. Seeing a shadow ahead or in front of you: you are "projecting" into the future. Seeing a shadow behind you: you are holding on to old fears and feelings of guilt. Or do you believe that you are standing in someone's shadow? Other dream images might tell the tale.

Shaft

V: Seeing a deep mine shaft: try to get to the bottom of things and explore what is hidden there—inside yourself and others.

D: See **Cave, Mine.**

Shark

D: A shark is always a warning not to harm others—control this impulse, even if it's difficult! Being bitten or even devoured by a shark: others are harming you and you let them! Sometimes the shark can also be a symbol of deceit: you are being deceived or you are trying to deceive others. See **Predator.**

Shaving, Shaver, Razor

V: If you are shaving: don't let others talk you into something; people are playing games with you. If someone else is shaving: deception is underfoot—someone is about to cheat you. Watching someone else shaving: don't get involved in a questionable project.

D: A razor stands for a keen, logical, analytical mind ("razor sharp"). Sharp-edged logic, however, can quickly deflate feelings, emotions, and intuitive talents. You are walking on the razor's edge. See **Beard, Hair.**

Sheep

V: Seeing one or more sheep means difficult times are on the way. Shearing a sheep: you are taking advantage of other people and you will have to account for your actions some day. Seeing a flock of sheep: you will be able to generate a good income, because you work diligently and are humble. See **Lamb.**

D: A sheep may reflect your easygoing nature, but also that you are easily influenced and let people take advantage of you. You are often too "soft" and can't say no when dealing with strong personalities. Do you feel like a "dumb" sheep? Do others call or treat you as if you were? Why? On the other hand, are you "a wolf in sheep's clothing"?

Sheets

V + D: Washing sheets means trying to make a quick decision about a very important matter, bringing order to your affairs. Sleeping in pure white sheets: a harmonious marriage. Seeing beautifully decorated or colorful sheets: improved social standing. Sleeping in dirty sheets: strong feelings of inferiority that need to be overcome. See **Bed, Laundry.**

Shepherd

V: Seeing a shepherd and his flock is a good omen: your prosperity will increase and someone will trust you with an important secret. A shepherd alone means losses or diminished prosperity.

D: The shepherd is your guide. He has the power to unite the contradictions in your personality. The dream is a challenge to accept your own conflicting attributes and strengthen your inner equilibrium.

Ship, Shipwreck

S: The ship is a symbol of your journey in life and from birth to death.

V: In a man's dream, the ship represents his longing to love a woman (a battleship stands for a prostitute, a sailboat for a young girl). A departing ship means a separation or change. Being a passenger on a ship: you are dissatisfied with your life and want a change. Boarding the wrong ship: take a close look at your professional and personal relationships and goals—you have made wrong decisions. The ship sinking: a serious warning about an unhealthy relationship.

D: The "ship of your life" can bring you to happy as well as unhappy places. Did the ship travel in "calm **Waters**"? Was it tossed about by waves or a violent **Storm**? Did you know its destination? The rest of the images are very important, because they might indicate if you are on the "right course" or if you should turn around. A shipwreck: a warning that dangers and difficulties that you have created yourself are threatening your life. See **Boat, Ocean, Yacht.**

Shirt

V: Putting on or washing a shirt: you are popular and people will be there when you are in need. Taking a shirt off: pay special attention to your health. Wearing a dirty shirt: people accuse you of having done something wrong and it will be hard to disprove it. Changing shirts means leaving a relationship and finding a new love. Putting on a new shirt: good luck in your love life. Having many beautiful shirts: you will either get married soon or find new friends. A torn shirt means carelessness!

D: The shirt in a dream might refer to erotic desires; it also indicates that you are afraid someone will expose something about you. See **Clothes, Pants.**

Shoemaker

V: Seeing a shoemaker: you will have to spend more money. Also, update the information you already have so that you can advance in your career. A shoemaker is repairing your shoes: a friend is helping you and a project that seemed hopeless is going to turn out okay after all.

D: With help from others you have a changed attitude and correcting a mistake gives you new insight.

Shoes

V: Looking at shoes: you have a lot of errands to run. Putting on a pair of comfortable shoes: you are going to be successful. Wearing shoes that are too tight: the road ahead is going to be hard. Finding a shoe: you will meet a stranger. Giving a pair of shoes as a gift: you either want to get rid of that person or that person is going to walk away from you. Buying a pair of shoes: you have a long way to go before you reach your goal; promises other people have made will not be kept. Looking at worn-down shoes: exercise great care when solving an unpleasant situation. The dream also means that you are unhappy or dissatisfied with your present situation. See **Running.**

Shooting

V: Shooting or hearing shots: extremely good news in the near future. You are speaking frankly in a certain situation. Watching other people shoot: you are pursuing ambitious goals, but need patience and energy to reach them. Hearing a volley of shots: turbulent times and unrest ahead.

D: Shooting means that you suddenly have to choose someone or something. Maybe you are struggling with two voices inside yourself and they are shouting at each other. If you are doing the shooting: if you share your worries and sorrows with someone else—you will be at peace again.

Shop

V: Seeing an empty shop: you don't trust yourself—be more assertive. A shop filled with merchandise: your plans will be met with good fortune and lots of success. Entering a shop: Determination will bring success, but it will cost money.

D: A shop filled with merchandise often represents the many opportunities you have been given in life. It is time now to make choices. See **Merchandise, Shopping.**

Shopping

V: Buying something for yourself: a wish will soon be fulfilled. Shopping for food: your financial situation is taking a turn for the better. Buying toiletries: an invitation to a dinner or a party. Buying a lot of things but not taking them home: you are buying a new business, but the contract has not yet been written. See **Shop.**

Shore

V: Spending time on shore: a mood change, sometimes even a life change, is imminent. Sitting on the bank of a **Brook**: pleasant hours will pass all too quickly.

D: The shore shows your hesitation, because you don't know what direction your life is supposed to take. The shore is the boundary between your ego and the unconscious. Have you found something on the shore? Are you feeling rudderless right now?

Shoulder

V: Someone putting his/her head on your shoulder: an appeal for sympathy and help. If you are putting your head on someone's shoulder: you need comfort or help from a friend.

D: Healthy shoulders are a sign of strength and the ability to master life. Crying on someone's shoulder: stop hiding your emotions—a good friend will support you.

Shovel

V: Working with a shovel: don't expect thanks or rewards, in spite of all your hard work and efforts. Seeing a shovel means someone asked you to do physical labor for them or needs help.

Shrew

V: Seeing a shrew: arguments with your loved one or in your marriage. You are longing for peace and harmony.

D: A shrew is a symbol of marital and relationship problems. Examine honestly if this symbol refers to you or your partner!

Shrinking

V: If something is shrinking: some personality traits are losing their influence over you, because you have changed your attitude. Sometimes this dream may suggest that you pay less attention to appearances; "shrink your need for them down to size." See **Small, Low.**

Siblings

D: Dreaming about your siblings means you are dealing with some of your own character traits that bother you. A fight among siblings means you have conflicting emotions and feelings. A brother is a symbol for the masculine side of you, a sister the feminine side.

Sickle

D: The sickle is a symbol of death.

V: Seeing a sickle: someone around you will insult you; also, a long-held desire will be fulfilled. Working with a sickle: a friend is going to die.

Sieve, Sifting

V: Looking at a sieve: you have acted foolishly and the result will be very unpleasant. Make sure that you keep an eye on things. If you are putting something through a sieve: something you want to do is turning out to be hopeless, and if you proceed you will only be wasting your energy. Using a sieve: somebody is asking you to account for your actions.

D: This is the time to "sift" through things and discard what is useless. The dream is an admonition to be more critical, especially about what you do, and change your materialistic view of the world.

Sigh

V + D: You or someone else is sighing: you can't or won't admit your most passionate longings to yourself.

Signal

V: Hearing a signal is a warning about impending events or certain people. See **Bell, Whistle.**

Signpost

V: Seeing a blank signpost on a house or door: you are facing a confusing situation—try to find a solution or alternate route. Somebody handing you a signpost means pay attention—someone is attacking you and you need to respond quickly. Seeing a sign above a door of a shop: friends are envious of your success and you are right to be annoyed.

D: A sign with instructions on it is a challenge to express more of your personality.

Signs of the Zodiac

D: The twelve signs of the Zodiac reflect your life and its developmental stages, possibilities, and experiences. If you meet any one of the following symbols in your dreams, the "central tasks" described below might be important for that month. See **Astrology, Planets, Star.**

Aries: learn patience and focused action, rein in anger.

Taurus: learn to be more flexible and find your place, rein in your urges.

Gemini: learn to be more sensitive and find a synthesis between that and your tendency to be superficial.

Cancer: learn to be independent and assertive—rein in your self-pity.

Leo: learn what true authority means—rein in your pride.

Virgo: learn to trust—rein in your skepticism toward everything and everybody.

Libra: learn to finally make a decision—rein in your tendency to be dishonest.

Scorpio: learn to say goodbye, to let go—rein in your desire for revenge.

Sagittarius: learn to face unpleasantness—rein in your arrogance.

Capricorn: learn to understand others—curb your tendency to generalize.

Aquarius: learn to do one thing at a time—rein in your restlessness.

Pisces: learn to be alone—rein in your fantasies and your tendency to "run."

Silence

D: Being silent: inner peace, serenity, and even wisdom. "Speech is silver but silence is golden." See **Speech, Speechless.**

Silk

V: Looking at silk fabric means a bright future and exciting events ahead. Buying silk: be honest, are you about to cheat on your lover? Wearing clothing made from silk: you would love to have the admiration of other people. Are you hiding feelings of inferiority? Weaving silk fabric, or spinning silk thread yourself: you will have to deal with many uncertainties in life. Are you living in a fantasy world?

D: Are you entertaining grandiose ideas? Would you like to "shine"? Don't overdo it—silk tears easily! See **Clothes, Velvet.**

Silver

V: Looking at things made from silver: your personal

affairs are proceeding extraordinarily well and your future looks promising.

D: Silver, ruled by the moon and the sign of Cancer, is a symbol of your soul and your feminine, emotional side. See **Signs of the Zodiac.**

Singing

V: Singing a song: right now you are at peace and happy. Hearing a choir: many meaningful hours ahead. Hearing or singing a happy song: expect good news. Hearing a sad song: bad news. Singing a sad song: you're melancholy and you worry too much.

D: Singing means that you are at peace with yourself and the world around you. A song in a dream: you are remembering past experiences and emotions. Was the song sad or happy? See **Music, Song, Yodeling.**

Sinking

Seeing a ship sinking: stay away from a risky enterprise. Dreaming about "the end of the world": a new phase in your life is beginning—let go of the old! See **Boat, Ship, Water.**

Sister

V: Seeing your sister in your dream: you are in the best of health. If you dream that your sister has died: your life will take a turn for the worse. Saying goodbye to your sister: you will be on your own in the near future. Seeing a nun: you will receive help in a dire situation. A woman dreaming about a nun: be more helpful to others. See **Nun.**

D: If you have a sister, the dream will reveal the real relationship you have with her. Sometimes the dream may refer to character traits that, while similar, do not quite match those of your sister. See **Siblings.**

Skeleton

S: The skeleton is the personification of death, as well as a promise and "instrument" of a new stage in life.

V: Seeing a skeleton is a reference to your innermost convictions and the essence of your personality—never ignore it. Ancient dream interpretations state that the skeleton is a promise of a very long life. See **Bones, Cadaver, Death.**

D: A skeleton is a symbol of the past and death and a sign of profound fear (fear of death, death wishes, etc.) Frequent dreams about skeletons might suggest that you need to consult with a psychotherapist.

Ski, Skier

V: A skier in a dream is a reminder that the best way to reach your goals is to be flexible and make use of your skills. Skiing downhill: sometimes things get worse faster than you think.

D: With skis, difficult situations are dealt with quickly. Are you going uphill on skis or down? Are you going as fast as you can without going out of control? The other images will tell you if the dream is positive or negative.

Skin

V: . Seeing wrinkled skin: count on living to a ripe old age. If the skin has a yellowish tint: you are too anxious about something. It also suggests you be prepared for intrigue.

D: The skin is a symbol of how the world sees you, what impressions you give. Has the past left traces in your face? Are you more thick-skinned? Thin-skinned?

Skirt

V: In men's dreams: seeing a beautiful skirt means winning the favor of a charming woman. Seeing a very short, tight skirt: you will meet a frivolous woman. Seeing a wide skirt: you are having an affair with a woman and the wheels of gossip are turning. In women's dreams: seeing a wide skirt: you are going to be faced with an embarrassing situation. Seeing a short, tight skirt: a man will make improper advances—but through no fault of your own. Seeing a worn-out skirt: right now you are not having much luck with the opposite sex—get ready for a disappointment. Seeing a beautiful skirt: good luck with the opposite sex. See **Clothes, Pants.**

D: A skirt, like pants, is a sign of your erotic desires and needs—a slip would be even more so: you clearly are ready for romance.

Skull

S: The skull is a symbol of the impermanence of life, and also of the uppermost part of the human body.

V: Seeing a skull: a reminder to be honest and to look at reality with a sober mind. If you can do that, you are going to succeed. Digging somewhere and finding a skull: you will receive a monetary gift.

D: See **Head, Skeleton.**

Sky

S: The sky is the seat of heavenly beings who are greater than humans; it is the manifestation of transcendence, a symbol for the sacred order of the universe.

V: Looking at a cloudless, blue sky: your plans will be successful; it also means great joy in the near future. A cloudy sky: worries, obstacles, or an uncertain future. If you are looking at **Stars**: a great desire is being fulfilled.

D: The sky stands for the emotional strength that influences your life, though you may not be aware of it. Dreaming about "being in heaven," or "seeing heaven" means you have either reached this state or are striving to get there. Do you feel like being in "seventh heaven" right now? See the chapter **"Colors in Dreams—Blue."**

Skyscraper

V: A skyscraper is a symbol of emotional frustration; the building itself is a phallic symbol and related to sexual desires. Do you feel isolated? Do you feel you are walking through life as a nameless person? If a woman dreams about a skyscraper without windows: her partner is emotionally unavailable.

D: Living in a skyscraper: you are in the wrong place, because the atmosphere is detrimental to your emotional health. In all other cases, the dream is a reminder: limit your expectations—you have set your hopes too high. See **House.**

Slave

D: Seeing male or female slaves is a sign of strong cravings, urges, and passions that have "enslaved" you. Only a courageous effort to free yourself will prevent more damage to your psyche.

Sled

V: Seeing a sled: adjust to the way things are now or you won't get ahead. Riding on a sled: a good omen for quick success—in love and work. If the sled flips over: your love will intensify. See **Ice, Snow.**

Sleeping, Bedroom

V: Looking at people sleeping means great happiness ahead. Looking at one person sleeping: your love relationship will deepen. Sleeping outdoors: a trip in the near future is possible. Sleeping in a wagon or boat: restless days are ahead; be on guard and don't let people talk you into anything. Looking at a bedroom: your greatest wish is not to be alone anymore—to find someone.

D: Sleep is the symbol of your unconscious fear of or flight from reality. Do you have unknown talents you need to "wake up" ? A bedroom is a sign of your sexual needs. Bedroom dreams usually appear when something is wrong in an intimate relationship. See **House, Room.**

Slide (Children's)

V: Seeing a slide: the pleasure you are pursuing is a waste of time. The dream is also a warning: don't get involved in "slippery" adventures, you could end up "going down the chute."

Slime

V: Thick slime might indicate intellectual laziness or a general lack of vitality, or that your personal growth is stagnating. On the other hand, are you hiding needs and desires you find disgusting? Such "emotional slime" should be "coughed up" quickly!

Sling, Noose

V: Having a noose around your neck: you have acted unethically and are now faced with the consequences. Try to find an honest solution quickly. A sling lying in the road: be cautious in business transactions—someone is setting a trap.

D: Are you trying to catch something or someone? Are you afraid someone is trying to catch you? Paying attention is now the best way to avoid danger, and stick to your agenda.

Slingshot

V + D: Using a slingshot: someone is planning a nasty attack. Watching others use a slingshot: somebody is planning something treacherous, and your defenses are not what they should be.

Slipper

V: Wearing torn slippers: a crisis in your relationship or marriage. Wearing worn-out slippers: are you planning to break out of your marriage or a relationship? It would be wise to stay—you won't manage your "new life" any better. Looking at slippers: don't be timid—be more assertive. Buying slippers: you are about to do something very stupid. Wearing wooden clogs: you are too domineering.

D: You either live with an overbearing partner or you are looking for a secure and comfortable life: which it is, you need to figure out for yourself. See **Clothes, Shoes.**

Slope

V: Sliding down a slope: expect unpleasant events; also possible defeat as a result of your own actions. Looking up a steep slope: you still have time to change your present course of action. Standing at the edge of a cliff: fear of a personal failing or future problems. See **Abyss, Cliff, Precipice.**

Small

D: Seeing yourself as small is a sign of your inferiority feelings. If other things or people appear small: you did not make a great impression on them. See **Tall, Big.** Are you making yourself smaller than you really are? And if so, why? Are you trying to make problems smaller than they are in reality? See **Midget, Shrinking.**

Smell

V: Pleasant smells/fragrances are a sign of positive emotions, while foul smells indicate that the feelings you have for another person are dying—or that something in your environment—or your life—"stinks to high heaven."

Smoke

V: Watching smoke rise: you will either enjoy domestic bliss or find refuge at someone else's place. Seeing thick, biting smoke: resistance from others and a fight you can't avoid. Seeing white smoke: you are lucky now, but know that it will last only a short time.

D: Dark smoke is a sign of trouble to come; light smoke means temporary happiness. Sometimes smoke indicates nervousness and anxiety, or that tendencies lurking under the surface have become habitual.

Smoking

V: If you are the one smoking: you are dissatisfied with yourself and the world. Smoking in smoke-free areas: you are bent on getting your own way, regardless of the consequences. Watching others smoke: someone's behavior is bothering you. Offering cigarettes to someone: you are getting closer to a person you have admired for a long time.

D: See **Cigar, Smoke, Tobacco.**

Snail, Snail Shell

S: The snail is a symbol of resurrection and also virginity.

V: Seeing a snail: your motto should be "slowly but surely"! A snail retreating into its shell: you expect something from someone, but are being kept in suspense. Eating snails: you are trying the patience of another person to the limit! Crushing a snail underfoot: your carelessness is putting you at a great disadvantage—serves you right!

D: The snail symbolizes your sensitivity and vulnerability. The snail shell is a sign that you are looking for a retreat or just to be left alone. See **Turtle.**

Sneezing

V: Dreaming about sneezing means that you are correct in your assumption that something is not quite right after all.

D: Sneezing is a sign of a sudden self-cleansing process that you have initiated. Suddenly everything becomes clear, your head is clear. You have new insights or a new idea is going to solve a problem. See **Nose.**

Snout, Trunk

V: Seeing an elephant's trunk: you want to cast a wide net and take something that is not yours. In men's dreams, it is often a desire to start an affair with a married, or otherwise "already attached" woman. The trunk, however, also suggests you look inside and find out who you really are.

D: The trunk is usually a symbol of sexual energies that need to surface soon. See **Elephant.**

Snow, Snowstorm, Snowman

V: Seeing snow: some of your desires are not being fulfilled. Seeing thick snowflakes: you have to solve quite a few problems in your private life. Melting snow: you will solve a crucial problem; the whole matter is disappearing. Seeing a snowman: a warning about being indifferent and "frosty" to the people around you, or your partner may be emotionally cold. A snowstorm; difficult times are ahead, but don't worry—you'll get through. See **Storm.**

D: Sleeping in the snow: things from your unconscious will be known as soon as the "snow has melted." People who are emotionally cold often dream of snow. Seeing a snowman may symbolize aging, or cold, frozen emotions. A snowstorm: a warning of dangers and conflicts to come, which are made worse by your emotional coldness.

Snuff

V: Snuff is a sign of troubles to come. Are things or events stuck right now? Vent your anger and things will move along much better.

Soap, Soap Bubbles, Foam

V: Looking at soap: take better care of your reputation and appearance. Seeing soap bubbles: you are living too much in fantasy land. Washing your hands with soap: you feel very guilty and need to make amends; in another matter, however, you are being wrongfully accused of something. See **Bathing, Washing.**

D: A soap dream encourages a process of self-cleansing and freeing yourself from an old guilt. Soap bubbles mean you are entertaining too many illusions and the bubbles will burst soon. The dream wants to warn you that there is nothing there for you to hold on to—the illusions will come to an end. Foam is a symbol of churning emotions like **Aggression, Anger,** or **Rage.**

Soccer

D: Dreaming about playing soccer is always a warning that you are too casual in your private and professional life.

Socks

See **Stocking.**

Sofa

D: This piece of furniture stands for comfort or the memory of past, happy events. See **Furniture, Chair (Upholstered).**

Soldier

V: Seeing a soldier: be steadfast and stand faithfully by your decision. Being pursued by soldiers: you need to deal with and solve many difficult problems. Women dreaming about a soldier: they are about to have an affair. Men dreaming about a soldier: difficult times are ahead. Dreaming about soldiers at war: fierce confrontations are ahead.

D: The soldier suggests being more disciplined and fitting in better. Practicing self-discipline right now would solve many problems. In women's dreams, a soldier often expresses sexual needs. See **Military, Officer, Recruit, War.**

Son

V: A father dreaming about a son: he wants someone to acknowledge that he is a good father. If you are the son: put your trust in your "higher power" and don't resist when someone asks or demands something from you. Seeing your own son: it is either a "telepathic" moment or a premonition about your son.

D: If the above does not apply, the dream might suggest that you are emotionally off center, because you are developing new traits (in the case of a son: more masculine traits, if a **Daughter**, more feminine traits). See **Child.**

Song

V: Hearing a song in a dream is an indication of great mood swings. Is it a serious or a happy song? Does it come from a distance or from near by? Do you hear solo voices or a choir? Pay more attention to your emotional state of mind. See **Singing.**

D: A happy song might mean emotional well-being. But it might also suggest you want to cover up unpleasant feelings with a lot of words.

Soot

V: Seeing soot: you have to finish an unpleasant task, but you will be successful. Cleaning a sooty **Oven** or **Chimney**:

you have trusted people and have been bitterly disappointed—or is it the other way around?

D: Soot is a warning: others are trying to slander and gossip about you. You are losing faith—or have you "soiled" yourself (See the chapter **"Colors in Dreams—Black"**). Sometimes the dream refers to an unpleasant task—"a dirty job"—that needs to be finished. See **Pitch.**

Soul

D: Are you selling your soul in the dream? To whom or why? Your overly materialistic attitude may go as far as you selling yourself. Are you losing your soul? If that is true, you are losing a vital part of your individuality. How did it come about? The dream is a serious warning, demanding your attention and countermeasures—as soon as possible. See **Name.**

Soup

V: Eating soup: you have "made your bed—now lie in it"! Soup is often a symbol of difficulties or problems you have either caused or initiated. Or has someone else "put too much salt into your soup? See **Salt.**

South

D: This "corner of the compass" is a symbol of consciousness that is primarily formed by spiritual experiences and insights. The South is the land of warmth and will powerfully influence your life. See **Four Corners of the Compass.**

Spade

V: With a spade we unearth things that hide beneath the surface—the side of our personality that is invisible to the world. In a positive sense the dream symbolizes the continued hard work you do in order to grow. See **Pickax, Shovel.**

Sparrow

V: Seeing a flock of sparrows: ugly gossip is the cause of many quarrels. Catching a sparrow: you are a frugal person. Listening to a sparrow twittering: you will have a fun get-together with friends.

D: Are you looking for diversion and company? Is the sparrow warning you about the gossip in your neighborhood? Find out!

Speaking, Talking

V: This points to your social skills or your wish to be better understood by the people around you. Pay attention to what is said and by whom! See **Deafness, Stuttering.**

Spear

D: The dream is a symbol of your tendency, when angry, to hurt other people. But it may also indicate that you need to defend yourself vigorously against unjust criticism. See **Arrow, Weapon.**

Speech

V: Speaking aloud in your dream: you are having an argument with yourself. If someone is talking to you: you are getting on people's nerves. Giving a speech: you are too ambitious. Listening to someone else's speech: a warning not to let other people talk you into things. See **Speaking.**

D: Are you trying to make others understand you better? Have you decided finally to speak your mind, express your opinion? Do you feel misunderstood or ignored right now? For a person who normally is not talkative, the dream is a challenge to be more courageous and assertive. For more outgoing people, it is a warning about being too ambitious, too talkative, and too pushy. You know which of the above applies to you!

Speechless

V: Being speechless: you are unable to express your emotions and desires. This dream warns of your inability to "speak out" in real life. See **Silence, Speaking.**

Sphinx

S: The sphinx is a mysterious creature with a human head and an animal body.

V: Seeing a sphinx: this puzzling creature poses a question: have you proven yourself reliable and worthy or are you living blissfully without concern for others? Take an honest look at how you live your life.

D: A sphinx always symbolizes the puzzling nature of human life, the meaning of life and the question of life after death. Maybe this dream will provide answers to some of these questions for you.

Spice

D: The "spice of life" is often diversion, change, adventure, or fun of all kinds. Do you wish for any of the above? Or is the dream a warning that there is too much "spice" in your life?

Spider, Spiderweb

S: The spider is a symbol of sinful, poisonous cravings.

V: Seeing a spider: honest efforts and hard work promise you happiness. Dreaming about a spider on your skin: be prepared for worries and provocation. Much of what matters to you right now is hanging on a "thin thread."

D: On one hand, the spider is skillful and creative—a symbol of good luck, but on the other, it represents female seduction and the "devouring" of the male! Which of the two fits you? The spider is often a sign of your self-hatred because of your sexual desires. The spiderweb may indicate an over-protective mother who interferes with her child's (usually the dreamer's) chances to develop and grow up. If the latter scenario fits, do something about it—and do it soon.

Spilling

V: Spilling a drink: you are either very careless or have wasted your energies.

Spinning Wheel

V: A woman dreaming about a spinning wheel: she will make a good housewife, find a good husband, or both. A man dreaming about a spinning wheel: a matter is coming to a quick end, but he will think about it for some time to come.

D: You are either enjoying comfort and security at home or you are looking for a life where all parts are woven into a harmonious whole!

Spiral

S: The spiral is a symbol of eternal renewal, repetition, and the cyclical nature of evolution.

Spiral Staircase

V: Seeing a spiral staircase: this complicated structure is always forcing us to move in tight circles. You will be thrown back on your own devices. Try to get off the merry-go-round.

D: See **Stairs, Steps.**

Splinters

V: Seeing a splinter: others want something from you and you are resisting. See **Thorn.**

D: Dreams about splinters are a sure sign of quarrels ahead and mean you are either rebelling against everyday problems or against sexual practices you find masochistic or sadistic and therefore unnatural.

Spoon

V: Looking at one or several spoons means you will receive an invitation soon. You are being fed with a spoon: somebody is treating you like a child. Looking at a silver spoon: you are envious of others who are better off than you. Eating something with a spoon: you have to eat the soup you have cooked yourself. Looking at a big wooden spoon: you have little say-so at home—someone else is "wearing the pants."

D: The spoon is usually a sign that you have maneuvered yourself into a limiting situation or position and only you can get yourself out of it!

Spring (as in Source)

S: A spring is a symbol of femininity and fertility. It represents eternal life and rebirth.

V: In a woman's dream, the spring is a symbol of virtue and purity. Either the dream is an expression of fear of losing your virginity; or you feel guilty (are there several lovers in your life?) because you lost it. Looking at a spring: direct your ideas into the proper channels and the waters will refresh and rejuvenate you. Drinking from a spring: you will reach old age in good health. Taking water from a muddy spring: you will have to deal with dishonest people. Drinking from a clear spring: the successful completion of a project.

D: The spring is a symbol of your striving for emotional clarity. See **Brook, River, Water.**

Springtime

V: Dreaming about spring indicates the beginning of a very pleasant period, a new love, or your wishes come true. A man dreaming about spring, when he is either in or has come through a mid-life crisis, means he is looking in vain for something very specific.

D: Often dreams about spring express sexual feelings and

desires. On a spiritual level it means your positive qualities are breaking through. Everything right now is blessed with success; the outlook is good.

Sprout, Sprouting

D: The sprout stands for your potential. Sprouting represents the "inner seed," which will grow because of your efforts or external influences. See **Seed.**

Spy

D: A dream about a spy is a serious warning: your distrust of people is almost pathological—bordering on feelings of persecution. Or the dream may be pointing to a situation in which people are actually spying on you. If you are the spy: you want to explore your unconscious and get a better understanding of other people and situations.

Square

V: Seeing a square: you are caught up in a serious problem—take care of it as soon as possible. Stay calm and collected and things are going to work out just fine.

D: The square is a symbol of a certain emotional strength and stability. See the chapter **"Numbers in Dreams—Four."**

Squirrel

V: Seeing a squirrel: single people will get married soon; married people will have children. Seeing a dead squirrel: a relative will come down with an illness. Watching a squirrel eating: a symbol of a happy, quiet family life. Being bitten by a squirrel: a problem-prone family member is giving reasons for worry. Watching a squirrel "squirrel away" food: you, too, should prepare soon for "lean" times.

D: Usually this animal is a symbol of your private life—marriage, pregnancy, or family life in general—(depending on the rest of the dream). Since the squirrel is a master in providing for the future, the dream might encourage you to do likewise!

Stag

V: Seeing a stag means you have been given an opportunity to assert yourself. Shooting a stag: receiving an inheritance or something else of value. Hunting or pursuing a stag: you are chasing a hopeless situation—use your time more wisely. Standing next to a killed stag: you will successfully defeat your enemies or rivals. A woman dreaming about a stag with large antlers means she is looking for sexual adventures. See **Antler.**

Stage

V: Being on stage: do you want to be successful on the job without working for it? Seeing other people on stage: you are envious and don't want to admit it! Take a good look at yourself: are you really honest and forthright—with yourself and others?

D: A stage might indicate that you want more respect; or you are recognizing your desires, interests, and hopes as a "stage of your life." Do you want more attention—do you want to be in the limelight? Is there a drama in progress on stage? See **Actor.**

Stain

V: Dreaming that your clothes are stained: take a close look at your habits and behaviors—the impression you make on others is very negative. Grease stains on your clothes: a marriage might make you prosperous. Soiling your clothes: you are about to make a mistake. See **Fat.**

D: Stains are often signs of a bad conscience, feelings of

guilt, or too casual an attitude toward life. Which is it in your case?

Stairs

V: Climbing stairs: you are on a spiritual journey that will lift you above the common confusions of everyday life, but here, too, you will have to deal with obstacles. Walking down a flight of stairs: after much effort, relief is in sight; you are getting back on solid ground. Falling down a flight of stairs: you are either waking up from a dream or will receive painful, sobering news. See **Ladder, Steps, Spiral Staircase.**

D: Stairs are either a sign of your desire for ecstatic sex or for more influence, power, and authority. Do you want to get to the top? If your climb up the stairs is easy, you will gain new insights.

Stall (as in a stable)

V: Seeing stalls with healthy animals is a promise of future wealth. A stall with healthy **Horses** means that you will win a substantial amount of money.

Stallion

V: Seeing a stallion: you are attracting the wrong people and are in for a disappointment. For men as well as for women, dreaming about riding a stallion stands for the desire for an intense love life.

D: The stallion is a symbol of male vitality, but more controlled than is implied in a dream about a **Steer**. In a woman's dream, it stands for the hope of finding a dynamic love relationship. In a man's dream it expresses the hope for more intense sexual experiences, increased vitality, and energy. See **Horse.**

Stamp

D: You have made a final decision in a certain matter—given it your stamp of approval. See **Seal**. Does the stamp have your **Name** on it?

Star, Shooting Star

S: The star is the symbol of the bringer of light.

V: Seeing stars in the sky: you will receive good news. Seeing one star right in front of you: listen to the voice within you—it is the guide of your fate. You have a good chance of succeeding but be careful, you have enemies! A star-filled sky is a promise of good fortune, if you don't set your goals too high. Seeing a shooting star: your most ardent wishes will be granted. Stars hidden behind clouds: a possible accident. The dream is a sign that you have lost your inner compass and are on the wrong path. See **Heaven.**

D: Dreaming about stars means you have set high goals for yourself and are searching for greater spiritual awareness. If you are "reaching for the stars," your actions will have negative consequences. A falling star: your hopes and dreams will come true.

Staring

V: Staring at someone: you want to influence that person's opinion and behavior to your advantage. Staring into space: a sign of the dreamer concentrating. See **Hypnosis, Stiff.**

Starving

V: Dreaming that you are starving: you are hungry for food or for love.

D: You are "hungry" for affection and love, neither of which have you found yet. Do something that will nourish you—don't "starve" your soul! Draw the attention of other people to you!

Statue

V: Looking at a marble statue: you are hopelessly in love with someone who is not in love with you. If you are the statue: you are too uptight and rigid, particularly at times when it would be wise to be much more approachable.

D: The statue stands for insensitivity, emotional coldness, or arrogance. Taken all together, these character traits will inevitably cause conflicts with others and within yourself.

Steam

V: Billowing steam means that the goals you have set for yourself are ill defined and the dream symbolizes your insecurities and **Aggression**. Your work may have been all for naught and worthless. The steam of a locomotive is a promise of great projects to come your way. Steam from a boiling pot on the stove; pay attention—family differences are about to surface.

D: Steam represents the amount of energy you invest in what you do; it also might be symbolic of anger you have repressed. Maybe you invested more energy in a project than was called for? The dream is a warning to release stress and tension to prevent the "pot" from boiling over or exploding. See **Fire, Water.**

Steep

D: Looking up at a steep road ahead: great efforts on your part will result in spiritual insight. Walking down a steep slope: your morals have gone "downhill." The dream might also indicate failure. See **Abyss, Mountain, Path, Road.**

Steering Wheel, Helmsman

V: Seeing the wheel of a boat or ship means that you are pursuing the wrong path—turn back!

D: Your personality is determining the direction of your

life's journey. The steering wheel stands for your will power. If the helmsman you see is a teacher or clergyman: you are pursuing intellectual and spiritual goals; if it is a businessman, your interests are mainly monetary. If an artist is holding the steering wheel: you want to be creative in your search for self-determination.

Step

D: Stepping toward something: reaching your goal will be easy—but don't become arrogant along the way. Taking one step at a time: you are approaching your goal systematically. See **Walking.**

Steps

V: Seeing steps: you hope that your boss will support you in your attempts to get a promotion, or that he will help protect you in your present position. Steps may also be a symbol of the stages of your personal growth—the dream is encouraging you to take the "next step." See **Climbing, Stairs.**

Stiff

D: Your principles are too rigid. You are also too formal in your dealings with other people. Stay cool and be tolerant. See **Staring, Statue**.

Stocking

V: Knitting stockings: you will uncover the source of the ugly gossip that is going around. Tearing a stocking while putting it on: you have wronged someone and need to apologize now. Losing a stocking: a planned love affair will cause trouble and tension in the days ahead. Socks are a sign of lax attitudes or questionable desires. See **Foot.**

D: The stocking stands for a desire for sex and an intimate relationship.

Stocks

V: Dealing with or buying stocks points to insecurities about business related issues. It is a warning about taking risks. Dreaming about calmly selling stocks indicates improvement in your financial situation. Stocks burning up in dark smoke: expect losses. If they are burning up in bright flames, you will be successful in your profession. See **Fire, Money.**

D: Dreaming about stocks is usually a sign of financial problems. The dream wants you to be very careful when it comes to financial transactions, like buying and selling!

Stomach, Belly

S: The stomach usually symbolizes sensuality and sexual passion.

V: Seeing yourself with a round, fat belly means change for the better in your economic situation . It is also a sign that your sexual desires are very strong. Dreaming about a flat or receding stomach: pay more attention to nutrition and your eating habits (you are not getting proper nourishment). Also, stop taking too many risks and chances right now.

D: In depth psychology, a belly or stomach is considered the "kitchen of the soul," which means that belly-dreams always have something to do with the "digestion" of past emotional experiences—it is time to start "digesting" them. In other cases, it is a purely sexual symbol and refers to erotic passions.

Stomach Trouble

V: Dreaming about having stomach trouble: slow down, you need to "digest" old emotional problems. Don't overreact to a certain situation. Having a stomachache is a warning: you are too materialistic and too focused on sex. If you are actually suffering from stomach problems, you are in a weak position right now and might have to face losses.

D: The stomach represents your "emotional digestion" and the ability to "take in" new things and situations. Stomach problems in a dream are a warning about not overdoing it. What has spoiled your "dinner"? What is "irritating" your stomach?

Stone Wall

S: A stone wall is a symbol of protection and safety.

V: Looking at a stone wall: something is holding you back or obstacles are put in your way (pay attention to the rest of the dream symbols). Climbing over a stone wall: you will find a solution to a confusing situation. Jumping off a stone wall: you are involved in a risky project. Standing on top of a tall stone wall: you have set important and worthwhile goals and you will succeed. See **Mountain, Rock.**

Stones

V: Throwing stones: you have been unfair to someone and this is payback time. Stones lying on the street: start to do something that should either have been completed already or that you have abandoned. You have passed up many opportunities. Was it you who threw the stones in your path? Looking at stones: you will have to put up with people who are very stubborn.

D: Stones are often a sign of emotional coldness, disgust, or lack of empathy. Analyze carefully whether you are on the receiving or giving end. Stones often appear when others have "thrown stones" or other obstacles in your path. See **Rock.**

Stork

S: The stork symbolizes the love of children.

V: Seeing a stork: you will be blessed with many children or have to deal with many children—not necessarily your own. Seeing a stork's nest: peace and harmony reigns in your house. A nest with young storks: you will visit a kindergarten, a children's home, or organize a children's party.

D: The stork is a symbol of the soul and your early childhood. For young people, the dream means they want to have children—for older people, they want grandchildren. See **Swallow.**

Storm

V: Being in a storm: you will face a hard fight and the best defense is good preparation. Struggling through a storm: be prepared for problems and losses. Listening to a storm roaring outside: bad news ahead. See **Air, Hurricane, Thunderstorm, Wind.**

D: The storm is a symbol of strong feelings and fears that have your emotions in an uproar. Storms are usually a sign that you feel your livelihood is in danger. Do something to calm the "inner turmoil" so that you can return to calm and tranquil waters! Getting caught in a storm: expect an emotional storm—you have ignored all warnings so far.

Stove/Heater

V: In a woman's dreams, the stove is the symbol of her partner. Was the oven hot or cold? No fire in the stove: fears that your present relationship is ending. Seeing only one stove: you want to find a partner. Sitting next to a warm stove: your friends always welcome you; you have a partner who loves you. Getting burned means "getting burned" in your love relationship. The oven grill means that love relationships or passions also have adverse effects. See **Fireplace, Oven.**

D: Generally speaking, the stove expresses your need for warmth and safety, but it also indicates sexual desires. Do you have "warm" feelings for someone? Is the stove "cold"? See **Baker, Cook.**

Stove/Range

V: In women's dreams, the image of a stove or range means that everything is well with the family, particularly if a bright fire (without smoke) is burning in the stove. In men's dreams, it means a steady love relationship. Watching the fire slowly burn down: a love relationship or marriage is soon coming to an end. See **Oven.**

D: The stove or range is seen in terms similar to **Fire** and always stands for your emotions. Is the flame of love still burning bright? Are you seeing only "silent embers"? An ice-cold stove indicates a similar condition—ice-cold emotions.

Straw, Straw Hat

V: Seeing a straw hat: you are wasting your time on unimportant things. Also—you are too talkative! Lying on straw: your financial situation will take a turn for the worse. Wearing a straw hat: you will enjoy a few happy, carefree days.

D: The dream warns about taking material risks or indicates an impending crisis. See **Hay.**

Strawberries

S: Strawberries, like violets, are symbols of humility, but also temptation.

V: Enjoying a bowl of strawberries means luck in your love life. See **Apple, Berries, Pear.** Looking at strawberries: the affection you have for another person is growing. Collecting wild strawberries: you would like to have a love affair. Spilling strawberries: disappointment in matters of love. See **Berries, Fruit.**

D: Strawberries symbolize your need for friendship as well as an intimate relationship.

Stream

V: Seeing a stream: important changes are ahead and they

are not necessarily what you would like. Traveling on or swimming in a stream: while not directly involved, you will be dragged into things that create unrest and problems. See **Ocean, River, Water.**

Street

V: Seeing a dark street: many difficulties lie ahead, but they can be overcome with courage. Walking on a road that stretches far into the distance: life may be tough, but patience and perseverance will get you through. Walking on a winding road: check first to see if you are on the right path. A deserted street: you must accomplish the task ahead of you on your own. See **Path, Road.**

D: The street is a symbol of the direction, fate, and goals of your life. The rest of the symbols will tell you if you are on the right road and if you will continue to grow. This dream symbol is important, because it makes you aware of options and possibilities.

Streetcar, Trolley

V: Driving a streetcar: the safety of many people is in your hands—and you are doing a great job. Jumping off a streetcar while it is moving: a sign of risky behavior. Seeing a streetcar: somebody is reminding you of a task you wish you had completed long ago.

D: See **Train.**

Stretcher

S: Seeing a stretcher: don't be too sure you will succeed in a certain matter! Seeing somebody else on a stretcher: somebody in your circle is going to be ill. If somebody is approaching you with a stretcher, an inheritance may change your life. If you are lying on a stretcher: you feel that you are not up to the task at hand; you are helpless, but—even without doing anything—you are receiving help. Being carried on a stretcher: the chances for success are good and the road will be easy. Carrying a stretcher: in an unhappy situation you might be able to salvage something.

D: A stretcher is a symbol of life changes. Being carried on a stretcher means your fate will literally "carry" you; if somebody else is on the stretcher, it usually means illness or death.

String

V: Tying a knot: even if a certain matter looks very difficult right now, the confusion will be resolved soon. Cutting string: you will be painfully disappointed. Looking at a tangled-up ball of string: it's time to bring order into a chaotic situation. Untangling a string: you will have to "grin and bear it" right now. Looking at a straight piece of string: the next few days will be uneventful.

D: A string could be a symbol of the "guidelines" that are giving direction to your life. A string wrapped around a package: success in a certain project. If the string is cut: the project will fail. See **Thread.**

Stuttering

V: Dreaming about stuttering is a sign of feelings of inferiority that influence your relationships in a negative way. Maybe you find it difficult—or you lack the courage—to explain yourself to others or voice your opinion. Speak freely and from your heart—it's easier than you think. See **Speaking.**

Submarine

D: The submarine is a symbol of instincts that (usually unnoticed) are influencing your behavior and life. See **Boat, Diving, Ship.**

Sugar

V: Eating sugar: you are very susceptible to flattery. Buying sugar: you want to win someone over to your side. See **Salt.**

D: What do you want to "sweeten"? Negative experiences, your weaknesses, your life in general? Examine honestly if this is a case of self-deception or if it makes sense!

Suitcase

V: Looking at a suitcase: you are going on a trip soon or you'll get bad news. Buying a suitcase: you will uncover a secret (about yourself or someone else). Getting a suitcase as a gift: prepare for a pleasant surprise. See **Luggage.**

Summer

V: Seeing a summer landscape: you are very optimistic and trusting and both qualities are helping you to succeed in your endeavors.

D: Summer represents the "prime of life." You are full of vigor and vitality, enjoying the best years of your life (in sexual terms as well). You have matured.

Sun

S: The sun is the symbol of prophecy, revelation, and infinity. As the source of light, it gives warmth and makes things visible.

V: The sun is probably the most enduring dream symbol of human beings. It is a symbol of vitality, strength, and optimism. Seeing a sunrise: your future is filled with promises. Seeing a sunset: a certain matter needs to be brought to its conclusion; or you can look forward to a quiet, happy old age. Reflection, peacefulness, and contemplation will enrich you on your journey through life. A "golden" sun is a promise of happiness and good fortune. A red sun means conflicts ahead. The sun shining through a window: your happiness resides within your own four walls. The sun hiding behind clouds: emotional upset and sorrow.

D: The sun is the brightest and most powerful dream symbol and often points to outside influences that affect your life. It is a promise of happiness, success, and joy. A sunset might indicate a serious impending crisis, or that a phase in your life is coming to an end. See **Light.** An eclipse of the sun means you feel temporarily depleted (you are either uncertain or just tired).

Sunday

V: This day of the week might illustrate your religious and spiritual connection to a higher power (See **God, Guru**), or it may simply be a sign that you need some peace and quiet.

Sundial

V: Seeing a sundial is a reminder that nothing ever stays the same. You would do well to enjoy the happy hours while they last. The sundial is a symbol of change, mortality, and the universal laws that govern our lives. Hold the "great moments" in your life in your heart! See **Clock.**

Sunrise

Seeing a red sunrise means a personal situation will slowly take a turn for the better. If you have been suffering for a long time, recovery or relief or emotional renewal is in sight.

D: Something "is dawning" on you! You begin to have a better understanding of other people, obligations, or circumstances. You are finding reasons to be more hopeful. The dream might also symbolize increasing awareness. This is a very beautiful and promising dream symbol.

Sunset

V: Seeing a sunset: the beginning of a "darker" period in your life. A sunset with clouds in the sky: sorrow, trouble, or unpleasantness. A sunset in a cloudless sky at the end of a pleasant dream: contentment and recovery from a present illness.

D: Go within yourself and search for more quiet and relaxation in order to replenish diminished energies.

Surgery

V: Dreaming about surgery could mean physical or emotional problems that need treatment. It could also mean help in your present situation. Someone else in surgery: a sad or even tragic event. See **Hospital, Illness.**

D: Surgery indicates the need to remove something from your emotional life. While the dream sometimes reveals a fear of illness, most of the time it means drastic changes because of something you did.

Surprise

V: A surprise is a reminder to be careful—unexpected problems could suddenly appear.

Suspended Animation

D: Being in suspended animation: repressed emotions have been temporarily lost from consciousness, but they will return and need your attention. In any case, begin changing harmful character attributes (let go of the old) and make room for new and positive attributes. See **Death.**

Swallow, Swallow's Nest

S: In antiquity the swallow was a symbol of light, and in the Middle Ages, a symbol of resurrection.

V: Seeing a swallow means that prospects are good for your love relationship and sometimes also for your professional life. Hearing the sound of swallows: you will finally receive a letter you have longed for for a long time. Looking at a swallow's nest: you will either establish your own little family or create additional space in your home. Seeing a swallow's nest with eggs inside: for younger people it means a child is on its way, and for older people, grandchildren. Destroying a nest: destroying your happiness. See **Stork.**

D: Both symbols are a clear sign of your longing to have a family, love, security, and a happy home. If you are already married, make sure you discuss this dream with your spouse.

Swamp

V: Looking at a swamp: a plan or project already started should be abandoned as quickly as possible—the chances of success are nil. If you are stuck in a swamp and sinking: you are on the wrong path. If you decide on a path that is wrong, it's never too late to turn back!

D: See **Mud, Quagmire.**

Swan

S: The swan is a symbol of light. There is a folk belief that a swan will sing when we die.

V: Seeing a swan: a happy and harmonious marriage. Hearing the cry of a swan: often announces the death of someone. Feeding swans: you will find someone who will be a faithful friend for life.

D: The swan often indicates that others don't understand you or don't reciprocate your feelings (particularly if you see a single swan).

Swimming

V: Dreaming about swimming: you will be successful in life if you let yourself be guided by the strength of your character. Struggling with large waves: difficult tasks are ahead, but don't be discouraged. You'll make it.

D: The water is a symbol of emotions, feelings, instincts, and urges. You have the ability (if you are a good swimmer in the dream) to live in harmony with them, or (as a nonswimmer) have yet to integrate them into your personality. See **Bathing, Water.**

Swing, Rocking Horse

V: Sitting or swinging on a swing: you are too easily influenced by others, have a hard time making decisions and, generally speaking, may be fickle and sometimes downright unreliable. Looking at a swing: it is time to look at your inconsistency. Rocking on a rocking horse: you are frittering away your time; also, what you call love is really infatuation.

D: A swing means your moods are constantly "swinging back and forth." In a man's dream, it also might imply that—if married and having an affair—he can't decide between his wife and his lover. The dream is a warning: make a decision now and be more assertive.

Switch

V: Looking at a switch means you have forgotten something important. It might also be a sign of marital infidelity. Hitting someone with a switch: beware, don't treat others harshly. Making a switch: thoughtless actions on your part will result in a difficult situation.

D: See **Whip, Rod, Cane.**

Sword

D: The sword could be a symbol of your courage, determination, character, chivalry, or love of truth. The way you use the sword is a reflection of how negatively or positively you use these character traits in your life. See **Dagger, Weapon.**

S = Symbol V = Vision D = Depth psychology

Table

V: Looking at an empty table: start taking better care of your family and house. Looking at a table set for dinner: domestic bliss and prosperity.

D: The table usually represents your responsibilities and obligations at work. Are you working at the table? See **Altar, Furniture.**

Tail

S: The tail is a phallic symbol.

V: Seeing a curly tail: you love to tease other people and play practical jokes. Seeing an animal with a long tail: many difficulties lie ahead; everything is dragging out. Holding an animal by the tail: you are "putting the cart before the horse"! Watching an animal wag its tail: happiness is ahead.

D: The tail is usually a sign of sexual needs, instincts, and urges, but also of vigor, and vitality. See the chapter on **"Colors in Dreams—Black."**

Tailcoat

V: Somebody or you yourself wearing tails: your efforts at work are going to be recognized (though the party given in your honor will be boring!). See **Clothes.**

Tailor

V: If you are the tailor: put more effort into staying in shape and be alert to what others expect from you. If you are involved with other people, it is time to pay more attention to your appearance. Sewing your own clothes: your love relationship is going well.

D: You are determined to change your opinions, appearance, or your social conduct. This dream frequently means that you are giving too much weight to outward appearances. See **Clothes.**

Tall, Big

D: Everything that appears to be very tall and very big has made an extraordinary impression on you. Are you feeling small in comparison to what you see? Are you making yourself smaller than you really are? Is something in the dream much larger than it is in reality? Are you "making a mountain out of a molehill"? See **Small.**

Tango

D: This dance is a symbol of an exciting romance, but not a serious one. See **Dance.**

Tank, Armored Car

V: Seeing a tank means difficulties are piling up. Somebody on the job wants to "roll over you"—look for safety. Riding in a tank: you are reminded—rather cruelly—of promises or responsibilities you made some time ago—you need to fulfill them, even if it is difficult.

D: As a weapon, the tank is a symbol of **Aggression.**

Tassel

V: Seeing a tassel: you might be awarded a prize and receive recognition.

D: Tassels usually are a sign of vanity and ambitions. See **Medal.**

Tatters

V: Collecting tattered clothes: painful experiences and melancholy moods. Dealing in old, tattered clothing: you are receiving money under highly unlikely circumstances. Wearing tattered clothes: your social and financial situation is taking a turn for the worse; you have embarrassed yourself, which has made you unpopular.

D: See **Clothing, Garbage, Refuse.**

Taxes

V: Having to pay taxes: you will be very restricted in the near future and feel a loss of self-determination.

Tea

V: Drinking tea: a call for reflection, because you are being pulled into a very confusing situation that can only be resolved with patience and tranquility. See **Coffee.**

D: Tea might be a symbol of your need for peace and quiet, companionship, or relaxation. Your immediate future will bring interesting experiences, new ideas, and new people into your life.

Teacher

S: A teacher in a man's dream represents his father.

V: If a man dreams about a female teacher, it means he has a repressed, sadistic streak—the craving to physically punish, even brutalize others. Seeing a teacher is a warning about thoughtless and frivolous behavior. Talking with a teacher: it is not only the best but also right time to solve long neg-lected problems. If you are the teacher, it means you think you know everything better than anybody else and have a tendency to lecture other people. See **Exam, Test.**

D: The teacher is usually your inner guide who is standing by with helpful advice. The teacher reminds you that life is a continuous test and challenge. The dream is also addressing your self-doubt, challenging you to trust yourself. See **Steering Wheel.**

Tears

V: Shedding tears: sorrowful times are ahead, but they will unexpectedly turn into joy. See **Crying.**

D: Are you depressed right now, crying in your dream? Are you too soft-hearted, with many feelings and too much sympathy?

Telegram

V: A telegram usually announces a surprise—whether positive or negative depends on the rest of the symbols in the dream.

Telephone

V: The telephone says a lot about your personal "connections." A telephone ringing: you will "get the message" about a certain matter. Are you calling long-distance? Are you told the number has been disconnected? Both possibilities are a sign of relationship problems. Being unable to make a connection means that—in real life—you "can't connect" either! Hearing a phone ring: you will soon get a negative reply or cancellation. Having a positive conversation on the phone: expect an important contract. The party you are calling is not answering: you made arrangements for a meeting, but the other party will not show up. Hearing the phone ring in your sleep but you are not answering: you are afraid of your innermost feelings or denying them.

D: The telephone reflects your personal relationships and your contact with your unconscious. Are you feeling lonely? Do you receive few or no phone calls during the day? The rest of the dream symbols are very important because they may give you useful insights or helpful hints.

Television

V: Watching TV: you are easily misled or are entertaining illusions about the future.

D: The TV indicates callous and impersonal coldness, negative emotions that will only spoil your day.

Temple

V: The temple is a place of refuge, a reminder that there is another (invisible) side to life besides the external, everyday world!

D: The temple is your body, the place where spirit and soul reside. The appearance of the temple will tell you how important you think your body, your soul, and your spirit are to you. See **House.**

Tent

S: A tent is a shelter for the shepherd, nomad, soldier, and hiker.

V: Sleeping in a tent: try to live more humbly and be more frugal. Crawling into a tent: someone is providing shelter for you in a desperate situation.

D: The tent is a symbol of the uncertain, impermanent life you have created for yourself. Are you a "nomad," always looking for an emotionally safe place? Or do you simply like risks and adventures, wanting to go through life with as little baggage as possible—since you "can't take it with you" anyhow?

Test

D: Are your abilities about to be "tested? Or do you have to demonstrate your skills? Make sure you examine your attitudes and expectations so that you can pass the challenge with flying colors.

Thaw, Thawing

D: You are at the beginning of an emotional "thaw." Your old habitual behavior, rigid principles, and hardened emotions are beginning to thaw out. The result is more emotional warmth and empathy (for yourself and others). A wonderful symbol, because your soul is thawing out!

Theater

V: Being in the theater: you still have too many illusions about life and the world.

If you have a part in a play on stage: people are looking at you with a critical eye.

D: See **Actor, Stage.**

Thermometer

V: If you are reading your temperature on a thermometer: the thermometer shows your present emotional state: passionate, dynamic people have a high temperature, calm people have a medium temperature, and very sensitive, soft-hearted people may feel cold.

Thermos Bottle

V: This practical device can keep "warm feelings" warm longer, or "cold feelings" cold longer. What is it in your case?

Thief

V: Watching a thief "at work": expect an unexpected

reward in the near future. If a thief has stolen something from you: examine the mistrust you harbor for certain colleagues. Dreaming that you stole something: you are feeling overtaxed either at the job or at home. Being discovered as you are stealing something means disappointment. See **Robbery.**

D: Behind this symbol are often hidden or unacknowledged desires—including for sexual adventures. The thief serves as warning to beware of your own foolishness.

Thirst

V: Dreaming about being thirsty means to beware of false friends. Drinking something and still being thirsty: you are hoping for something you can't have. Being thirsty and finding a bottle that is empty means much heartache in your love life. Giving a drink to a thirsty person: someone will be very grateful to you.

D: Thirst is always a symbol of a person's need for love. See **Drinking.**

Thistle

V: Getting stung by a thistle: don't expect people around you to agree with you. Watering a thistle: don't expect thanks from others right now.

D: The thistle tells you to except misfortunes and disappointments; you have only yourself to blame.

Thorn

V: Being surrounded by thorns: times will be difficult for a while. A woman dreaming about thorns is afraid of venereal disease. Looking at thorns: trouble in the love department. Getting pricked by a thorn: if you are a young girl it means fear of sexual contact. If you are an adult, a friendship might come to an end. Falling into a bush that has thorns: you are getting involved in a confusing situation—getting out of it will be difficult. Wearing a wreath of thorns on your head: you may be involved in much emotional hurt. See **Splinters.**

D: Thorns express your unconscious fear of the "hazards" that come with sexual relationships. Like Sleeping Beauty, the dream for some women indicates that they are waiting for a prince to rescue them.

Thread

V: Winding a thread into a ball: you'll need a lot of patience before you reach your goal. Unraveling a thread: with patience you will uncover a secret. A black thread: unpleasantness and frustration. A white thread: closer contact with some people. A red thread: you are constantly repeating something—find out what it is. Seeing a long thread: something is being dragged out endlessly.

D: The thread is a sign of nervous tension or emotional weakness, and also of shyness and insecurity. Have you lost the thread in a certain matter? Or is it a momentary lack of concentration? Do you have a bad habit that is a thread running through your life? See also the chapter **"Color in Dreams."**

Threat

D: Every threat in a dream confronts you with your insecurities and lack of assertiveness. You also feel uncertain about the future.

Threshold, Ramp

V: Stepping over a threshold: you are going to enter a new phase in your private and professional life, or build a new home. Standing in front of a doorsill: be careful and don't overlook a possibly difficult situation that might "trip you up."

D: You have finally come to a decision, making it possible to find a new direction in life. It is important to know whether you are standing in front of the threshold (still hesitating) or have already stepped across.

Throne

S: The throne is a symbol of authority.

V: Sitting on a throne: you are quite arrogant and would like to be "above" other people and give orders. Reassess your own conduct. Standing in front of a throne: you have set your goal too high.

D: The throne is a symbol of a hidden craving for power and acceptance. See **Castle, Emperor, King, Palace, Prince.**

Thumb

V: In women's dreams, the thumb is not a phallic symbol, but a sign of her productivity and ability to persevere. When the thumb is injured: you are unable to use your energies productively or you are repressing them. Having a very large thumb: you are fearful of losing your freedom; but it also symbolizes courage and a fighting spirit. Cutting your thumb: be prepared for obstacles that people will throw in your path. See **Cutting, Finger, Hand.**

Thunder

D: Thunder in a dream indicates that repressed emotions will soon "break loose." Sometimes it is a warning not to make such a fuss about nothing.

Thunderstorm

V: Seeing a thunderstorm and a dark sky: you are unsettled about something. Watching a thunderstorm from a safe place: you are about to vent your anger and things will change for the better. Getting caught in a thunderstorm means you are on the wrong path and need to turn back. See **Clouds, Hail, Rain, Storm, Thunder.**

D: A thunderstorm stands for a lightning-fast outburst of emotions and a far-reaching, sudden change in your life!

Ticket

Standing in line to buy a ticket: what you need most in the coming weeks is patience. Receiving a ticket to an event: you will meet an interesting person. Buying a ticket for a movie or play: you want to do something interesting with other people.

Tides

See **High Tide** and **Low Tide.**

Tiger, Tigress

V: In women's dreams, this beautiful animal is always a symbol of the longing for powerful erotic sexuality, but at the same time fear (if you are fearful in the dream) of such an experience. This is similar to dreams about a lion. Dreaming about a tiger: be very careful, somebody is sneaking up, waiting for an opportunity to "pounce" on you. Being pursued by a tiger, watch out: a vengeful person is waiting to get even with you. See **Animals, Lion, Predator.**

D: The tiger is the symbol of urges that are beyond your control. This overdeveloped "animalistic drive" is potentially dangerous, unless you can rein it in. The tigress is a symbol of aggressive sexuality in a woman—the tiger of male sexual drives, aggression, and sexual potency.

Toad

V: The toad in a dream has the same meaning as in fairy tales: it means unpleasantness ahead, but when transformed, can be unexpected good luck. The rest of the dream images are very important here. Holding a toad in your hand: you have a good chance of winning something. Killing a toad:

injury or loss that you have caused yourself. Eating a toad: an illness is coming your way.

Tobacco

V: If you are smoking: you are afraid and apprehensive about reality and would rather live in a fantasy world. Inhaling tobacco smoke: you are literally "inhaling" negative thoughts. Smoking a pipe: you are greatly surprised by the realization that home can be very pleasing.

D: A pipe and a cigar are phallic symbols. Other than that, tobacco is a sign that all your efforts are for naught—they are "going up in smoke." See **Cigar, Pipe.**

Toes

V: Looking at toes: make sure your feet are in good shape, because you have to do a lot of walking; or a trip will turn out to be stressful.

D: See **Finger, Foot, Legs.**

Toilet

V: Seeing a toilet: honestly analyze your feelings. Sitting on a toilet: you are getting rid of an emotional or an external burden. Seeing human excrement or producing it: expect a win or additional income. Seeing an empty toilet, on the other hand, means disaster.

D: The toilet is a symbol of relief from emotional ballast, of getting the internal household in order, of unloading unwanted pressure. See **Excrement.**

Tomato

S: The tomato is a symbol of love.

V: Looking at a tomato: your love for someone is growing stronger, and your chances are improving! Eating tomatoes:

you are about to have an affair, but you are taking a risk—it could have disastrous consequences. See **Vegetables,** and the chapter **"Colors in Dreams."**

D: The tomato is a symbol of mature love or passion. If you are ashamed of something, do you turn red like a tomato?

Tomb, Vault

V: Looking into a tomb: repressed fears may be coming up. Digging in a tomb: possibly news of a death. If a tomb is caving in: an illness in the family. See **Cave.**

D: A tomb always points to character traits or fears that you are denying—and that are the reason for present conflicts.

Tone, Sound

V: If you hear a tone: now is the time to "look inside" and discover your true self.

D: See **Music, Signal.**

Tongue

V: Someone is sticking his/her tongue out at you: be careful, you are rather clumsy and about to make a fool of yourself. Avoid all gossip. Seeing a tongue: "watch your tongue." Burning your tongue: your gossip is arousing a negative reaction from others.

D: Sometimes, as a phallic symbol, the tongue may refer to sexual needs, but it is more often related to speaking and cultivating social contact. The dream could mean that you need to share more about yourself. Or maybe talk less? See **Mouth.**

Tools

V: Tools are always a symbol of manual dexterity and practical sense. Have you repaired, improved, or made something more beautiful? Do you need to "improve" something in your life? Do you have talents you didn't know about? You know which of the above fits you! Dreaming about using tools: your work right now will turn a good profit. This dream is also a challenge to become more active in "repairing" something—including a relationship.

Tooth, Dentist

V: Looking at healthy teeth: you are struggling with a certain issue, but success is guaranteed. Teeth falling out: losses are imminent. Loose teeth: you are afraid of losing things or people who you thought were your "property." Looking at the teeth of others: friends or relatives are in a dangerous situation or are aggressive. Going to a dentist: you are in need of professional advice. A tooth has to be pulled: miscalculations on your part are the reason for losses in the near future. You have a toothache: a huge expense is creating havoc in your bank account. A tooth needs to be filled: you made a mistake when trying to solve a problem. Wearing false teeth: pseudo-success is all you will get unless you change your arrogant (hypocritical) attitude. Other people pulling teeth: you want to profit from someone else's misfortune.

D: A woman dreaming about losing her teeth means she is afraid of losing the man she loves. In the case of a man, it means fear of becoming impotent. Teeth are a symbol of either sexual prowess or material goals. Has someone "bared his teeth"? Have remarks you have made been "biting"? People who have a hard time getting through life often dream about teeth! Dreaming about a dentist means that you are afraid that someone is going to hurt you, or that you are hoping that someone is coming to help you in a difficult situation.

Top

D: Moving to the top: you have set lofty goals (hopefully, not too lofty). However, the dream might also mean that you are living too much "in your head." See **Lowly.**

Top Hat, Cylinder

V: The top hat in a man's dream is a phallic symbol. A cylinder appears often, in a man's dream, if he feels he cannot perform sexually as well as he used to. Wearing a top hat: success will bring recognition from friends and the public. See **Hat.**

D: The cylinder from a motor is an indication of your strength and vitality—and you will need both to reach the goals you have set for yourself.

Torch

S: The torch is a symbol of victory, joy, freedom, and liberation. If you see a torch: a secret will be unveiled, or love is knocking on your door. Witnessing or taking part in a torchlight parade: be careful, don't get involved in a hasty love affair. Watching a torch go out or watching one being doused; a dashed hope, or a death in your circle of friends is imminent. See **Fire, Light.**

D: The torch represents a change in your personality, because it illuminates the darkness of the unconscious.

Torture

V: Dreaming about being tortured means either strong emotions or an unhappy love affair. Torturing another person: you are about to do an injustice to another person. Looking at a torture chamber: you are afraid of the consequences of your actions.

D: Dreaming about torture is a sign of a bad conscience; you made a mistake and feel guilty. Sometimes it expresses empathy: you feel "tortured" knowing about people in need and not being able to help.

Towel

V: If you are drying your hands on a towel: you want to get

out of an unpleasant situation. Looking at a clean towel: be sure that you conclude a matter "cleanly"! A dirty towel means more pressure in your life.

Tower, Tower Clock

S: A tower is an artificial axis between heaven and earth.

V: Standing on top of a tower: a good position is within reach. A collapsing tower: your hopes will be dashed. Hearing the clock in the tower ring: time to make an important decision. If a woman is looking at a high tower (phallic symbol), it might be expressing her positive attitude toward male sexuality. Dreaming of being locked up in a tower: she is troubled about male sexuality. See **Clock, Pillar.**

Town Hall

Looking at Town Hall: your chances are good for an honorary appointment or a good job. Walking into Town Hall: you need to deal with a difficult official situation. Doing business in Town Hall: like it or not, you will get a chance to learn from your mistakes!

D: You have to make an important decision. Go slow and think things through before you act! Sometimes Town Hall or its equivalent is a sign that you will receive helpful expert advice. See **Government.**

Traffic

V: Seeing a traffic sign: changes are already in progress and great demands are being made on you. Looking at big-city traffic: a sign that you should avoid turmoil and stress. See **Auto, Train.**

Traffic Accident

V: Dreaming about having an accident: you might be in danger (not necessarily in traffic). Be careful when dealing with others; you also have to face setbacks at work. See **Misfortune.**

D: Are you preoccupied with the idea of having an accident? Or have you hurt or injured someone by your actions?

Train

V: In a man's dream, a train is often a sign of fear—fear of having missed something. The train you have missed in the dream is the equivalent of a missed opportunity in real life. Traveling in a train: you are advancing quickly in life. Watching a train leaving the station: a separation is unavoidable. Seeing a train: you will have to say goodbye to someone. Being on a train that goes through a tunnel: you are giving away one of your secrets. In a woman's dream, a train is a sexual symbol, particularly if it is driving into a tunnel.

D: Riding in a train is symbolic of your life's journey. You are changing your emotional bearings—don't miss your connections! The lead engine symbolizes your vitality; the railroad cars your experiences and adventures: the tracks the values that guide you and give you direction. The trip itself is a symbol of how your life will unfold. See **Train Station.**

Train Station

S: A train station is always a symbol of changes to come in your life or in interpersonal relationships.

V: Arriving at a train station: a decision made previously was correct. If you want to go to the train station but the road is blocked: a few hurdles have to be overcome before change is possible. Leaving a train station: try to determine if you have postponed an important decision for too long; it is time to make that decision now! If you are looking at a train station: a change in your life is imminent. Missing your train: you have also missed an opportunity in your life.

D: Train stations are important dream images. They show us a starting point for examining different goals we have set ourselves in life. Usually a train station means a new phase in your life is about to start. If the train station is under renovation or it is difficult to find the train you want: things you have planned might be in question. See **Train.**

Trap

V: Dreaming about a trap means caution! A questionable person is setting a trap but you will recognize it in time. Stepping into a trap: you fell in love with an unworthy person. Catching someone else in a trap: a long-held wish will be granted.

D: The trap is a warning that a wrong decision could be harmful; hopes and ideals are misplaced.

Travel, Traveler

V: If you dream about traveling, expect things to change, possibly a separation from a close friend will take place, or a break with old habits. Seeing other people travel: you are either going on a trip or someone from out of town is coming to visit.

D: Dreaming about a trip expresses your desire to find a new base from which to continue your life's journey, a new mission, and new projects. Maybe the trip is a journey of exploration—not of the world outside but of the world within—a search for deeper self-knowledge.

Treasure

V: Digging for treasure; you are pursuing a totally useless matter; your motto right now should be "hands off," because you are being hoodwinked. Burying a treasure: your behavior is turning people away and is the reason for your present troubles.

Finding a treasure: keep your eyes and ears open; otherwise, you will walk right past a very promising opportunity.

D: A treasure dream means you are questioning the meaning of your life. You might find a "treasure"—externally or internally. See **Gold.**

Tree

S: An upright structure reaching for the heavens and symbolizing vitality (victory over death), the tree is a symbol of your energies and strengths, ideas, attitudes, and behavior.

V: Sitting under a flowering tree means great personal good fortune. A tree laden with fruit is a sign of a successful life. A leafless, rotten tree means bad luck. A cut-down tree is a warning of illness or disappointment to come. Climbing a tree means you are overly ambitious, so people may not like you much; you are making enemies. Falling out of a tree: disappointments and ridicule from your colleagues. Owning a tree (or several): a long life and good health.

D: The tree is the tree of life. The health, quality, and shape of the dream-tree is an indication of your constitution and vitality. The tree is not only a symbol of physical energy and strength (including your potential) but also the inner strength that dictates your actions. See **Branch.**

Tree Limb

Dreaming about climbing a tree means professional advancement in some unusual way (or via a detour). If limbs are in your way: expect difficulty on the job. A limb breaking off while you're climbing: pay more attention, be more careful. A woman seeing a bare limb: unconscious fear of not being able to have children.

D: A branch is always a part of your personal "tree of life"—the stronger the branch, the more leaves and fruit it has, the more stable your present situation. See **Tree.**

Trial

V: If you are taking someone to court: you will get involved in a nasty business that comes to a "happy" ending only at the last minute. If you are taken to court: your selfish behavior will be your undoing. Winning a court case: and you thought you didn't have a chance! Losing a court case: try to make peace with your adversary or find a compromise.

D: See **Court, Lawyer.**

Triangle

Looking at, stepping into, or having a triangle thrown at you: you have a hidden talent for scientific research. As a spiritual sign, the triangle represents a heightened sense of serenity. In a man's dream the triangle is usually a symbol of female genitalia.

D: The triangle is the symbol for a "triangulated" affair. It may, however, also indicate that contradictory traits in your personality can be balanced in order to create something new. See also the chapter **"Numbers in Dreams—Number 3."**

Trip, Ticket

V: Whether you are driving yourself or someone else is driving you: your emotions are "on the move." It also indicates that you want to change the present situation in your life. Leaving on a trip suddenly and packing helter-skelter fashion: you are trying to run away from a responsibility. See **Auto, Train.** Preparing for a trip: you soon have to make an important decision. Looking forward to a trip with great anticipation: your present situation will soon change for the better. Buying a train/bus/plane ticket: you have the strength and opportunity to overcome a long-standing problem or obstacle. Missing a train at the last minute: fear of a missed opportunity. See **Train.**

D: The trip you are dreaming about is a metaphor for

your future. Pay attention to the direction you are going, the type of transportation, and possible passengers. The price of the ticket relates to the price (the experiences in your life) of getting ahead.

Trombone

V: Seeing a trombone: your bad conscience wants your attention. Hearing a trombone: you deeply regret a stupid thing you did a long time ago. Playing a trombone: you will soon take a certain person to task. Looking at several trombones: you are now making several commitments. See **Trumpet.**

Trophy

V: You earned a trophy: a project will be a rousing success. A gold or silver trophy: high honors or an inheritance are possible. Drinking from a valuable trophy: you will regain complete health. Breaking a trophy means illness.

D: See **Cup.**

Trotting

V: Seeing a horse trotting: you need to hurry if you want to reach your goal. A slow "gate" could mean losses. See **Horse, Racetrack, Riding.**

Trout

V: Watching a trout in a clear stream means a joyful experience or event. The dream also indicates that you are very healthy. Catching a trout means prosperity or good luck in the lottery. See **Fish, Photo, Picture, Water.**

Truck

D: Compared to a car, a truck is designed to move heavy objects. The dream, therefore, shows that you have the strength to handle difficult tasks. A van indicates that you are either going to move, change your personal situation, or change your mind.

Trumpet

V: Playing the trumpet is a warning to be careful about what you say—you might get in trouble with your neighbors. Hearing several trumpets: you will either get good news or celebrate a happy reunion with a dear friend. See **Trombone.**

Tube, Pipe

D: Are you "stuck" right know? Are you dreaming "pipe dreams"? If so, the tube (something you could get "stuck" in) or the pipe would means difficulties and failure. Sometimes it may be a memory of your birth.

Tulip

V: Dreaming about a tulip means valuable connections in the near future. Picking tulips: in a man's dream, it is a sign of a relationship with a beautiful woman.

D: See **Flower.**

Tunnel

V: Driving through a tunnel: don't be afraid, things are not as bad as you thought—the "end of the tunnel" is in sight.

D: The dream might be a memory of your own birth. It may also mean that you want to explore you unconscious so that you can understand yourself better. Are you afraid of uncertainty, of the future?

Turtle

S: The turtle is a symbol of Aphrodite (Venus), and of fertility, health, vitality, and immortality.

V: Seeing a turtle means you are well protected and have valuable friends. But it also means that you are easily taken advantage of because you react too slowly. Killing a turtle: you will lose the support of a benefactor. Finding a dead turtle: you are losing—through no fault of yours—a good friend or supporter.

D: If you are a very sensitive person, the turtle is a symbol of the "hard shell you wear" as a protection against being hurt. While the turtle itself is a symbol of inertia, the dream also means that you will travel through life with determination.

Twins

V: Seeing twins: an actual situation presents two equally good possibilities. Make up your mind . . . A twin may also be a symbol of your "shadow" ("two voices but one soul").

S = Symbol V = Vision D = Depth psychology

Umbrella

V: Looking at an open umbrella: speak and act carefully right now—even if you can't undo the damage that has been done. Seeing a closed umbrella: you are unnecessarily worried. Opening an umbrella: you won't find luck by walking blindly past it.

D: Are you afraid of something? Are you afraid of your passions? Don't deny your emotions—deal with them and you will feel much better. Are you afraid that things will only get worse and you will, like rain in some places, end up in the gutter? See **Parasol.**

Uncle

D: The uncle is a symbol of your own masculine traits and may refer to the actual relationship you have with your own uncle or another male relative.

Uniform

V: Seeing yourself or others in uniform: don't be deceived by appearances and try to be less arrogant and shallow. In a man's dream, a uniform indicates a lack of order and being uncomfortable in a chaotic situation.

D: Are you conforming too easily to conventional standards? The uniform may be a sign of intolerance and rigidity.

Do you want more influence and power? See **General, Military, Officer.**

University

V: The university represents experiences from which you have already learned (or should learn from now). What activities are going on at the university? See **School, Teacher.**

Uranus

D: This planet represents your ingenuity, intuition, creative spirit, pioneering spirit, and reform-mindedness. This energy can open horizons and safeguard technical or scientific systems. The negative side of Uranus can cause restlessness, resistance, and/or fanaticism. See **Planets, Signs of the Zodiac.**

Urine, Urinating

V: Dreaming about urinating: it may just be an actual need to relieve yourself. If that's not it, relief from a difficult situation is in sight. Dreaming about wetting your bed: practice more abstinence. Drinking urine in a dream: the urine is a symbol of the medicine you need to take to improve your health.

D: Excrement and human waste products are a symbol of relief, of letting go, and setting oneself free. Reacting with disgust means that you're afraid others will not accept you. See **Excrement.**

Urn

V: The urn usually "announces" someone's illness or death. See **Coffin.**

S = Symbol V = Vision D = Depth psychology

Vacation

V: Dreaming about a vacation: you are sick of your job, or you do need a break, but the boss is not eager to see you go. Dreaming about going on vacation: you were looking forward to a fun event, but can't take part.

D: The dream is a sign that you really need a break—it is high time you stopped putting in so much overtime. You are exhausted! See **Park.**

Vaccination

V: Dreaming about being vaccinated: people are dishonest and trying to make life difficult for you—defend yourself! Watching a child being vaccinated: you are protecting a defenseless person from being attacked (with a sharp, "piercing tongue").

D: The dream is a sign that you want to immunize yourself against other people's hostilities, nastiness, and malice. These people are not important—don't take them seriously. Besides, everyone is entitled to his own brand of meanness!

Vagabond

V: Dreaming about a vagabond or being one: you are traveling in "loose" company and prefer to live a nonstructured life with little work and lots of fun. Having a vagabond as a friend:

your moral standards are weak—you are in bad company.

D: The vagabond is a symbol of an unstructured life and weak morals that will cause conflicts. Maybe morally indefensible character traits have emerged that you want to suppress as quickly as possible.

Valet

V: Seeing a valet in your dream: if you work hard for it you will earn a good income. You will also see an old friend again. See **Servant.**

Valley

V: Finding yourself in a valley: you have set your goals much too high; with more humility reasonable goals can be reached. Seeing a dark valley: your extravagant lifestyle is literally asking for losses.

D: A valley can be a symbol of female sexuality or sexual needs. The dream might also mean that you are at a low point in your life and depressed. See **Cave, Mountain.**

Vampire

V: Seeing a vampire: unbridled passions are taking over and depleting you or another person.

D: Fears, instincts, and primitive urges are producing a "cold" heart and depleting your strength. They will make your life difficult in the future—unless you can control them quickly. See **Monster.**

Vase

V: Looking at a flower vase: you have a sense of beauty, creative taste, and talent. Might love be behind it all? Do you want to impress someone? Breaking a vase: you will lose a good friend.

D: See **Chalice.**

Vault

V: Seeing or walking through a vault indicates a difficult task ahead; this is the time to show courage. A vault is also often a sign of emotional anxiety and depression. See **Cave, Tomb.**

D: A vault can also be a symbol of emotional anxiety and depression. Did you wander aimlessly inside the vault or did you find your way out?

Vegetables

V: Looking at vegetables suggests that you need to take better care of your health. Eating vegetables: reexamine your conduct toward children and friends; you are either asking too much of them or taking advantage of them. Planting vegetables: pleasant hours with friends or a pleasant event.

D: Particularly in women's dreams, vegetables are a symbol of erotic needs and desires. As a man, do you prefer a young and fresh "thing"?

Vegetarian

D: Being a vegetarian could be a sign that you are working on transforming your cravings, instincts, or urges into more spiritual strength. This can be done if anger, aggression, and sexual desires are not suppressed but confronted and worked with when they arise.

Vegetation

V: Seeing an overgrown field: your future will be uncertain. Seeing young green shoots is a good omen: you might win something. See **Fruit, Grain.**

D: The dream indicates your hope that your efforts and hard work will "flourish," and that you will receive just rewards for your labor.

Veil

V: Do you want to hide something—from yourself or others? Women who pretend to have orgasms often dream about a veil. Wearing a veil: someone wants to hide something from you that you are dying to know, but don't believe everything you've been told. A torn veil: your relationship is in danger of breaking up.

D: Are you walking through life "veiled"—are you isolating or do you feel alone? Are others hiding behind a veil to deceive you? Is there a veil between you and the person you love? See **Curtain.**

Vein

V: Dreaming about veins: your heart, circulatory system, or blood pressure is not in good shape. If you are anxious in the dream, you need to see your doctor. If blood-letting is performed on you: you will have a fight with somebody. Blood-letting performed on someone else: somebody might die or get sick.

D: Veins are a symbol of vitality and "life's juices." It is important what your veins looked like, their condition, and what you felt during the dream.

Velvet

V: Looking at velvet cloth or clothing made from velvet: you will increase in stature. Wearing or stroking velvet clothes: you would like to escape from the daily grind and yearn for a loving relationship. Seeing others in velvet clothes: you will meet powerful people who will be helpful to you.

D: Wearing velvet clothes: you are a bit vain and arrogant. Are you trying to impress people with what you wear? It won't work! See **Clothes, Silk.**

Venus

D: Venus, the "blue" planet, is a symbol of erotic, emotional, sexual, beautiful, esthetic, harmonious, feminine, maternal, and creative things. On the negative side, it stands for gluttony, excessive sex, and laziness. What do you want to achieve? What do you want to conquer? See **Planets, Signs of the Zodiac.**

Vermin, Pests

V: In women's dreams, vermin are a sign of unsatisfied sexual desires. They may also express fear of an unwanted pregnancy. Seeing vermin in the immediate surroundings: people are bothering you. If the dream is pleasant overall, it means good fortune or money coming in. See **Insects.**

Vessel, Container

D: Looking at a full vessel or container is a sign of success; an empty vessel means failure. Might looking at a "full glass" be an indication that your fears are unfounded? See **Bowl, Bucket, Chalice, Cup.**

Vinegar

V + D: Seeing or even drinking vinegar: things are apt to turn sour in the near future; your goals won't be realized as planned. Making your own vinegar: unpleasant feelings (frustration, anger) toward others.

Violence

D: Dreaming about violence is a sign of hidden **Aggression,** or shows your negative feelings toward another person. Are you doing violence—in some form or other—to yourself or others? An honest evaluation is in order here and would be helpful.

Violets

V: Seeing violets in your dream: happiness is possible if you continue to be humble. Do you think you are a "shy violet," because you have been overlooked so often? Picking violets means luck in love without wasting a lot of words. See **Flower.**

D: The violet is a reminder of past experiences. Sometimes it is a sign of a happy marriage or family—enjoy it!

Violin

S: In men's dreams the violin is often a symbol for sexual vigor.

V: Playing the violin: you still have very romantic ideas about life and love, but this is one of the things people like about you. Listening to others play the violin: be honest, aren't you just a little jealous of other people's talents and successes? Looking at a violin in your dream means pleasant conversations with nice people. Hearing a violin: you are unconsciously yearning for something; it also means you have hidden talents. See **Bass Viol, Music.**

D: A dream about a violin may be suggesting that you reexamine your hopes and dreams. Have you set your sights too high? Do you want to make "beautiful music"—have a romantic affair ?

Virgin

V: A virgin in a man's dream may refer to a project he has in mind at work; or it might mean that he would like to get to know a specific woman. Insulting a virgin with suggestive remarks: you will be punished soon for something you did. A woman dreaming about a virgin: she would like to have more self-restraint and moderation in her life.

D: A virgin dream suggests that you have already taken the first step in your determination to change. Sometimes the virgin is a sign that you have remained true to yourself in love relationships. In spite of the influences around you, your soul remained unmarred. Your very essence remained healthy in spite of the troubles in your life.

Volcano

V: Dreaming about a volcano: dangerous passions are boiling—find an appropriate outlet or pay the consequences of making bad choices.

D: The dream is a warning about extreme emotional outbursts, because suppressed feelings and urges want attention. You are experiencing a powerful self-cleansing. The process will be painful at times, because awareness does not come without pain. See **Crater, Explosion, Fire, Mountain.**

Vomiting

D: Vomiting in a dream, just like **Diarrhea,** is a symbol of self-cleansing. Are there things in your life that make you want to "throw up"?

Vulture

V: Seeing one or more vultures indicates the fear of being used or deceived by others. Your enemies are only waiting for the right moment! Watching a vulture in flight: somebody is, indeed, doing you an injustice. Killing a vulture: you will defeat your enemy.

D: The vulture has a keen, sharp mind. He can immediately spot the weaknesses of others and take advantage of them. This can be true for the victim as well as the "perpetrator." You are asked to show more sympathy and altruism.

S = Symbol V = Vision D = Depth psychology

Wafer, Host

V: Looking at or eating a wafer means pleasant news. Seeing or eating a host in church, on the other hand, is a sign of reflection, high goals, and spiritual guidance.

Wagon

V: Riding in a wagon: chances for quick advancement at the job are good. Losing a wheel: you will be faced with an embarrassing situation—someone's thickheadedness makes you mad. Falling out of a wagon: you are very clumsy and are not doing well; you could lose your job. A mule is pulling the wagon: you are influenced by people who are dangerous or stupid. If people are pulling the wagon (a rickshaw): you want to influence other people or take advantage of them.

D: See **Auto,** and, in the case of a horse-drawn wagon, see **Horse.**

Waiter, Waitress

V: Seeing a waiter or waitress: you are spending time with questionable people. This is also a sign of laziness; you would like someone to cater to you. In a man's dream, this also hold true in matters of sex. If you yourself are the waiter or waitress: you are making sacrifices for someone, and in the process you will lose your independence.

D: The waiter or waitress shows your willingness to serve, your humility, or concern for others. If you are being served: you can expect to get help soon. Dreaming about waiters and waitresses often is a sign that you do too much for others!

Waiting Room

V: Sitting in a waiting room: you are phlegmatic and can't make decisions. Take the initiative—your chances are good.

D: See **Outer Office.**

Walking

V: You are walking backward: past experiences and events are holding you back. Walking forward with purpose: your self-confidence and vitality make great things possible. Are you climbing stairs with great effort? Are you (or things) "going downhill"? Observe the other images in the dream to interpret and understand the meaning of the dream. See **Step.**

T: The act of walking in a dream always represents your life at present. Where are you headed (see **Four Points of the Compass**)? What do you see? See **Path, Street.** Are you healthy? See **Foot.** What have you planned for the future? Analyze this dream carefully because it will provide good insight and tell you if your life is "moving" in the right direction!

Wall

V: Standing in front of a wall: insurmountable obstacles are in your way—turn back!. See **Barrier, Rock.**

D: A wall provides safety (protection) or is an obstacle (obstruction). Are you beating your head against a wall? If so, you are trying to solve your problems the wrong way—find a more effective way! The rest of the dream is important if you want to gain deeper insight.

Wallet

S: The wallet is a symbol of **Greed.**

V: Being given a wallet as a gift promises a pleasant surprise. Looking at an empty wallet: expect financial losses. Finding an empty wallet: disappointed hopes. Suddenly finding a wallet full of money: good luck or even a win. A wallet full of money is also a symbol of powerful sexuality. Men dreaming about losing their wallet face problems with impotence. In women's dreams, it means don't speculate in the near future.

D: The wallet is a symbol of worries about property and the desire for financial security. Maybe the dream is a warning not to let material considerations run your life. The wallet is always a warning to be careful of losses to come. While the wallet is a sign of influence, power (and potency), but the dream is warning you not to squander its contents.

Wallpaper

V: If you are wallpapering one or more rooms: you would like to change something in your life, but the desire is still residing in your unconscious.

D: A dream about wallpaper is a challenge to express more feelings, intentions, and thoughts, and to throw away the mask you've been hiding behind. See **Mask, Painting.**

Walnut Tree

V: Looking at a green walnut tree is a good omen for a long and healthy life. Climbing or sitting under a walnut tree means obstacles have to be overcome before you can enjoy a secure retirement.

D: See **Tree.**

Waltz

V: Dancing the waltz: look forward to a romantic adventure, which will come to a rather "unromantic" end.

D: See **Dance, Music, Tango.**

War

V: Being in the midst of a war: you have to face official business, and perseverance is the only way to get through. If you are taken prisoner: you will meet a powerful adversary who could harm you. Looking at war machinery: extremely difficult times are ahead. If the war machinery is damaged: your present dilemma is going to ease.

D: Dreaming about war means that you are in a difficult situation: you are fighting with yourself. But the dream may also be an indication that you are "at war" with others—spouses, parents, colleagues, business partners, officials, etc. All these conflicts—the result of unrealistic hopes and/or expectations—will come to an end if you make a firm decision. See **Fight.**

Wart

V: Seeing warts: get ready, things are going to be unpleasant for the next few days and the problems will make you angry. Having warts: people have found your weak spots and don't hesitate to point them out to you.

D: A wart symbolizes a weakness you would like to hide from others. Sometimes warts symbolize "dark things" from the past of which you are shamed.

Washing

V: Washing hands: you are feeling remorse because of something you did. Washing dirty things: others caused problems, because they insisted on something that was wrong. Washing yourself or taking a bath: traits that "stain" your character need to be removed. See **Bathing, Soap, Water.**

D: Dreams about washing are a reminder to "wash away" bad habits. See **Laundry.**

Wasp

V: Seeing a wasp: you have a devious "friend"—don't get "stung." Getting stung by a wasp: you have betrayed a friend, who is taking revenge by spreading stories about you.

D: The wasp—unlike the bee—is lazy, hurtful, and often vicious. This describes you or someone in your surroundings who is mean and angry or who hates and wants revenge—defend yourself! See **Insects.**

Wastefulness

V: Dreaming about being wasteful: you have been too generous or you should give more freely.

Water

V: Water dreams are always a symbol of a cleansing process and emotional stirrings. If the water is clear, it means luck at work and in your private life. If the water is muddy: don't get involved in a questionable transaction—you are fishing in murky waters. Drinking freshwater: you are very healthy and will reach a ripe old age. If the water is unsettled: expect the next few days to be likewise. Seeing your image reflected in the water: you are only fooling yourself. In a woman's dream, luxuriating in water is a sign of a healthy attitude toward sex and an overall positive disposition. See **Fish, Lake, Ocean, Pond, River.**

D: Water is the symbol of life-giving and life-preserving energies and always a sign of your emotional state. The condition of the water tells whether your emotional state is positive or negative. The color of the water is also important (see the chapter **"Colors in Dreams"**). See **Swimming.**

Wax, Putty

V: If you are working with putty: you would like to win others over to your side, but you are not firm enough in your approach. A burning candle: a solemn occasion is observed; listen more to your inner voice and "find yourself."

D: Putty stands for your soft, impressionable side that is easily influenced. You are controlled by outer forces and inner ones from your unconscious. Are you "putty" in the hands of others? Would you like to "reshape" someone's attitude in accordance with your own? Figure which of the two applies here. See **Candle, Clay.**

Wealth

D: Dreaming about being wealthy means you are looking for more material possessions; it is also a sign that you want more power and influence over others. See **Bank, Million.**

Weapon

V: Dreaming about a sharp, pointed weapon: people around you are ready for a fight. Owning a weapon: you need others to respect you more and be a bit afraid of you. A damaged weapon means your attempts to defend yourself are futile. See **Cannon, Dagger, Pistol, Revolver, Rifle.**

D: The dream usually indicates that an important emotional decision needs to made. Because the weapon is a symbol of aggression, and the desire is to solve problems by force, it also stands for aggressive, male sexuality.

Weather

V: The weather is the barometer of your present state of mind: sunshine means lots of energy, optimism, vitality, and self-confidence. Cloudy skies mean fear, depression, pessimism; heavy, dark clouds mean deep despair. Rain is "cleaning out" suppressed emotions. Wind and storms always indicate emotional temper tantrums. Lightning means changes are imminent, which could be very satisfying. See **Air, Rain, Sun, Water, Wind.**

Weaving, Weaving Loom

D: Weaving is a symbol of hard work, patience, and thrift—you either have these qualities already or need to acquire them. The weaver is showing you the intricate connections (experiences, adventures), that give "pattern" and structure to your life. Should you put your weaving skills into your personal relationships? See **Carpet, String, Wool.**

Wedding

V: Being in a wedding party means good news. If single, you might be ready to make a lasting commitment to someone. Are you married? Get ready, children are on the way. Dreaming about a honeymoon means big surprises. You see many wedding guests: you are spending way too much money—or losing it.

D: If you are young, a wedding dream may indicate sexual needs you are unable to live out. If you are married, the people in the dream remind you of your own wedding and the expectations connected with it, expectations that either have been fulfilled or have not—depending on the rest of the dream symbols.

Wedding Ring

V: Seeing a wedding ring: you might get engaged or married; or your marriage is based on trust and love. Losing the ring: you have become careless in your marriage or contemplate a separation. Putting a wedding band on your finger: you have to wait a long time before you will get engaged or married. Taking the ring off: your love relationship is coming to an end.

D: See **Ring.**

Weeds

V: If you are pulling weeds: a messed-up situation can be resolved, but pay attention only to what is essential.

D: Cravings, wild urges, out-of-control emotions, and desires are "pushing up" and taking over "the garden of your life." Remove these" wild plants" quickly and thoroughly—pull the weeds from your soul!

Well

S: "The Well is the source of seeking and finding."

V: A dried-up well is a negative sign for all your personal affairs and their possibilities. A well filled with clear water: your emotions and your soul are in balance and alive and promise much success. Falling into a well: you are passionate—but beware, this could end up hurting you! Taking water out of a deep well: you are obsessed with desires, but are denying that they exist; or you have become attached to someone (if the water in the well is clear, a good person, if the water is murky, a false friend). Giving water from the well to someone else: a warning that not everybody is worth your abiding confidence.

D: A well is a symbol of "the fountain of youth." People who draw or drink the water are reaching unconsciously for inner strength while, at the same time, undergoing a spiritual renewal. The well is the place where the experiences of your life are "stored" and from which you can draw again and again. See **Fountain, Water.**

West

D: This direction of the compass is a symbol for the connection between light and dark, body and spirit, consciousness and unconsciousness. What happened when you looked toward the West? What did you see? See **Four Corners of the Compass.**

Whale

V: Seeing a whale in your dream: a profitable enterprise is coming to a successful conclusion. See **Elephant.**

D: This dream is a warning not to be too self-confident or feel so self-important. See **Fish.**

Wheat, Wheat Kernel

V: Looking at wheat: hard work will bring prosperity. Growing wheat: rewards will be proportional to the amount of work you did. Looking at wheat kernels means money will be coming in soon. Wheat flour: you are going to have a wonderful party or enjoy culinary delights.

D: See **Corn, Grain.**

Wheel

S: The moving wheel is the symbol of the road to wholeness, the path to the future. It predicts change of residence and freedom.

V: Looking at a moving wheel: your life is changing; something you started is going forward. Sitting on a bicycle: a certain matter is proceeding faster than expected. If the wheel is not moving: changes that had been planned have fallen through.

D: The wheel represents the constant ups and downs of life. A pleasant dream is a sign of a "rounded" personality. See **Bicycle.**

Wheel of Fortune

V: Seeing a wheel of fortune means something unpleasant is ahead. Turning a wheel of fortune: you hope in vain for good luck—but success is possible only if you take action.

D: The wheel of fortune is a sign that you count too much on Lady Luck—luck only comes to people who are active and work hard.

Whip

V: Seeing a whip or being whipped: your masochistic tendencies have no outlet. A woman dreaming about a whip: she would like to subjugate herself sexually and intellectually to her partner. Wielding a whip: you have secret, aggressive tendencies that other people hate or find repulsive. Listening to the sound of a whip: you will go far in life.

D: Whippings may point to an aberrant personality that needs professional attention, particularly if the dream appears frequently. A whip by itself is a sign of aggression, hate, contempt, as well as arrogance. Examine honestly if you are the perpetrator or the victim right now.

Whisk

V: Receiving a whisk as a gift: you are a restless spirit; find a way to relax (with yoga, self-hypnosis, or meditation). A broken whisk means the end of a relationship.

Whistling

V: Hearing a shrill whistle: be careful for the next couple of days, you might be in danger.

D: The sound of a piercing whistle warns of danger.

Widow, Widower

V + D: Would you like to withdraw from human contact for a while? Are you still attached to past experiences? Are you a "merry widow" or "widower" in the dream? Are you sad and grieving? See **Man, Woman.**

Wig

V: Seeing a person wearing a wig: you are falling victim to the deceit of others; be careful in the presence of arrogant people. Seeing a wig: you are too gullible. Wearing a wig yourself: you are suffering from feelings of inferiority.

D: A wig may stand for wrong attitudes and behaviors—occasionally also of feelings of inferiority. See **Hair, Powder.**

Wind, Windmill

V: Feeling a warm, soft wind: let go of the daily grind for now and indulge in the softer side of life. A sharp, strong wind: find strength within you and the hurdles can be taken! Pieces of paper twirling in the wind: expect to receive news soon. See **Paper.** Having the wind at your back: projects at work are going well. Looking at a windmill: don't be selfish—only hard work and patience will get you through.

D: The wind is a symbol of spiritual energies that unconsciously influence your life. Wind blowing in your face means problems ahead. See **Air.**

Window

V: Standing in front of a closed window: be less distant around others and more thoughtful. You have no real reason to isolate as much as you do. An open window: a positive sign—don't give up your optimism. It helps you achieve success. If you break a window, your actions have created havoc. Looking out a window: expectations have been dashed, but the future still looks good.

D: The window is a symbol of your attitude about the world and the expectations you have of others. What did you see when you looked out the window? See **Glass.**

Wine, Wine Bottle

V: Seeing a wine bottle: fun people are coming to visit you. An empty or broken wine bottle: a melancholy mood and lots of worries. Spilling wine: be more careful; don't open your mouth so quickly. Sour wine: you can't handle noisy company; you need peace and quiet. Drinking a good wine: you will meet interesting and intelligent people. See **Alcohol, Grapes, Mug.**

Winter

V: Dreaming about winter: stagnation and worries will be over soon—spring is close at hand in all areas of your life. Experiencing winter: stay put—now is not the time to make new plans or start big projects. See **Cold, Ice.**

D: A bitter, cold winter reflects loneliness and emotional stress. Maybe your feelings are running cold right now (you have been putting them on hold)? Often dreams about winter are a sign that you need to step back for a while—but spring will always follow!

Wire

V: Stumbling or falling over a wire: be careful, somebody has set a trap. Seeing barbed wire: a clear warning to be patient until a predicament resolves itself without any effort on your part. Getting caught on a barbed wire fence: a legal argument, or a fight with someone will be very frustrating. See **Rope, String.**

D: The wire is a symbol of the difficulties and obstacles you may encounter in the next few weeks.

Wise Man, Wisdom

D: Dreaming about a "wise man": first remember that wisdom has nothing to do with intelligence but is born of inner strength. The dream asks you to make use of this strength so that you can live more effectively. It could also indicate that you are already living in harmony with your inner wisdom. See **Guru.**

Witch

V: Dreaming about a witch: plans you have made are proceeding well.

D: The witch represents people with ill intentions—and

perhaps also your own nastiness. It is a sign of your fear of the irrational, and suspicion of the unconscious forces that often influence your actions. Was the witch in the dream good or evil? Is there a witch inside of you? If so, what part of you does she represent? The witch might also stand for certain, strictly sexual emotions.

Witness

V: Appearing as a witness in a trial: someone will demand that you account for your actions. Be careful—the matter could turn on you. See **Court, Oath, Perjury.**

Wolf

V: In men's dreams, the wolf indicates difficulties in controlling his sex drive; he may be out of control. Seeing a wolf: a warning of false friends. A wolf attacking: a well-known person will make a lot of trouble.

D: The wolf indicates that the dreamer is fighting his sexual urges. This animal is primarily guided by instincts, cravings, and aggression (see **Predator**), and the human, emotional side of you should be safe from it (see **Animals**). Learn to control these instinctive urges. This is an important dream. See **Aggression.**

Woman

V: If you are a woman dreaming about a female sex-symbol; you are unsure of your partner and questioning your own femininity. If you dream about a "motherly" type of person, you are anxious for more emotional security. Seeing a woman you know: good news. Seeing a strange woman: quarrels, envy, and frustration.

If you are a man flirting with a woman: be careful with your spending habits. A woman with a child warns of worries to come. A pregnant woman means unexpected pleasure. If a woman is flirting with you: you have acted foolishly and your finances are tight—nothing will save you except being more frugal. Meeting a strange woman: you are meeting a new friend. If you see several women together: people are gossiping about you. Hugging a woman: avoid a superficial love affair. A woman with black hair: you are envious and don't know it. A woman with red hair: somebody is setting a trap for you. A woman with long hair: a relationship will intensify. A naked woman: you are unconsciously passionate about somebody; it might also be a sign that you have acted foolishly. A woman laughing: worry and despair about your love relationship is draining your strength.

D: Dreams about old women or old men are regarded as memories of your mother whom you have idealized. Women (particularly in men's dreams) could be a symbol of erotic needs, expectations, and desires, or may represent emotions or the irrational in the man's personality. Dreams about women who are pleasant and peaceful are a sign of devotion to other people and objects, and sensitivity to external impressions and influences. See **Old Man.**

Wood

V: Watching someone splitting logs: bad news or even a death. Looking for wood: you may experience sorrow and sad conditions. Cutting wood: hard work must come before a reward. Working in a wood shop is a very good sign and means positive changes ahead. Carving a piece of wood: you have hidden artistic talents. Throwing wood in the fire: you tend to be wasteful in several areas in your life. Dragging wood around: be prepared for a downturn in your financial situation. See **Beam.**

D: Wood is a symbol of the habits, opinions, and ideas that you have been raised with; they are a part of your personality. A dream about wood is a challenge: think critically about your traits (or they will become "petrified"). Begin now building a new life (like building new furniture from old wood). Is the wood in the dream still green or dried and knotty? Is the wood already decaying"? If it is—it is high time to start building something new!

Wool

V: Looking at wool means financial gain. Shearing a sheep: hard work and thrift will bring prosperity.

D: Either your life is proceeding "soft and gently" or you have a gentle personality. Both are pleasant possibilities. What did you do with the wool in your dream? See **Sheep, Yarn.**

Words

V: If you hear words being spoken, pay close attention: it is a message from your soul—providing important information and advice. Hearing your name spoken: see **Name.** Seeing individual letters: see the chapter **"Letters in Dreams."**

Work

V + D: Dreaming about working (regardless of the kind of work) is a sign of success in life. Seeing others working for you: you are working hard and are being manipulated by others. If you are delegating jobs to others: you can now make a profit.

World, Universe

V: Dreaming about the universe: your hopes that something is going to change won't come true. See **Planets, Star.**

D: The world represents the thoughts and ideals that guide your everyday life—your existence. What does your world look like? The rest of the images, the condition, and the color of this world or universe is important here. See **Earth.**

Worm

V: Seeing a worm: you find a friend or acquaintance becoming increasingly unfriendly. Somebody might try to undermine your position. You have a strange premonition—but you are still in the dark.

D: Worms are a symbol of intense nervousness or sexual needs. They are also considered a symbol of lower, instinctive urges. See **Earth.**

Worship

V: Dreaming about being part of a worship service: you are looking for spiritual guidance and reflection. An external problem can be solved with the help of spiritual guidance. Praying reverently: your soul is pleading for help. Find an impartial counselor, or pay more attention to your religious needs and/or attitudes. Listening reverently to a worship service expresses the need for a deeper, more spiritual life.

D: See **Altar, Confession, Praying.**

Wound

V: If you are injured: someone has insulted or hurt you and the emotional wound has not healed. See **Band Aid.**

D: A wound is a symbol of your present ambivalent and "pained" situation. You unconscious is clamoring for attention, clarity, or healing. See **Injury, Pain.**

Wreath

V: Making a wreath: your future looks good. Looking at a wreath made of myrrh: a wedding, possibly your own or the wedding of a close friend. Wearing a wreath on your head: you or someone else will soon be honored and take part in the celebration. Placing a wreath on a grave: it is time to bury a hope and make peace with a friend.

Wreck

V: Seeing a wreck: a big venture will not succeed, and work already in progress is going to be interrupted. It is important whether the wreck was an **Auto** or **Ship.** Or are you a physical wreck?

D: A wreck implies that an important project is headed for trouble. Often it is a sign that you feel like a "wreck" and have no energy. See **Rubble, Ruins.**

Wrestling Match

V: A wrestling match symbolizes the fight you have with yourself—even if it seems that you are just bothered by others. Losing the fight: a peaceful conclusion to a bitter argument. Winning the match: you are having an important argument with someone and a separation is the result.

D: You are looking for a confrontation with another person. Winning the match: you are going to prevail in an argument, but the result will be a separation. Losing the match: you will find a compromise and remain friends. Pay attention to the rest of the dream images. See **Fight.**

Wrinkles

V: Dreaming that your face is wrinkled: not to panic, you are going to be young all the way into a ripe old age, even if something painful makes you doubt it. Looking at wrinkled-faced people: try not to be so arrogant. The dream might also indicate that one of your projects will "stretch out" longer than you thought.

D: The wrinkles in your face are a testament to all your experiences and disappointments. What you do today (negative or positive) is influenced by the past. The rest of the dream images would be important here.

Wristwatch

V: Looking at your wristwatch: a warning to make better use of your time.

D: The wristwatch represents the way your life is going and how you spend your time. This symbol is either a challenge to manage your own time better or to be more decisive. See **Clock.**

Writing

V: Watching someone else write: do not sign a contract—you would only regret it later. If you do the writing: don't take an oral agreement seriously—insist that it be done in writing.

D: Writing is often the best way to bring clarity to your thoughts, emotions, and ideas. Are you confused about something at present? Do you want to see something in "black and white"? What are you writing about? What are others writing? See **Bill, Leaf, Paper, Receipt.**

S = Symbol V = Vision D = Depth psychology

X-Rays

V: Seeing an x-ray of yourself: the unpleasant situation you are facing right now is entirely your fault. Seeing an x-ray of someone else: a person you have known for a long time is suddenly showing a side of which you were completely unaware.

D: Are you afraid that someone will look "through you"? Are you suddenly able to "look through" another person or a certain situation? The x-ray could also mean that you're afraid of getting sick or that you would like to understand yourself better—to understand what is going on "inside." If the x-ray is very clear and the images sharp, the dream is the sign of a keen mind that will greatly enhance your personal growth.

Xylophone

D: Either people are playing tricks on you (you are the victim) or you are playing with the emotions of others (you are the perpetrator). Both scenarios are unacceptable.

S = SYMBOL   V = VISION   D = DEPTH PSYCHOLOGY

Yacht

V: It is not by accident that the figurehead of large ships was always a voluptuous woman. In a man's dream, the yacht means he wants to meet a beautiful woman (usually a woman with large breasts). Looking at or being on a yacht: having important connections. Owning a yacht: a supposedly useful connection turns out to be totally useless.

D: The yacht represents a more elegant means of transportation. See **Boat** or **Ship.**

Yarn

V: Be careful, someone wants to "ensnare" or tangle with you. Winding yarn: a confusing issue is slowly becoming untangled and dealt with in an orderly way. See **String, Thread.**

Yoga

V: In a woman's dream, assuming and remaining in a specific yoga position, or watch others doing yoga exercises, reveals dissatisfaction with her sex life.

Yogi

Seeing a Yogi means you need to work more on yourself in order to find peace and contentment.

Young Girl

V: Men dreaming of being surrounded and idolized by young girls: a warning to control your desires or others will make fun of you. Kissing a young girl: don't overestimate your strength; you might cause harm. Young girls are kissing you: the euphoria of love might initially be beautiful, but disillusion is bound to follow. Seeing a beautiful girl: be careful with your money.

D: Older men dreaming about young girls: they want to have an affair with a young girl. Other than that, the dream is a sign of the dreamer's feminine side and indicates that he is maturing sexually. A woman dreaming about being a young girl or being in the company of a young girl: she would like to escape from her adult role and all its responsibilities; or she wants to return to the "innocence" of earlier years.

Young People, Adolescents

V: If an adolescent girl dreams about a young man: she will soon fall in love or get married. A grown-up dreaming about a young boy is a sign of immaturity and the desire to be forever young and without responsibility; it can also be a suggestion that honest work and commitment to duty is the only road to prosperity. Meeting a young person who is very attached to you: you are admired or loved by a stranger.

D: A young man represents the masculine/intellectual side of your personality.

See **Youth.**

Youth

V: Seeing yourself as a young person: you keep trying to turn back the clock—but to no avail. The dream is a warning: your rigid and narcissistic attempts "to remain young" is causing you to miss out on today's possibilities and making you look foolish.

D: Youth is the symbol of continued spiritual growth and increasing maturity. Older people dreaming about youth often want to ignore the reality of aging. The dream is a warning against living in the past.

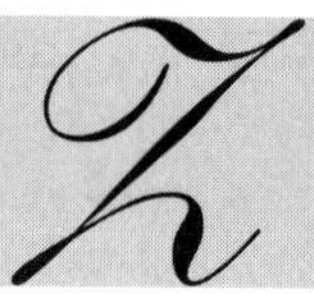

S = Symbol V = Vision D = Depth psychology

Zeppelin

V: Seeing a zeppelin: you will reach great heights. Flying in a zeppelin: you are climbing to the top of your profession. If the zeppelin is crashing: beware, your livelihood is in danger! See **Blimp, Flying.**

D: Transforming sexual needs into spiritual energy increases creativity and allows you to rise above everyday monotony and achieve something special.

Zero

V: Looking at the number "0" in a dream is a good sign for all business transactions. You have a good chance for success and may even win the lottery.

D: See the chapter **"Numbers in Dreams."**

Zipper

D: The zipper stands for the loving connection you have with other people. If the zipper is broken, expect disappointments in a relationship. See **Sewing.**

Zither

V: Seeing or playing the zither: you have begun to get control over an unpleasant project—see it through to its completion!

D: A beautifully played zither may be a sign of a harmonious relationship with another person.

Zoo

D: The zoo is the place where all your instincts and urges reside. You are either suppressing or controlling them. Caged animals in the zoo are often a sign that you are suppressing your urges. See **Animals.** The rest of the dream is an indication of your actual situation.

Colors in Dreams

C= Color Therapy D= Depth Psychology

Blue

Blue always has something to do with intellectual or spiritual events, insights, experiences, and mental processes. It is the opposite of the emotional red, because it is "cool" and "analytical." A soft, gentle blue is typically a female color. Blue is a symbol of the emotional calm and contentment that we all would like to attain. It indicates that you live wisely and with compassion. Blue stands for intellectual goals and insight, faith, and spiritual maturity.

C: Blue has antiseptic, cooling, and constricting qualities. It supports healing in case of hyperthyroidism, sore throat, inflammation, fever, ear infection, mental exhaustion, nervousness, high blood pressure, and anxiety.

D: The color of "faraway places" and of infinity, blue is a symbol of faith, longing, and relaxation—but also of turning within, back to the true self, back to the "I."

Red

Red is an active, affective color, full of passion and emotion. It is also the color of blood and fire. A softer red is also a symbol of love, as well as mercy, brotherly love, and compassion. When intense, red can also indicate hate. If red flashes through our dreams, our soul is ready for action; it indicates either admiration or suffering. A "passionately" red dress we put on in a dream is a sign of strong sexual desire. But red can also mean sin, rage, and the devil. Dark red is a symbol of passion, greed, energy, and anger. Light red stands for warmth and affection.

C: Red is a good color to use in cases of depression, lack of energy, bladder infection, pale skin, anemia, circulatory problems, impotence, and frigidity.

D: Red can mean luck, joy, happiness, energy, action, but also hate, blood, greed, irritability, temper tantrums, and will power.

Green

Green has always stood for vegetation, nature, and growing (deep green in astrology relates to Taurus, ruled by Venus). Green reminds us of spring; only a "poison" green is ugly. When the green color in the dream is stark, it refers to overwhelming emotions (is hope all you have in your life?). Green is the color of sensitivity. Dreaming about this color frequently means that we need to pay attention to a more natural lifestyle.

C: Green is growth, connection to nature, and innocence. Dark green calls up a negative attitude toward life, exhaustion, breathing difficulties, tension, sleep disorders, troubles, cancer, and paranoia.

D: Green relaxes, refreshes, is friendly, represents nature, hope, vitality, self-confidence, and contentment.

Yellow

Yellow is a happy, encouraging color. In spite of its gentleness, however, it can easily slide into unpleasantness, because only the slightest addition can quickly make it look dirty, unattractive, greenish, or caustic. Yellow is the color of intuition, premonitions, and perceptions, however much it is easily irritated. A warm yellow is the color of the radiant energy of the sun, enlightening and warming at the same time.

C: Yellow is a good color in cases of digestive problems, liver and gallbladder problems, diabetes, food allergies, low blood sugar, too much sexual energy, muscle tension and spasms, asthma, and depression.

D: Yellow is a symbol of your optimism, sunny disposition, the light, joy, spirit, and your interest in new things. But it is also irritation, envy, extroversion, extreme motivation, and activity.

Orange

Orange is the color of youthful idealism and enthusiasm. Dark orange indicates prejudice and cynicism.

C: Orange works well in cases of kidney weaknesses, constipation, low energy, environmental allergies, muscle cramps and tension, suppression, and emotional tension.

D: Orange is a mixture of red and yellow—and points to fun, refreshment, conviviality, warmth, energy, and fire.

Indigo

Indigo is a symbol of an alert mind and the desire to be fully aware. The vibrations of indigo are located in the "third eye."

C: Indigo is good for the eyes, nose, ears, and for all types of pain, diarrhea, asthma, bronchitis, lung ailments, nervous and emotional exhaustion.

D: The color indicates strong spiritual energies, without which you cannot build a deeper, more positive, or expanded awareness. You either have built that deeper awareness or you need to do it now!

Violet

Violet—a combination of red and blue—symbolizes emotional attitudes. It can indicate resignation, but it is also the color of introspection, religious beliefs, penance, and atonement. It is a sign of your desire for self-knowledge and spiritual guidance.

C: Violet is particularly effective in the areas of mind and spirit. It controls the pituitary gland, and works well in cases of depression, migraine, parasitic conditions, baldness, and dandruff.

D: This combination of red and blue symbolizes faith, extravagance, magic, dualism, and femininity.

White

White really is not a color at all, but we see it as a symbol of purity—usually beyond the realm of the earthly. The white horse appears where death is waiting or when we have a premonition. White in a dream might possibly be a reminder to resolve special situations or problems. White is feminine, symbolizing virginity, but also emotional coldness and immaturity.

D: White is the color of the bride. It stands for completeness, idealism, purity, innocence, elegance, openness, and the beginning and end of all colors.

Black

Black is the color of the unconscious, of sinking into darkness, or mourning. Black is masculine, night, unsettling, and unconscious.

D: Black is the color of limitation, mourning, taboo, magic, hardness, conservatism, old age, inhibition, restriction, melancholy, defense, and sacrifice.

Brown

Brown has always been the color of earth. The tone is warm, calm, and motherly, feminine. Dressing in a brown dress in a dream means the dreamer has chosen a natural lifestyle or would like to live that way.

D: Brown is a mixture of orange and black. It is the color that symbolizes a connection to the earth, humility, indestructibility, nature, earth, excrement, and emotional stamina. It is passive but persistent.

Silver

Silver stands for restraint, politeness, quiet, coolness, the moon.

Gold

Gold stands for wealth, power, pride, luxuries, fame, elegance, festivities.

Numbers in Dreams

Dreaming about numbers often reveals connections to past or future events. Numbers can mean a birth date, house number, or the number of a year. They always refer to important events—or our unconscious would not use them as reminders. Numbers are also visionary inspirations that we can use playing the lottery or other number-games.

And last but not least, each individual number has its own profound meaning that has been interpreted by numerology and the Kabala and are categorized as follows:

One

One means fundamental wholeness, and is the symbol for all that is godly. As an organizing number, it is the starting point and has the highest ranking; it is the symbolic number for the SUN.

One stands for strength, but also for what you do with it. The One points to strong willpower, mental power, and control, as well as drives, urges, and the desire for independence. The One type of person is the typical hermit who "goes it alone"—usually very successfully, but with a fierce determination can also destroy his/her life. Friendships are pleasant but not a necessity. One is creative, has powerful traits, and is an "original"—tough, assertive, stubborn, and ambitious. In general, the One always means a new beginning, something primary that can't be shared with others. One is a part of everything—it symbolizes masculinity, individuality, and an independent personality. The mind and reasoning ability are strong. They are risk-takers. Do you want to become "One with yourself"? Or with another person? Do you want to create a base from which to operate? Then just "do it"! See **Sun.**

One-people have birthdays on the first, tenth, and 28th day of the month.

Two

The number Two is a symbol of partnership, dualism, contrasts, light and dark, polarity, the Light and the Darkness. Two is the symbol of the moon and regarded as feminine. It stands for gentleness, sensitivity, rich imagination, creative talents, idealism, and romance. Two-type people are less strong than One-people, but they have patience and perseverance. They are not very assertive, are overly sensitive, and tend to be melancholy. Two-people are balanced, thrive on harmony, are restrained, passive, and give in easily. Friendships are important to them and are nurtured.

Generally speaking, Two might be a symbol of polarity—contradictions, good versus evil, spirit versus matter. It represents femininity, the ability to give and receive, and freedom of decision. This number tells you that everything has two sides and encourages you to reconcile contradictions and opposites or to balance them. See **Moon.**

Two-people have birthdays on the second, 11th (the master number), and 29th of the month.

Three

Three refers to something combative and masculine. Religions see in the number Three the trinity (God the Father, the Son, and the Holy Ghost). Wherever the Three appears there is also energy. Three is an effective, holy, but also dangerous number. In many dreams Three announces that something new is happening—when, for instance, you look at a watch or clock in your dream and it is 3 o'clock. Three is the number of Jupiter. Three-people strive for success, but will follow instructions from a boss without complaining. They carry out assignments responsibly and are very ambitious. The Three-person is creative and steadfast, loves partying, dancing, and being in love. Three-ness produces all things.

In general, Three always points to something new that is created from things that have already existed. Negatives and positives can be united—in the external as well as in your personality. It could possibly indicate a desire to have a child (two want to create something new), or might start a new business or a new project together with other people. See **Jupiter.**

Three-people have birthdays on the third, 12th, or the 30th day of a month.

Four

Four in a dream is usually a positive symbol. There are Four earth elements, Four seasons, and Four psychological functions in the human system. The Four is where the change in the human personality takes place. The number Four belongs to Uranus. Four-people want to revolutionize the world: they are scientists, clerics, social reformers, nonconformists, and artists. They brood, attack problems, and have a quick wit. Four analyzes and organizes. It stands against the carefree mentality of the Three—having received the Divine one. Four-people have the clarity needed to understand the center, the "I," and what holds life together. But a Four-person can also suffocate in this orderliness. Four-people have staying-power and willpower, as well as a tendency to be melancholy.

Generally speaking, the Four represents immense inner strength, energy, vitality, and a great love for and connection with nature. You are asked to either support and advance these qualities, or you need them in greater measure in order to fulfill your life's work. See **Uranus.**

Four-people have birthdays on the 4th, 13th, 22nd (a master number), or 31st of the month.

Five

Five is the number of a naturally playful life. If it appears in a dream, the dreamer's spirit will choose a life that is soothing, active, and bright. The Five in China is an undisputedly lucky number. A Five-person is impulsive, quick, and has business intelligence. Lacking perseverance and easily annoyed or angered, Five-people need to learn to be more selective in their choice of friends. Symbolically, the Five stands for Mercury. The Five in people points to drives and lusts. It is the sum of all kinds of qualities—packaged in a restless, nervous, and unpredictable mold.

In general, it can be said that a variety of things is behind the Five, the results of a combination of different character traits. Five represents the human body: the head, two arms, and two legs. Sometimes the Five is seen as a symbol for marriage or for the desire to have children. See **Mercury.**

Five-people have birthdays on the 5th, 14th, or 23rd day of the month.

Six

Six appears only rarely in dreams. It is the symbol of Venus. Six directions (four on a flat surface, one pointing up, and the other down) represent the highest form of possibilities. Six-people have an unusual radiance and "love" is mirrored everywhere. The idealistic and motherly aspects of love are particularly strong, but also the sensual. Creativity, harmonious family life, diplomacy, romance, and enthusiasm are their strengths; they look for absolute union in sex, love, or in friendship. Negative elements are their tendency to be complicated and to prefer conventional, often trivial solutions.

In general, the Six is a shield for the need for harmony and symmetry. It is the symbol for the unity of body, mind, and soul. For that reason, the Six might be a symbol for your health or a warning against illness or harm. See **Venus.**

Six-people have birthdays on the 6th, 15th, or 24th day of the month.

Seven

The Seven wears a halo—in mythology as well. The week has Seven days, four times Seven is the month of the moon. There are Seven deadly sins and Seven virtues. Seven is the symbol for Neptune. Seven-people long for adventure—from pure lust and traveling and discovery, to cultivated, intellectual pleasures. They love company, but deep down they are loners with curious interests (mysticism, philosophy, religion, and art). They have a strong intuitive sense and great imagination, which often appears reserved or introverted. The mind rules over matter, and the soul fascinates them just as much. Their strong sensibilities often lead them to become mystics—or daydreamers.

Generally speaking, the Seven often hides inner or universal vibrations. Human development is divided into Seven stages (childhood, adolescence, puberty, etc.). Chinese medicine speaks of Seven energy centers. The Seven is also connected to colors and notes. See **Neptune.**

Seven-people have birthdays on the 7th, 16th, or 25th day of the month.

Eight

Eight is always connected with Four—since it is the "double" of Four, and also seems to be a lucky number. Eight is the symbol of Saturn and is always connected with "Karma." Eight-people are often misunderstood, but tend to be loners with a tendency to fanaticism. They are often unfairly seen as emotionally cold and unapproachable, because the Eight does not like to show emotions. Eight-people are achievers, industrious, and dynamic, keeping an eye on success in every situation. The sheer amount of energy they invest in their goals can turn into ruthlessness and combativeness.

In general, behind the number Eight might be elements of death and rebirth, the moving downward of the lower part so that the upper part can move upward. But the Eight may also be a symbol of the highest point of development from which something new can be created—because after reaching the summit, the old can't develop any further. The number Eight often stands for decay and procreation. See **Saturn.**

Eight-people have birthdays on the 8th, 17th, and 26th of the month.

Nine

The number Nine is a triple of Three, and therefore, close to creation. It is also the planet Mars. Nine-people are fighters and don't avoid conflicts. Willpower, assertiveness, and the desire for independence is the key to their life. On the negative side, Nine-people have a tendency to be domineering, have a violent temper, are often careless, and—in a subordinate position—easily discouraged. Their impulsiveness and thoughtless, sharp words often inflict emotional pain on sensitive people. They have enormous strength—and are passionate and impulsive. Many exceptional traits could be developed, if concentration and a strong will would work together.

In general, the number Nine is a symbol for the end of a certain developmental and growing phase in your life. Nine is the end of the numbers—after that come numbers on a higher plane. For instance, a pregnancy is completed after the ninth month. See **Mars.**

Nine-people have birthdays on the 9th, 18th, and 27th day of the month.

Ten

Ten appears seldom in dreams. Sometimes ten—1 and 0—indicates the dreamer's loneliness. A new, higher phase of development in life is beginning that is born of the emptiness of the zero (0). You are starting something new, but need to build on the experiences of the past. The Ten is the symbol for rebirth and perhaps of a new career.

Ten—people: see **One.**

Eleven

Eleven is a master number, it strengthens the effect of Two. It is often the symbol of an illegal union of two people. Sometimes eleven is the symbol of your desire for a good, long-term relationship; it might also be the sign of a problem with or changes in your vegetative nervous system.

Twelve

Twelve is the number of the signs of the zodiac and the symbol for a complete year, Twelve months, as well as the number of disciples of Jesus. There are Twelve animals in the sign of the zodiac, Twelve knights at Arthur's round table, Twelve chosen tribes of Israel. Twelve is a very important number. If it is Twelve o'clock in your dream, it really is "high time"! Twelve refers to the knowledge you have gained, serving as a guide to enrich your soul. Twelve is the symbol of all that is possible, your hopes and desires, your instincts and urges, but also your higher ideals, reason, love, all doubts, and intuition—in other words, everything that makes up a human life.

What about the unlucky number 13?

Many people have a deeply rooted aversion against—even a fear of—the number Thirteen. Ancient cultures assigned great importance to it, considering it more positive than negative. It is stated in old writings that "he who knows the meaning of the number 13 has the key to power and control"!

Christianity, however, was opposed to any kind of occultism and had a lot to do with giving this number such a bad reputation. They insisted that 13 was an unlucky number because there were 13 people sitting at the table of the Last Supper. This gave rise, for instance, to the belief that when 13 people sat at a table, one of them would die in the same year. And to this day, there are hotels where no room is numbered 13. Theaters in Italy don't have a seat numbered 13. But this suspicion is rare in the rest of the world. It is only prevalent in places where the Christian Church is very influential.

Cheiro, in *The Book of Numbers*, wrote:

> In the Indian pantheon there are 13 Buddhas. The mystical discs which surmount Indian and Chinese pagodas are 13 in number. Enshrined in the Temple of Atsusa, in Japan, is a sacred sword with 13 objects of mystery forming its hilt. Turning westward, 13 was the sacred number of the Mexicans. They had 13 snake gods.
>
> The original states that formed the American Union were 13; its motto, *E Pluribus Unum*, has 13 letters, the American eagle has 13 feathers in each wing, and when George Washington raised the Republican standard he was saluted with 13 guns.

The sum of the number 13 is 4 (1+3=4), the number of "radicals," because Four-people often feel misunderstood and unconsciously invite secret envy and enemies. They are not inclined to recognize authorities who act as if the power is theirs alone and often misuse it. Challenging conventional standards, laws, and the powerful—and speaking out—has never been popular with the general public, least of all with the ruling authorities.

The number 13 is Four on a higher level and has thereby more gravity, increasing the intensity of any revolutionary conviction even more—including the struggle to bring about social reform and justice.

13 is a symbol of your whole person and your entire life. Don't let others drive you crazy—13 is not an unlucky number! On the contrary, it seeks to "revolutionize" in the sense of reforming a world that is in dire need of it.

Letters in Dreams

A Something unique, the beginning of a new event or project.

B Self-isolation, things hidden and not yet known.

C Matter that surrounds spirit, language, throat.

D Symbol for food and growth/development.

E Bridge between body and spirit, call for unity.

F Symbol for the outside and inner world, insight, hope, understanding.

G Weapon, staff, scepter—conquest and/or domination.

H Balanced, self-improvement.

I The human need for safety and severity.

J Adviser, admonishing or threatening index finger.

K Creative vitality, straightforward action, abundant energy.

L Reaching arm, striving for material and/or intellectual fortune.

M Mother, woman, fertility, creative energy.

N Masculine spirit stimulated by the feminine.

O The circle, insurmountable limits of fate.

P Mishaps, bad luck, accidents, disappointments, negative experiences.

Q The result of our action, our language.

R Male energy, used to pursue our goals.

S Weapons, tools, techniques, and support.

T The cross, origin of your power/energy.

U The cup, the chalice, the passing of life/time.

V Success, victory, the search for completeness.

W No specific symbols could be found, but possibly refers to the ups and downs of life.

X The ten, checkmarks, crossing out.

Y The unknown, sometimes also sexual needs.

Z Risky decisions, lightning, electricity.

Closing Remarks

Symbols, metaphors, and archetypes in your dream do not appear by accident but usually have a deeper and more powerful significance. Some dreams are simply a way for us to "digest" the previous day's events. Most of the time, however, they are messages from our soul, unresolved events and feelings that still reside in our unconscious; they also may provide "visionary" suggestions. That is the reason why we believe it is so important to try to decipher dreams. The best "specialist" to do this is you. An expert dream analyst or a psychotherapist would at best be a "midwife" or guide, and then only if your dream presented clear indications that there was emotional illness and that psychological support was important.

A dream symbol often points to several possibilities. For instance, the question of whether you are the victim or the perpetrator plays a major role that only honest self-examination can answer. Dream interpretation is not a game, something you do every now and then. It only makes sense if it becomes—like daily hygiene—a consistent part of your daily routine—a form of "emotional hygiene." The rewards are well worth the effort. Nothing can replace self-analysis followed by self-awareness. Only in this way can you lead a happy and productive life and be at peace with yourself.

Your unconscious is often the best friend you can have, because it provides advice and suggestions about how to deal with the problems that arise. The wisdom of your unconscious can even open a window into the future—allowing you to face the unknown with confidence.

The increase in the number of people who suffer from emotional problems can be laid at the door of today's culture, with its emphasis on acquiring money, property, and success. But those who are in touch with their unconscious and its messages won't easily violate the natural needs of their soul. The best protection we have against depression, anxieties, and countless other emotional problems is effective dream interpretation.

Index

All entries in this dictionary are alphabetical except for the following: